No One Will Let Her Live

The publisher gratefully acknowledges the generous support of the General Endowment Fund of the University of California Press Foundation.

No One Will Let Her Live

WOMEN'S STRUGGLE FOR WELL-BEING
IN A DELHI SLUM

Claire Snell-Rood

Photographs by Mayank Austen Soofi

UNIVERSITY OF CALIFORNIA PRESS

University of California Press, one of the most distinguished university presses in the United States, enriches lives around the world by advancing scholarship in the humanities, social sciences, and natural sciences. Its activities are supported by the UC Press Foundation and by philanthropic contributions from individuals and institutions. For more information, visit www.ucpress.edu.

University of California Press
Oakland, California

© 2015 by The Regents of the University of California

Library of Congress Cataloging-in-Publication Data

Snell-Rood, Claire Natalie, author.
    No one will let her live : women's struggle for well-being in a Delhi slum / Claire Snell-Rood.
        p. cm.
    Includes bibliographical references and index.
    ISBN 978-0-520-28480-7 (cloth : alk. paper)
    ISBN 978-0-520-28482-1 (pbk. : alk. paper)
    ISBN 978-0-520-96050-3 (ebook)
    1. Poor women—India—Delhi—Social conditions. 2. Poor women—Health and hygiene—India—Delhi. 3. Well-being—India—Delhi. I. Title.
    HQ1745.D4S64 2015
    362.83′985—dc23

                                                                2014045950

Manufactured in the United States of America

24   23   22   21   20   19   18   17   16   15
10   9   8   7   6   5   4   3   2   1

To Dad

Contents

Illustrations

Acknowledgments

There are times when saying "thank you" is met with recoil. My friends in India have taught me you're not supposed to say thank you—at least not to the ones you hold dearest. It shows how little you expected from them and implies perhaps that you are eager to seal the exchange, rather than be there to give back. So as much gratitude as I have, here I will not say thank you, but instead explain how this project has been collaborative from start to finish. Despite the lone author's name written on this book's title page, it has grown, developed, and been pushed further through the generous labors of many people.

This project has been generously funded by a number of different sources. I am grateful to the U.S. Department of Education for Foreign Language and Area Studies (FLAS) grants in the academic year of 2005–2006 and summer 2006 that enabled me to study Hindi at University of Virginia and the American Institute of Indian Studies Intermediate Hindi Summer Program in Jaipur, India. The Anthropology Department at the University of Virginia funded a summer of pre–field research in 2007 and supported the final stage of writing and revising the dissertation that was the basis for this book. The U.S. Department of Education provided a generous Fulbright-Hays Doctoral Dissertation Grant that enabled me to conduct a year of fieldwork in Delhi and hire a research assistant. The financial support of Moriel Vandsburger, my husband, enabled me to write up my dissertation, making a critical difference when I did not receive other grants. And the University of Kentucky's College of Medicine supported me and gave me a home during the final write-up of the book manuscript.

At the University of California Press, I have been lucky to work with Naomi Schneider and Rob Borofsky, who first considered this project and gave it a chance. Their belief in this work has been vital. As I have gone farther in the process, Ally Power has given patient support to me as a confused, first-time author. I am grateful to Ted Lowe, editor of *Ethos*, for allowing me to publish a revised version of "To Know the Field" in this book as chapter 4. Finally, Mayank Austen Soofi's photos of Delhi so well capture the range of feelings that Delhi provokes. I appreciate his participation in this project, knowing that his photos can bring readers closer to Delhi and its extraordinary residents.

My academic journey began with Dr. Alan Dundes, from the University of California, Berkeley, who is sadly no longer with us. I never would have begun graduate school and done this research if he had not told me I was a dummy not to. I ended my undergraduate career frustrated with anthropology and academia and convinced I would never return. He convinced me not to renounce the true pleasure of learning. I miss him, his desk piled with papers, and his grand, mischievous smile. I have been blessed with an amazing dissertation committee who guided me from the beginning of this project: R. S. Khare, Susan McKinnon, Kath Weston, Wende Marshall, and Norman Oliver. At the University of Virginia, R. S. Khare has been an incredible mentor from the beginning of my graduate career. He has prodded me to extend my explorations further, holding me to high standards, while accepting my ability to comprehend from a limited position at any point in time. His enthusiasm for this project has kept me inspired and made me believe it was possible for a naïve white woman to do this research; he never questioned it. Susan McKinnon has taught me the importance of careful argumentation, urging me to patiently understand how all the pieces fit together. When my tendency was to argue a point impatiently, she suggested thoughtful rearrangement that profoundly shifted meanings. Through fieldwork and analysis, Susie's kind words have motivated me to find my own potential and have let me believe that indeed maybe there was something to all of this. Kath Weston pushed me to consider how my research might point in new directions. She encouraged me to pull this project beyond the walls in which I had micromanaged it. As intimidated as I have been at times by her theoretical precision, I am so grateful for it and know that I will only continue to learn from it. I appreciate her support for me to further develop my writing. Wende Marshall urged that learning must always occur in unexpected, intimate places. She has conveyed to me that scholarship must be passionately inspired—it should feel, not just know. Wende taught me to carefully consider the politics of research, both whom it is for and what it can and should do. Norm Oliver has been an ardent mentor, suggesting fruitful ways that I bring this research back off the paper and into the real, messy world. He has led me to believe that I can be honest about women's lives in ways that also honor the political stakes of research. Philip McEldowney, the librarian for South Asia and anthropology at the University of Virginia's Alderman library, taught me the true excitement of thinking historically and across disciplines. Nancy Schoenberg and Carl Leukefeld of University of Kentucky's Department of Behavioral Science encouraged me to finish this project as even as the new demands of my postdoc emerged; without their backing, it would not have been possible. Claire Renzetti provided essential guidance as I put together the book proposal for this work.

At Delhi University's Department of Sociology in the Delhi School of Economics, Rabindra Ray was my mentor during fieldwork. I could not have been luckier to have a guide who I have trusted since my first trip to India in 2003. For those who know the delight of working with Dr. Ray, we are blessed by his impassioned advice that is as incisive as it is far ranging. In Delhi, staff at the Centre for Women's Development Studies, the National Institute for Urban Affairs, and the library at Jagori were generous in helping me access their collections. A steadfast group of people helped me in my continued study of Hindi: Griff Chaussee, Bimla Gaur, and Mehr Farooqi at the University of Virginia; Rakesh Ranjan, Bimla-ji, Reshmi-ji, and Upma-ji at the American Institute of Indian Studies Intermediate Hindi Summer Program in Jaipur (2006); and, during the write-up of the book, I have turned to friends and colleagues to help me in translation, including Anmol Arora, Bindu Sharma, Sonal Upadhyaya, and Nivedita Naresh.

Fieldwork was the toughest thing I have ever done. It required extreme independence and fierce self-questioning that rocked me daily—and I could not have done it without an amazing community of friends and family. Whenever I visit India, my mother feels compelled to write to Pallavi and Adit Tandon to thank them for being my family in India. There is not enough room here to recount all of the times they have saved me. The Arora family in Jaipur were wonderful hosts during my language study in Jaipur. I am so grateful that their son Anmol has become my watchful brother in Delhi or wherever I am. There were so many times where I showed up on the front doorstep of Eileen Kelly and Sanjay Pahuja, sweaty and depressed. I'm so grateful for all of the times that Eileen reminded me of how much fieldwork demanded and that it was okay to acknowledge our limits and frustrations. During my time in Delhi, Bindu Sharma came to know everything about my fieldwork struggles. Bindu offered me her wonderful home for the majority of my fieldwork and is responsible for the fact that I stayed healthy and mentally sound. I counted on our daily counseling of each other and the personal standards for which we held each other accountable. There is no way to imagine the fieldwork experience—and my life afterwards—without her. Susan Johnson-Roehr was there for me every single day leading up to demolition and in the months afterwards, calling me to check up on me. A fellow Fulbrighter, Susan reminded me of all the life beyond the extreme things I got caught up with from day to day.

Numerous researchers and activists in Delhi were the impetus that pushed this project into being and made vital conceptual contributions to the project as a whole. Sadre Alam, of the Centre for Community Support and Social Development, helped me from the very beginning of this project, explaining the foundations of poverty in Delhi and the political landscape. He connected me to my fieldsite and never stopped checking up on my progress. He had faith in this project, no matter how far it seemed at times from his deeply important, grounded activist work in Delhi. Pushpa Pandey, quite possibly the sweetest and most determined activist in Delhi, has explained so much to me about Delhi in slow, deliberate Hindi with kind pauses ensuring that I understand everything. She and her family have welcomed me into their home so many times. Pushpa and her colleagues at the Bhaleswa Resettlement Colony Shakti Manch repeatedly opened the doors of their valuable work to me as a visitor, kindly answering all of my questions and sharing their very personal experiences. The staff at the Navjyoti Development Society—Rajinder-ji, Sonu, Kanta, Sadhna, and Pushpa—graciously introduced me to members of the community in Ghaziapuram. They ensured I did not get lost and answered so many of my questions as I got to know members of the community. I was lucky to meet several compassionate individuals who facilitated health and social services for my interlocutors, including Barbara Spencer at Kamalini; Sangeeta Sindhwani at Lady Hardinge Medical Institute; Dunu Roy and the staff at the Hazards Centre; Amita at the Delhi Shramik Sangathan (DSS); Anil Kumar Verma, a graduate student at Jawaharlal Nehru University; and V. Ramana Dhara, of the Centers for Disease Control and Emory University.

Numerous scholars throughout Delhi shared their individual and institutional work that provided essential background on this research project: Madhvi Misra and Krishna Rao at Public Health Foundation of India; Bertrand Lefebvre and Cyril Robin at the Centre de Sciences Humaines; Rajesh Chandra of the National Institute for Urban Affairs; Arup Mitra and Indrani Gupta at the Institute of Economic Growth; Meera Chatterjee, Jerry LaForgia, and Genevieve Connors at the World Bank; Purnima Menon of the International Food Policy Research Institute; Dr. Nandini Sharma at Maulana Azad Medical College; Geeta Gupta at UNIFEM; Anita Khokhar at Sardarjung Hospital; Renu Khosla at CURE; Isher Judge Ahluwalia; Sunita Reddy at Jawaharlal Nehru University's Community Health and Social Medicine; Harish Naraindas in Jawaharlal Nehru University's Centre for the Study of Social Systems; Dr. Savyasaachi of Jamia Milia University; Roma Chatterji and Deepak Mehta of the Department of Sociology in the Delhi School of Economics; Veena Das of Johns Hopkins University; and Dr. Shalini Grover of the Institute of Economic Growth, who was a consistent source of encouragement from the project's conception through fieldwork. Government officials also helped me, including Mr. Kundan Lal and Mr. Maggu at Delhi's Slum and JJ Department; and Mr. P. K. Jha of the Monitoring Committee for Sealing Commercial Establishments in Residential Areas. I had valuable conversations with other scholars doing research in Indian slums that helped generate new interesting questions: Adam Auerbach; Rityajyoti Bandyopadhyay; Alekya "Baba" Das; Shankar Ramaswami; and Richa Dhanju.

I was lucky to benefit from an extremely supportive community of graduate students during the research and write-up process, in particular Lydia Rodriguez, Holly Donahue Singh, Roberto Armengol, SherriLynn Colby-Bottel, Beth Bollwerk, Todne Chipumuro, Tal Shamur, and Sibylle Lustenberger. Lu Ann Williams will always be my scholarly knight in shining armor. She has picked up me when I am down, taught me much about the values of collegiality, and worked me through the dirty nitty-gritty of my theoretical arguments. Jennie Doberne gave me strength and sass to push this manuscript into a book when I thought it was not possible, and Na'amah Razon helped me focus on how we can define our own meaningful worlds of anthropology within the larger disciplinary world from which we sometimes feel alienated. Many friends, colleagues, and family members dedicated time to reading, commenting, and editing many different iterations of these chapters: Malini Sur, Uday Chandra, Ajay Gandhi, Julia Kowalski, Susan Johnson-Roehr, Abby Lowe, and Sarah Stefanos. My aunt Mary Ann Rood gave impeccable editing for versions of several chapters. I also received helpful feedback at conferences and presentations. Thanks to discussant Dr. Ritty Lukose and the participants of the 2009 AAA Panel on Transforming South Asian Publics, participants of the 2011 Yale University Modern South Asia Workshop, the University of Haifa sociology-anthropology department, participants of the 2011 Israeli Anthropological Association meetings (particularly Pnina Motzafi-Haller), Donald Seeman, and members of Nurit Vandsburger's professional women's group in Herzliya for all of their helpful comments.

I was lucky to have family and friends who not only encouraged me in my efforts, but were interested in learning about my research, and some even visiting me. I found inspiration in the excited questions of my dear friends Abby Lowe, Sarah Stefanos, and Jessie James, my Aunt Karen and Aunt Mary Ann, Uncle John, Uncle Sandy, Aunt Betty, Uncle Ricky, Cousin Melissa, my late great Uncle Alex, and the entire Vandsburger family. As I've crossed back and forth between India and the United States, they reinforced the connections between these worlds that I have felt so intimately.

My sister Emilie has been my graduate school guardian angel from before I even started this process. Her no-nonsense passion for learning has been a great inspiration to remind me what matters through all of this and cautioned me not to let academic drama ever get the best of me. With her butterfly net swinging and her refusal to be bored, Emilie will always be my role model. I am so grateful that my parents have shared so many of the mundane moments throughout these last years, letting me drop by their offices throughout the weeks, feeding me dinner, and welcoming so many of my graduate school friends into their lives. Listening to my mother talk with other scholars and her former students, I've also learned so much about the kind of colleague, teacher, and researcher I want to be: dedicated, empathetic, and passionate. My dad has been a great source of calm. When I grew frustrated with grant writing, communication, or the research process, he would always chuckle and assure me that everything was proceeding exactly on schedule. I appreciate the confidence that he had in me through all of these trips to India, never questioning my aims and always trusting my judgment. When I defended my dissertation in 2011, my dad made it clear that he was excited for me to turn it into a book. When he passed unexpectedly later that year, I was not sure if I would ever be able to do it. With him on my shoulder, I finished this. And for this reason, I dedicate this book to him. I miss you, Dad, and wish you could read this.

My husband, Moriel, has helped me through most of this process, since we met after the second year of graduate school. Moriel helped me to realize that work did not have to consume all of life and indeed that it should not. From our first date to now, he has always made every effort to understand why learning all of this is important to me and has told me to take myself more seriously than I knew how. In all of my own crises of faith, Moriel has always calmly made me believe that it will get done and I'm doing something valuable—all while taking care of me, feeding me, and giving me strength.

My gratitude is greatest for Saraswati, Neetu, Durga, Geeta, Sunita, Mrinalini, Padma, Jyoti, Shaista, Mohan, and their families—you have been my amazing gurus. As far away as I am from you now, I remember you every single day. You gave me everything, shared everything, and without hesitation. As different as I am, you took a chance on me, heard me, took care of me, explained to me, understood me, made me laugh, and made me your own. You taught me to recognize my mistakes and you forgave them. These are all things that, no matter what you say, cannot ever be forgotten.

Note on Translation and Transliteration

During my continued process of learning Hindi, I have found it useful to compare Hindi words with their English translations to gain a better sense of the nuances of different words and phrases. For this reason, where possible, I have included the Hindi transliteration of interview quotes. I have tried my best to translate the quotes to colloquial English that captures the sentiment of the conversations and have consulted numerous native Hindi speakers to verify and improve my translations. However, in some cases, Hindi speakers may find that they would have translated these quotes differently.

I have transliterated most of the Hindi words in this text according to the U.S. Library of Congress standards. However, I depart from these conventions with my transliterations of nasal sounds. For the ease of reading, I have indicated the nasal sounds (indicated in devanagari script through a dot or crescent above the letters) simply as *n* within the words where they appear. (One exception is the word *gaov* for village, in which I have removed the nasal in the transliteration to follow the more common transliteration of this word.) All Hindi words are written in italics throughout the text. However, proper names of people and places are indicated without italics. I have given pseudonyms to all of my interlocutors.

A few guidelines for the non-Hindi speakers eager to try sounding out Hindi words: vowels with a line over the top (like *ā* or *ī*) should be pronounced as a long vowel; letters with a dot underneath (like *ṭ* or *ḍ*) should be pronounced with the tongue against the palate of the mouth; the *ṛ*, reserved for those brave enough to try, should be attempted by flapping the tongue forward; "c" is pronounced as "ch"; the presence of "n" at the end of a word should be pronounced as a nasal rather than a hard "n"; and any consonant followed by an "h" (as in *bh* or *ch*) should be aspirated, or pronounced with an extra push of air.

Introduction

"I have my hands"—that is what the midwife Durga said, smiling, when I asked her if she was scared the night before the government demolished her home. Durga was used to uncertainty. She had built a life here in the Delhi slum of Ghaziapuram twenty-five years earlier, after fleeing an abusive husband. Living on her own as a single woman meant that it was written that she would have to earn for herself, she explained, while tracing a finger across her forehead—the place where destiny is inscribed. When business was slow, she grew anxious. When it was not, she counted her blessings. Even as she kept helping her family in the village, she was never sure what she could count on in return. The clunky government tankers that delivered water to her neighborhood were known to come days late and were hardly guaranteed to fill all the buckets of those who scrambled around their base. Now, even the home around her was about to be bulldozed.

Durga's neighbor and friend Neetu emphasized the vulnerability that women like the two of them shared: "God has given women such a fate that she has to depend on someone or another." The miserly care they received from family and neighbors, their homes that the Delhi government had demolished, and the poor environment they endured—their

1

Figure 1. Big-City Loneliness. Photo by Mayank Austen Soofi.

health was tied to their relationships, no matter how fragile. Research on the social production of health over the last few decades has focused on how social conditions shape health. Relationships, from the microscale of the family to the macroscale of community and politics, establish the social conditions in which health is forged. The inequalities that structure these relationships have left the health of women like Durga chronically vulnerable. But for women in contemporary India, especially those living in slums, there is no other option *but* to depend on others. And if women tried to do without these relationships, no matter how precarious? Then, Neetu contended, "No one will let her live." Women needed family, neighbors, and the powerful classes. Without these ties, Durga had no hope that politicians might intervene to stop demolition, she had no one to help her haul water, and she had no family to bolster her identity as a mother. Maintaining these ties was a social and cultural imperative.

Yet here was Durga displaying her hands that would remain, alongside her panic over what to do next and her frustration that it was all so fragile. Durga's last patient for the day sat on her bed in the back room. Her work continued as if on any other day, though by now she had gotten her neighbors to remove and sell her roof. Leaves, dust, and chunks of building material from the surrounding commotion of an uprooting community fell onto her floor. While I stood trying to make sense of her calm, she continued, "As long as I have my hands, I can keep eating. God gives everything. Why worry? There is no reason to be sad."

Based on fourteen months of intensive fieldwork with ten families in a Delhi slum, this book argues that women respond to the inequalities that threaten their health by fostering inner well-being. Exploring the centrality of the moral self, this book considers how cultural strategies of resilience buoyed women's mental health while enabling them to navigate their dubious relationships. Like Neetu, women accepted these conditions as their fate. But there were things beyond fate. What was in their hands, what God saw, the strength of their bodies, how they "got ahead," the purity of their hearts: these were words that women used to describe what they made of themselves in spite of their dependencies. I move beyond the reasons that "no one will let [them] live" to the ways that women living in slums continue to do so.

Contemporary advocates for health have endorsed widespread change through attention to the social conditions of health. Yet the large scale and policy orientation of this approach are less concerned with how women negotiate their social relationships every day. This book explores women's relationships with family, community, state, and the environment. While relationships were necessary channels to obtain the *dāl-roṭī* (lentils and bread) needed for survival, women remarked on their hidden consequences. Haphazardly played, relationships yielded disastrous effects on social reputation, piled on long-term obligation, and whittled away one's self-respect. Women could be left with no one to depend on and no moral reserve to sustain them. What was in their hands, they explained, were the boundaries they drew within relationships to maintain their independence and their capacity to define their meaning.

Attention to their moral selves left women with a form of well-being beyond the reach of those on whom they depended. Women intertwined spiritual values of asceticism and endurance with the values of mobility and citizenship endemic in contemporary urban India. Inner well-being did not ease physical ache or mental tension. But when women illuminated the personal strength they used to endure their suffering, they articulated inner well-being as a resource that outlasted present pain. In so doing, women reinterpreted the priorities that both biomedical and political-economic experts have elaborated for their health.

STARTING WITH SURVIVAL

Durga's hands, and the other things she intended to last, were not what I thought I would find when I met her. I came to her twenty-five-year-old slum settlement in the Ghaziapuram Industrial Area first in the summer of 2007 and then returned in November 2008 for a full year of research. I was fixated on Durga's neighbor who kept walking casually through the door, her sari tucked at the top of a pregnant belly that seemed too small on a body that seemed even smaller. Her son who trailed beside her was always sick. Rather than Durga's strong hands, I had pictured someone with her weak body when I first planned to come to Ghaziapuram.

In an atmosphere of such chronic structural violence, how women managed to continue surviving burned as the most urgent issue. The 2011 census figures estimated that 15 percent of Delhi's population lived in slums (Dash 2013), but other estimates pose that 50 percent of Delhi's population lives in slums (Hindu News Group 2009). By 2030, 550 million people in India—more than half the population—are predicted to be living in urban areas (Dhar 2009; Gupta, Arnold, and Lhungdim 2009). The people living in this increasingly common urban form have worse health than those living in the urban areas surrounding slums, often comparable to— or even worse than—the health of the extremely poor rural regions from where they originally migrated (Islam, Montgomery, and Taneja 2006). For the urban poor, there is a dual burden of risk: all of the classic illnesses of underdevelopment that haunted them in the village as well as diabetes and obesity that came from being cooped up in crowded communities (Gupta, Arnold, and Lhungdim 2009).

A large corpus of health and economic survey research on slums emphasizes how the social conditions of poverty intertwine with sexism, racism, and other forms of inequality to generate health disparities. "Such inequalities," writes Paul Farmer, "are embodied as differential risk for infection and, among those already infected, for adverse outcomes including death" (Farmer 2004: 305). Local manifestations of poor health are linked to broader geopolitical inequalities (Nguyen and Peschard 2003).

The residents of Ghaziapuram had seen the wealth of Delhi, like other Indian cities, surge with the onset of globalization. Yet urban planning decisions did little to alleviate slum conditions (Fernandes 2006). Two-thirds of Delhi's slums remained "non-notified." Unrecognized by the government, these slums had poorer water supply, sanitation, and power, and flimsy legal standing. Not only do they barely count as part of the city, their health needs are not counted within health policy needs (Gupta and Mondal 2014). People often lacked access to toilets yet their neighborhood was forced to accommodate a disproportionate amount of the city's waste. They fought and waited and strained their backs to get water, and the air they breathed was more likely to carry industrial pollutants (Shukla, Kumar, and Ory 1991; Tewari et al. 2004; Tovey 2002). The gleaming malls that rose up and highways that kept expanding cloistered the poor into smaller, more segregated spaces.

Before, the courts had ruled that rural migrants to India's cities deserved to have their homes protected in order to preserve their right to pursue a basic livelihood. Now, demolition had become the preferred method of urban development, encouraged by the public interest court settlements of middle-class people. They found slums threatening to their businesses, an eyesore to their aspirations of a "green Delhi," and an obstacle to their city's efforts to polish its shine as a world-class city (Bhan 2009; Ghertner 2010). Only a quarter of those whose homes are destroyed are resettled. People found themselves dumped on the edge of the city in settlements without electricity or water (Menon-Sen 2006; Bhan 2009: 128). To continue working, they rose before dawn to accommodate the ride to a now-distant Delhi. Those who were not resettled scrambled for a new roof over their heads, after their biggest financial asset was destroyed.

Life had always been difficult for migrants, but the present posed new frustrations. As Aamir sighed to me, "The average man runs after money for every single thing."[1] After all, now there was less work to be had. Since the 1990s, India's economic liberalization made secure factory jobs scarcer (Joshi 1999). For rural migrants who sought work in cities far wealthier than their rural villages, there were few options outside factory work. Their village homes had offered few opportunities for education, but now without education, what could they do (Joshi 1999; Papola 2007)? There was little room for negotiation with bosses who demanded more and gave less (Ramaswami 2006). So men sought casual labor and brought home little (Papola 2007), and the women in their households increasingly ventured out into middle-class homes as domestic servants, covering up their contributions in order to make the peace with underemployed husbands (Das 1994; Grover 2011).

Poor people in India have suffered as the state has pulled back its social welfare resources since economic liberalization. Geeta's experience trying to get help for a rash modeled a pattern of how poor Delhi residents tried to get help these days. To get a doctor's advice, she woke up early to battle through Delhi's waves of traffic to get to the hospital. Through the throng of bicyclists to the industrial area, across a maze of cars, to an overflowing bus, down through busy streets, she arrived at a hospital and pulled up her sari to show a nurse the huge rash that extended from her stomach to her back, legs, arms, and neck. "Come tomorrow at nine," the nurses said confidently. "The doctor you need to see will be here then, for sure." There was a vision for what should be available, but often it was not available when it was needed.

The large-scale infrastructure for public health was largely fractured, with urban health care facilities for the poor few and far between, environmental infrastructure woefully inadequate, and few preventive health programs. State welfare programs that were at the core of India's project of development since its independence were now just skeletons of their former robust selves (Gupta 2012). Public health programs that in past decades had been charged with eliminating epidemics had diminished, as if satisfied with extinguishing the outbreaks that threatened the middle class but apathetic about the environmental conditions that sustained health disparities (Chaplin 1999; Gupta 2005). There was room in public services for reproductive and child health and the "essential disease control programs" for HIV/AIDS, tuberculosis, and malaria (Qadeer 2009), but not for the diarrhea, malnutrition, and domestic violence that Durga saw so often in the families that sought her out. Instead of comprehensive health care for the poor, the public sector now limited health care services to the bare essentials (Qadeer 2009).

Other bedrocks to sustain population health and alleviate poverty crumbled. During my fieldwork, the government mysteriously cut thousands of people from the rolls of its government-subsidized ration program, an eerie sign of parliament's ongoing debate about doing away with ration cards all together. Meanwhile, in the stores and open-air markets beyond the ration store, prices of basic food supplies rose dramatically. In the absence of promised state services and protections, many poor people in India petitioned politicians and local leaders who mediated their access to municipal services, guaranteed their safety, and assisted with their personal needs (Blom Hansen 2005; Harriss 2005; Weinstein 2008). When these relationships did not facilitate the services that were needed, people in slums were left high and dry. They may drill wells for themselves (Anand 2011) or shell out precious cash for fake documents (Srivastava 2012). Or, like Durga, they may have no one to halt demolition.

Medical anthropologists describe "how harmful social conditions and injurious social connections" can lead to intertwined illnesses that reinforce one another (Singer and Clair 2003: 429). The social suffering that women experience makes them vulnerable to illness, and that illness in turn makes them vulnerable to more social suffering (Mendenhall 2012). Indeed this insecurity was manifested in the health of women living in slums. For people living in low-income neighborhoods, illness is considered "part of ordinary life" (Das and Das 2006). Illness can be a revolving door into which different family members step, so that at least one family member in 35 percent to 45 percent of slum households is always suffering from something (Karn and Harada 2002). Though fever, cough, and diarrhea receive less attention from public health campaigns, they are responsible for the greatest loss of productivity. Yet their chronic presence wears down the attention allotted to treating them. Over time, many people living in poverty have neither the time nor the money to treat them, waiting until they can take it no longer—incidentally, when it is often difficult to treat (Mitra 2009). For many of the families living in urban poverty in South Asia, there are tough decisions made about who would benefit from family resources for medical care and portions for food, with women often facing the short end of the stick (Cohen 1998; Das and Das 2006; Jesmin and Salway 2000; Palriwala and Pillai 2008; Rashid 2007b; Vera-Sanso 1999). When there is cash at home to treat poor health,

Table 1 National Family Health Survey (NFHS) Data on Delhi, 2005–2006

	Slum	Nonslum	Poorest Quartile
Infant mortality rate	54.1	36.1	55.7
Under-five mortality rate	72.8	40.4	70.8
Percentage of children (12–23 mo.) with all basic vaccinations	51.7	67.0	39.9
Percentage of births delivered in a health facility	33.4	68.4	17.0
Percentage of children with stunted height[1]	50.9	37.9	57.3
Percentage of children with stunted weight[2]	35.3	23.9	45.5
Nutritional status for women			
BMI <18.5 (thin)	21.2	12.8	32.0
BMI <17.0 (moderately or severely thin)	7.9	4.7	11.2
BMI ≥25 (overweight or obese)	20.3	28.9	7.9
BMI ≥30 (obese)	6.4	8.6	1.2
Nutritional status for men			
BMI <18.5 (thin)	22.4	13.0	26.9
BMI <17.0 (moderately or severely thin)	6.5	2.8	6.9
BMI ≥25 (overweight or obese)	10.5	20.0	6.5
BMI ≥30 (obese)	1.4	3.2	1.2
Number of women per 100,000 females who have medically treated TB[3]	376	206	549
Number of men per 100,000 males who have medically treated TB[3]	391	190	507
Women experiencing spousal abuse[4]			
Physical or sexual violence ever	28.0	12.4	37.2
Physical or sexual violence in last 12 months	21.9	8.8	29.2

NOTE: Figures are from the Census definition of slums, defined by the Office of the Registrar General and Census commissioner as areas specified a slum by state or local government (even those not formally notified): a "compact area of at least 300 population or about 60–70 households of poorly built congested tents, in unhygienic environment usually with inadequate infrastructure and lacking in proper sanitary and drinking water facilities." All data reported in Gupta, Arnold, and Lhungdim 2009.

1. Children under five years whose height-for-age index is two standard deviations below the median WHO child growth standards.
2. Children under five years whose weight-for-age index is two standard deviations below the median WHO child growth standards.
3. This measure is used to increase the reliability of reporting on TB, so that symptoms are not confused with another illness. However, these figures likely represent an underestimate of actual prevalence.
4. Percentage of ever-married women aged 15–49 experiencing violence from spouse.

symptoms can be read as illness. But when there is not, family members inadvertently may read even symptoms of severe illness as normal (Das and Das 2006: 193–94). With public hospitals overflowing, people living in slums tried to soothe their repeated illnesses through visits to the various medical practitioners who dot their communities. While the service of these local practitioners is sometimes reliable, often their expertise does not adequately address the complex conditions they face (Das and Hammer 2007; de Zoysa et al. 1988; Das and Das 2006).

Researchers have highlighted how women living in communities like Ghaziapuram are bound by patriarchal relationships that limit their autonomy and make them vulnerable to physical abuse (Haider 2000; Visaria 2000). The high incidence of domestic violence in their households is partly responsible for mental health problems that affect a full half of women living in slums, more than twice the rate of those living in urban nonslum areas (Kumar et al. 2005). Midwives like Durga, who respond to reproductive health problems, have ample work even though women seek treatment for not even a third of the reproductive health problems they face. From marriage onward, pain and reproductive illness persist for women, shaping the contours of their mental and physical health (Ramasubban and Rishyasringa 2008).

When fragile social conditions engender such bodily vulnerability, the word that researchers repeatedly use to describe people's basic existence is "survival," what is named "the most basic right" (Farmer 2005: 6). Many researchers have argued that the imperative of survival reorganizes the priorities of people living in poverty. As Susan Seymour writes in her comparative study on the family practices across classes in Orissa, "Whereas middle- and upper-status women usually responded 'being a wife and a mother' when asked what brought them the most satisfaction in life, lower-status women responded 'surviving'" (Seymour 1999: 145). Or, writing about women living in a slum in northern Delhi, Meenaski Thapan notes, "A woman's embodiment is rarely experienced for pleasure or joy; the body is an instrument for survival. In this sense, the body becomes the weapon with which there is a desperate attempt to contest the harsh realities of everyday life in the fight for survival" (2009: 133). In her writing about poor domestic workers and the higher-class women whose homes they clean, Sara Dickey comments that "they too are concerned with keeping inside spaces clean and protected," although generally these concerns are more extensively elaborated amongst higher-class women (2000: 480). However, domestic workers are preoccupied by other worries, she writes, "having insufficient resources to provide for their families' daily survival needs," worries that are "more 'real' than are employers' fears that their households and class standing will be dissolved" (2000: 481). Survival seems to peel away all else, from kinship to bodily meaning to household standing, in a bid for continued existence. As Haider (2000: 30) wrote, through her fieldwork with women in a Delhi slum she learned "their claustrophobia at being trapped in a heavily congested squatter settlement; their monotonous daily work in the effort to access basic minimum needs, especially water; their unending endeavor to make two ends meet some-how; their nagging fear that their hutment might be demolished at any time making them live in constant anxiety and insecurity; their curtailed freedom of movement; their muting; their reflections on their lives in an urban city—often only echoes of information given by their spouse; their almost non-existent relationships with their husbands; their alienation from the larger urban social and cultural milieu."

In this powerful passage, Haider encompasses the expansive scale of social determinants within individual experience. Every relationship that these women have—with environment, state and city, neighborhood, and family—is fragile. Across these four accounts, researchers describe "survival" as women's imperative, requiring work, fighting, and accepting relationships beyond their control.

IN SEARCH OF CHANGE

Researchers and reformers have articulated an ambitious agenda to make sure that survival would not be such a bruising fight for women living in India's poor urban communities. As much as the vulnerability of these women may be clear, no single public health agenda has been coalesced to address it. The priorities set and the means suggested to achieve them vary drastically by the researcher, policymaker, or activist recommending them. Some researchers and reformers draw from multiple perspectives to address the health of people in slums; others vehemently disagree with approaches that they felt misrepresented the problems and provided only shallow solutions. Here, I outline several of the main approaches and the forms they took in wider Delhi, though many of these efforts were not felt directly within the lives of people within Ghaziapuram.

Researchers of the social production of health school argue that any health system must be "placed within a national effort to provide food, water, shelter, sanitation, education, and other basic needs" (Narayan 2011). If basic needs do not take precedence, then public health efforts will be consumed in curing disease, rather than preventing and promoting it. For women like Durga and her neighbors, this needed to start with securing their basic citizenship (Sen 2011). When people living in slums are not counted as part of society, then neither are they provided with basic infrastructure for everyday life, much less provisions for health care (Shetty 2011). Delhi's urban policy, as well as the Indian government's approach to urban policy, must include poor people in its planning, rather than forever moving them to the side (Baviskar 2006; Menon-Sen and Bhan 2008). Counting poor urban communities as part of the city requires providing them with clean, reliable water, sewers that remove waste, provisions to create latrines in people's homes, and public toilets for those who cannot afford them in their homes. Once infrastructure is there, health and hygiene will follow (Renu Khosla, personal communication with the author, August 21, 2009). Further, some researchers argue that health will not improve without fundamental changes in economic policies. If Aamir is forever running behind every rupee, then how could he ever afford basic necessities, much less have any long-term security? Economic policies that encourage more stable employment are necessary to ensure that people like Aamir can escape repeated cycles of poverty (Menon-Sen and Bhan 2008). Without such basic changes to livelihood, government programs to support basic welfare can only have shallow effects (Gupta 2012). This broad grouping of reforms looks less at what is in Durga's hands and more at rebuilding the basic policy infrastructure that shaped her poverty and health: urban policies that provided security for the poor, basic environmental infrastructure, and economic policies that ensure more stable livelihood.

"If health is of the people and for the people," other researchers argued in a nod away from policymakers, "the people have to be at the centre of health action" (Paul et al. 2011). Communities themselves would power the reforms in this vision. Already research has shown that people living in urban low-income communities internationally helped themselves through resource-sharing relationships (Stack 1974; Gonzalez de la Rocha 1994) and providing protection from stigma (Mullings and Wali 2001). These reformers build on changes in public health and development programs since the late 1970s and early 1980s. As it became apparent that the global development agenda was slow in delivering its promises to improve health globally, activists gradually assembled the nongovernmental organization (NGO) model buoyed by concepts of community development and social change, Paulo Freire's work on critical pedagogy, and feminism (Gupta and Sharma 2006). NGOs could provide services in gaps where public efforts have fallen short, while empowering communities to initiate social change themselves (Nadkarni, Sinha, and D'Mello 2009). In Delhi, *mahilā pañchāyats* (women's councils) exemplify this approach. Women facing domestic violence, dowry harassment, or a lack of support can bring their husbands before a community-based council to have their dispute heard and receive recommendations for its resolution. With the legal system operating at a sluggish pace and police a threat more than a resource, *mahilā pañchāyats* are often the lead institutional players in adjudicating family disputes for low-income urban families (Grover 2011; Magar 2000). In the process, members generate community-based solutions for a key health problem. Beyond women's councils, reformers and researchers suggested that community members could play an active role in community education, planning health programming at the local level, and promoting healthy behaviors (Paul et al. 2011). Advocates of this approach reason that because people in low-income communities struggled through the same challenges and possessed collective social resources for health, health development would benefit from institutionalizing their homegrown expertise.

A number of researchers assert that grassroots activism leads the charge for change. These researchers see community-based activists as distinct from community work within established health development programs. Now institutionalized within the development establishment, NGOs did not address the more fundamental forces of inequality that threatened low-income communities. By fighting "against the process of economic adjustment and the intensification of their own exploitation by demanding the right to work, reservation in jobs, political participation, education and welfare for the poor," grassroots organizations "assert their entitlements of equality and improved health" (Qadeer 2009: 247). While some organizations fight for the large policy changes forwarded by advocates for the social determinants of health, many others push for change through piecemeal efforts that make changes one community at a time. Citizens' organizations have enabled poorer residents to lobby for electricity and land claims (Chatterjee 2004), negotiate with international developers about sanitation projects (Appadurai 2000), and arbitrate for control over illegal space (Anjaria 2011: 63). These organizations' resistance to professionalism gives them greater freedom in the demands they can make. Where political restrictions tied the hands of policymakers and programmatic obligations distracted community NGOs, researchers and reformers believed that grassroots activism could promote policy change from the ground up.

Other advocates argued that focusing on communities as a whole did not account for the way that gender inequity weighed women with more health problems than men (Raj 2011). Stronger laws could help women advocate for their rights, but even more so, researchers have noted "societal norms that tolerate and accept violence are widely prevalent in Indian society" (Visaria 2008). These entrenched norms reverberate in women's overall access to care: their needs have little priority within families, and they have little power to make their own decisions about the care they want (Jejeebhoy and Varkey 2004; Mishra and Tripathi 2011). Researchers argue that educational efforts should further women's ability to voice their needs within families as much as spread awareness among their husbands, families, and broader communities that violence is wrong and that women deserve better support (Jejeebhoy and Varkey 2004; Koenig et al. 2006; Nidadavolu 2004).

Finally, many health researchers left the macroscale of social conditions in favor of improving the health care through which people in slums tried to alleviate their health problems. To address the broad range of illnesses that they faced, women like Geeta and her neighbors were faced with a dizzying array of health care practitioners (Indrani Gupta, personal communication with the author, August 12, 2009). They were not all affordable or accessible, nor were they all good. Consequently, researchers suggest people living in slums would benefit from increased awareness about good care, so that they can differentiate their options and choose best (Agarwal et al. 2007). Reformers have stressed how the quality of practitioners and the accessibility of public hospitals are in dire need of improvement (Das and Hammer 2007; de Zoysa et al. 1998), particularly so that people in slums have more options than the community-based registered medical practitioners (RMPs) that they depend on (Das and Das 2006; Kamat and Nichter 1998). In this way, Geeta should be able to get care when she needed it, having hospitals ready to serve her, and practitioners close by to avoid her taxing trek. In addition to improved health care, researchers felt that people living in slums needed better awareness of preventive care before they became weak or sick. Educational initiatives could play a vital role in promoting early childhood development, reproductive health, and good nutrition (Paul et al. 2011). Women living in slums face considerable reproductive demands, these researchers argue, but may not realize how their decisions to receive pre- and postnatal care, delay childbirth, or use contraception have huge advantages for preventing health complications (Jejeebhoy and Varkey 2004; Ramasubban and Rishyasringa 2008). Often, women living in slums may not understand the severity of particular symptoms that they or their family members may face, leading to escalation of illnesses that could be readily addressed (de Zoysa et al. 1998; Jejeebhoy and Varkey 2004). Improving the options for health care and expanding families' awareness of when health care was needed would ease the suffering of people living in India's low-income urban communities.

Weaving their way through many of these approaches are several key threads. First, housing, food access, infrastructure, livelihood, and access to health care are basic necessities without which people living in urban communities will continue to be chronically vulnerable to ill health. The challenges of poverty are experienced in a particular way in Ghaziapuram, let alone India, but overall, the basic ingredients that people in Ghaziapuram lack for their health are those which are necessary for health everywhere. Efforts that do not address this on a large scale will have limited impact. Second, people living in urban slums *collectively* face many of the same obstacles to health, even as women bear a distinct set of challenges that men do not. Because many of the threats are collectively experienced, communities are well poised to improve health through providing small-scale resources (savings groups and informal courts) that substitute for that which they lack, adapting programs to their particular needs, and demanding the services that they need the most. Third, if women knew that they deserved good care within the household and their families supported them in this, then domestic violence could decrease, maternal and child health would improve, and women's overall health would be strengthened. Collectively, these approaches prioritize health outcomes, agreeing on the goals of improved mortality and decreased burden of disease, though they debate the steps to get there.

BEYOND SURVIVAL: WELL-BEING AND THE SELF

From Ghaziapuram, the old public health structure was felt through the government hospitals where Jyoti trekked with little hope, the billboards announcing messages of disease prevention that dotted occasional roads, and the women's and child development centers that they had heard about in other neighborhoods, but not this one. Closer to home, however, was the area NGO with its savings group, *mahilā maṇḍal* to hear domestic violence disputes, and rotating public health campaigns. Other small organizations sat in surrounding communities, rich in services but dwarfed by all of the homes and families they were charged with serving.

When I came to Durga's neighborhood, I had hoped to learn just how she managed to survive. I asked women about the community resources through which they helped themselves and the impacts of the social conditions they lived in. "Yes, we help each other out," agreed Padma. But the conversations I had expected to have about neighborly assistance often just led to gossipy tirades. This person was lying about abuse at home or that person was responsible for clogging the local drains. Rather than joining efforts for collective action, I was brought along to discreetly lobby for special rights in front of policemen and to political rallies that would later be deemed "useless." Even the poor health status that seemed so clear in researchers' concerned words gradually disintegrated. When, from her perch on Durga's stoop, Padma solemnly told me that she was *ūpr-jānīwālā*—about to go to heaven—because of her poor health, Durga yelled back out, "she's not going anywhere!" Saraswati complained of her chronic weakness from constant work, poverty, and abuse. Yet after meeting a middle-class friend of mine who came to visit, she proclaimed her comparative strength. Where was the community? Why was health status confusing?

As I became more involved in family and community life, I observed a number of women's decisions in everyday life that seemed disconnected from their well-being. At least that was how it seemed to me. I became wrapped up with particular situations that made no sense to me in the context of women's regular reports of weakness and financial insecurity. Saraswati's wrists became increasingly thinner as she stopped eating in the wake of her husband's violence. When Neetu's fights with her husband reached their peak, she announced her seemingly sudden distrust of her dear friend Durga—her one option for intervention. As the date posted on demolition notices drew near, Geeta and her neighbors seemed ambivalent about whether it would actually happen. And Durga made a point to comment on how dirty other women's homes were—even as they seemed to share the exact same barriers to water and sanitation.

In the midst of so many physical threats, I grew frustrated with the stories that women told me every day about their complicated relationships. They seemed less important than issues related to their survival (i.e., Farmer 2004). I was unsatisfied with Saraswati's explanation for why she would not eat, angry with Neetu for cutting off the one friend who could talk sense into her husband, frustrated at the lack of urgency as demolition approached, and annoyed with the fact that hygiene seemed an opportunity to differentiate oneself.

But my urgency to focus on what I saw as essential for their survival did not acknowledge these women as "fully embodied and affective interlocutors" (Jackson Jr. 2010: 285). I had a hard time understanding that daily concerns were just as important as the weighty matters (Khare 1995: 148). I was interested in using the personal experiences of people living in poverty in the name of international moralities about the social determinants of health. Yet focusing on the structural violence that I saw at the heart of their lives abstracted their lives from the complex moral systems in which they lived (Butt 2002). I did not know what well-being meant to them, nor did I understand what they did to create it.

While social conditions explained the vulnerability of women's health, they did little to explain the decisions that women made daily. Like others,

I had inadvertently relegated well-being to distinct domains and sidelined strategies I deemed less productive of survival. Because I had separated the shared conditions of poverty from the realities of social diversity, I had felt that political matters that promote survival should not be distracted by private personal grudges. Because I saw individual well-being apart from the social meaning of family, I was sure that women's efforts for well-being should not be compromised by their social need for families. My concern for physical survival threatened by social conditions failed to explain the meaning of the fear of evil magic between neighbors, the desire to promote family relations even if they are abusive, the disdain of neighbors' hygiene, and the retreat from collective political action. These decisions mattered too. I had dismissed important axes of meaning in slum life because of the type of well-being for which I searched.

For women, the constrictions of the social determinants for health were paired with what they saw "in their hands" every day. What was "in their hands" was what *they* could do. Only through months of analysis did it occur to me that the "me" and the "I," the *jīv* or *man* (self) in Hindi, the "good" or "bad" person in gossip, the person women described in relationship to God—that these all outlined a cultural model of personhood that shaped their notions of "body, soul, mind, and emotion" (McHugh 1989: 77) as much as of well-being. In all of the situations that made no sense to me, women articulated different stakes of well-being by elaborating a moral self. In this way, women challenged social determinants of health perspectives that "tacitly assume that agency and will are themselves socially scripted" (Greenough 2009: 31). Their perspectives questioned several of the key assumptions of efforts set out to improve their health.

Following what women shared of their lives, I consider two intertwined forms of well-being: that which is relational, and that which is outside of relationships, alluding to otherworldly unity. The moral principles that guided them urged me to see beyond their physical vulnerability to consider the consequences their social conditions had on their self-respect (Bourgois and Scheper-Hughes 2004: 318). They lived anxiously, assaulted by legal, social, cultural, and moral stigma (Baviskar 2006; Bhan 2009; Chandola 2010; Ramanathan 2006). Their prescriptions for well-being urged protection in their social interactions, discipline in their mobility, generosity in their families, and creativity in their environment.

Much of what was in their hands were the relationships through which they lived in these precarious structural conditions (i.e., Parson 2010)—the relationships without which, as Neetu said, women could not live. For people living in poverty, power operates through their relationships in their daily lives: both their relationships with the powerful that generated their poverty as well as those through which they act in the world (Green 2004; Harriss 2007: 3). In South Asia, though women's relational well-being has been considered first and foremost through the family, I follow other scholars who point to the lived dynamics of relationships beyond the immediate family (Han 2011: 12; Povinelli 2006; Stack 1974) that are equally a part of daily life even as their cultural value may be diminished. I explore the social relationships—family, neighborly, political, and environmental—in which Durga and her neighbors were embedded through Janet Carsten's formulation of relatedness, as "indigenous ways of acting out and conceptualizing relations between people" (1995: 224). Throughout, women described how they retained their individuality within sociality (Ewing 1991; McHugh 1989; Raval 2009; Trawick 1992b).

When women espoused hard and fast expectations for their relationships, they seemed to confirm the formal "symbols and systems" of kinship, caste, and society frozen in social anthropology (Donner 2008: 4). However, as I looked more carefully over all that women had shared, it was clear how much ambivalence guided their relationships, so I began analyzing the widely divergent feelings they expressed about each of their relationships (Ewing 1990; Peletz 2001; Trawick 1992b). I reconstructed the practices and feelings of particular relationships to capture the fine distinctions that women drew between the ways they were engaging with others, the permanence or ephemerality of their engagements, and the meaning they attributed to their relationships (Weston 2001).

Yet as women negotiated the relationships that they needed for survival, they looked inward and upward. These women were not simply Hindu, Muslim, or Sikh. Among them was a Sikh woman who worshipped Sai Baba, a woman born Muslim but now Hindu, Hindus who went to Muslim saints' graves and lower-caste magic healers, and those who refused to speak about God. Yet there were commonalities in how women indicated their gaze upward as they named God, judgment after death, and right action, or *karmā*. I asked less who God was and paid more attention to what women said God did and meant.

In this paired gaze—toward the relationships in front of them and to the deeper spiritual resources within and beyond themselves—Hindus engage their selves within two levels of reality, one worldly and one other-worldly. The "worldly" consists of the reality before them: the body, the caste, the family, and the social status into which they are born (Khare 1993: 201) and the social conditions they lived in now. For instance, Mrinalini explained that God was called upon to help in the life before her, to "make the sadness less, erase the sadness, [for this] we put our hands together to pray to God."

Yet as she continued in her description, her requests gradually disappeared and God subsumed her within something larger:

> God you are the giver, you are the eraser, of our children, of our people, the one who gives us sadness. This is why we go to God's door. God gives people startled breathlessness, upon having faith in God. Because the one who gives life is him. That is why people take God's name at the time of dying and the time of living as well. Only in the name of God are words given and the one who gives is only you. Only you erase our sadness, decide the moment of our death, only you do good. The days are only yours, as you keep us in this *karm*. This is the faith that man has in God.[2]

Rather than her self as the giver of birth to her children, God was the giver of her children. Rather than Mrinalini as the caregiver of her family, preserving and nurturing life, God was the sustainer and eraser of life. Rather than her own ability to give or seek comfort, to make good or even cause harm in this world, Mrinalini argued that God was the giver of sadness, suffering, and goodness. Rather than marking her personal history through days, Mrinalini argues that the days in which she lives, and the *karmā* (action) through which she lives them, are not hers. A true understanding of God, in Mrinalini's description, requires erasure of the self.

Scholars have written that all individuals, whether they realize or not, are also part of another existence in which their individuality is dissolved, earthly distinctions and desires are nonexistent, and the self is subsumed within the Universal (Khandelwal 2004; Khare 1993; Parry 1994). To realize the dissolved self is to adopt acceptance of God's will rather than seek action and realize one's impulses (Krause 1989: 566), acknowledging how "much of this life still remained unknown and unseen" (Khare 1993: 201). Geeta's take on what was unknown and unseen was more cynical. (After all, that was Geeta.) Geeta posed with irritation, "What does God do for health? He does nothing for health. Everything is according to his wants." But what began as her annoyance balanced out to a wider portrait of God. "Everything is in his hands. He keeps us happy; he annoys us. Everything is in his hands alone. There is nothing in the hands of people."[3]

Within this world, it was assumed that people living in slums as much as those in "hi-fi" apartments will act for their own prosperity and success. I should study and get a good job, said Saraswati, and she and her family should *āge baṛhānā*, get ahead. But this should be done in the right way, warned Neetu. She explained, "God gave us existence from several sides, so God said to do *karm*" (right action). Channeling this voice, she narrated, "'I am giving you your very existence, so with this hand do your *karm*. Do not do anyone wrong, do not touch anyone, do not look at anyone and be jealous, do not steal from anyone. . . . You need *roṭī* (bread) and salt so in this spend your time, in this remain happy.' God said this."[4] Though karma is associated with the accumulation of merit for the next life, Neetu argued that one's obligation to act well in this life was reciprocity to God for the life you were initially given.

But Hindus and Muslims alike believe that their actions in this world would resonate beyond this moment. In the aftermath of demolition, Padma (born Muslim, and now identifying as Hindu) put it this way: "This is why they say that you give your hand to someone, it is that very hand that will take you ahead. If you give someone one thing, then God will give you ten more. I am telling you the truth. If you give someone on your doorstep one rupee, God will give you ten. If you keep that one to yourself, then someone will say, 'Look, what a horrible person. Take it, bastard, you'll die of hunger.' That's what is said."[5] Collectively, actions will be evaluated through a day of judgment (for Muslims) (Rahman 1989: 167) or through karmic reward or punishment in rebirth (for Hindus) (Babb 1983b). In either case, the intentions behind one's actions will be known (Babb 1983b: 180; Rahman 1989: 167). By doing good action (*karmā*) unattached to outcome throughout their worldly lives, people cultivate their souls. Muslim thought offers a related prescription, to protect the inside, divine self by controlling one's outer bodily senses (Ring 2006: 150).

Looking in both directions, people commonly oscillate between worldly distinctions and otherworldly unity. As Sarala put it, "There is no difference between the wealthy and the poor. There are differences between the things [that they have]."[6] And, in parallel, they alternated between the poles of individual action and acceptance (Khandelwal 2004; Khare 1993; Khare 1984),[7] allowing Mrinalini to pray to God for intervention and to accept that God decides everything. Thus, as much careful reflection on action is exacted through the self, there is also an acceptance of action's limits in favor of accepting divine control (Khare 1993: 204; see also Shweder 2008: 75–76). Because dissolving the ego allowed women to let go of the anxiety of when to accept and when to act, it brought them peace. "In taking the name of God," reflected Neetu, "you find peace. . . . God stands by you in every crisis. In every crisis, in sadness, in happiness, in everything is my God. Everyone's God."[8]

Describing women's cultivation of their selves in such challenging circumstances requires ethnography, for only ethnography can demonstrate how women's everyday decisions represented varied forms of action, negotiated ambiguous feelings about relatedness, and acted through multiple selves. Other studies have explored the self as an object of development and the state, elaborating the types of moral qualities that are deliberately inculcated through state programming, and articulating the ways that people respond to and incorporate such concepts within their subjectivity or self (Biehl, Byron, and Kleinman 2007; Karp 2002; Pandian 2008). Although I acknowledge that state and development programs have shaped, in some ways, the different forms of self that I write about, I contest the "remarkably persistent" notion of third world people's "over determined lives" (Khandelwal 2004: 4; Mohanty 1984). They surely were interacting with the moral projects of the state and development that they encountered in the television serials they watched, in the strict language of the doctors and NGOs that served them, and in the expectations of their family members and neighbors to consume and to present themselves in particular ways. Yet my aims are different. For a group of people whose circumstances have been defined by what is beyond their control, I ask what they determined through their selves and how their selves reflected their well-being. Women's concepts of well-being inadvertently interacted with the varied institutional moralities of the public health, often agreeing with or tempering these viewpoints but sometimes representing parallel moral worlds with different stakes and priorities (i.e., Zigon 2009).

Following others who argue that well-being in South Asia draws together moral, social, cosmological, and physical worlds (Kakar 1989; Khare 1996; Lambert 2000), I examine how women built well-being from the inside through negotiating their relationships and cultivating their selves. Alongside the social conditions that made them sick, women living in South Asian slums faced other profound changes in the present that shaped the context in which they seek well-being.[9] In the following four sections, I explore the broader terrain in which women made sense of their lives and defined their priorities.

RELATIONAL WELL-BEING AND FAMILY SECRETS

When I had begun my research with my field assistant Saraswati, I explained that part of my interest was the role that families played in health. That was fine, she responded, but then she cautioned that "No one will tell you the truth about their families." In a place where initial introductions began with an iteration of one's family members and daily conversations began with how they were, the extreme interest in family seemed incongruent with her allegations of widespread secrecy.

Scholars have long pointed to how personhood, and also well-being, in South Asia is "relational." Being part of the family, and being nourished by the collective, is core to well-being (Kakar 1978). Many feminists have argued that relationality is particularly significant for women, and that their "well-being thus depends not only on a woman's sense of herself as an individual, but also on her relationship with others in her extended family and community" (Thapan 2009: 132). Rather than seeking autonomy, women grew personally as they became further intertwined within family relationships and activities (Menon and Shweder 1998; Seymour 1999: 279; Trawick 1992b). If all of this was true, then women depended on someone else to live not just because they needed to, but because being intertwined with others contributed to their well-being. Was the secrecy that Saraswati alleged due to women's desire to obscure their ambiguous feelings about family? Or was it because they were unsure of who their families were? It gradually became apparent that women's silences were connected to their own questions about what their family changes might have said about themselves.

Like most other South Asian women, Saraswati moved between her natal and her married family households over the course of her lifetime. From physical posture to daily routine and form of address, she adjusted every detail between these worlds. Women defined their lives and their selves through the adjustments these transitions required. In contrast, men often stayed within the same family over time, a family that gradually enveloped new family members (Lamb 2000; Menon and Shweder 1998; Raval and Kral 2004; Vatuk 1990). The ability of women to "maintain enduring mental representations of sources of self-esteem and comfort" is what enables them to adjust to the extended family they make their own (Ewing 1991: 132). In this sense, the well-being of women's relational self depends on their ability to maintain an individual self within these relationships. But in contemporary South Asia, as household forms have changed over time, they have demanded a new definition of relational well-being. No longer did women always have to adjust to living with their husband's extended family. No longer did men always remain at home.[10] How could women become increasingly intertwined with relationships when city life truncated their families?

The way that women told their family histories changed as women got to know me. Marriage breakup is increasingly common, particularly in poor urban settings, with women often as the initiators (Parry 2001; Grover 2009; Jesmin and Salway 2000: 693; Rashid 2007b: 116). For women, being sick, their husbands' affairs, unpaid dowry, and not having children were all factors that they felt put them at risk for being abandoned (Das and Das 2006: 81; Jesmin and Salway 2000: 694; Rashid 2007b: 111). They, in turn, considered abandoning their husbands because of their lack of employment or inability to provide (Rashid 2007b: 116; Jesmin and Salway 2000: 694). Whereas usually women continue to rely on their parents to arbitrate disputes after marriage, women who chose their own love marriages retreat from kin, feeling "hesitant about complaining, approaching and bringing their marital grievances to their natal kin, as they feel they cannot hold their parents accountable for their current situation" (Grover 2009: 26; see also Das and Das 2004: 53). Because leaving family even in the case of abuse was stigmatized, I tried to minimize my questions about leaving and respected women's silences. In some cases, I chose to follow up with questions later, finding that with increased time and changed circumstances, women might be willing to share their experiences.

Outside the question of whether relations would last was the question of the type of support that relationships provided. To whom was what owed? Women's rights to family resources in both their affinal and natal families—from maintenance to land—were contingent on their interpersonal relations and investments, such as sending remittances and investing in village land (Palriwala 1993: 54; Das and Das 2004: 72; Jesmin and Salway 2000: 698). Older women sometimes traded the security of living with their children with control of the household budget, which they relinquished to sons and daughters-in-law—who did not necessarily have their best interests in mind (Vera-Sanso 1999: 589). At times, families made efforts to cut off poorer relatives through marriage or movement (Bear 2007: 187). Migration introduced new inequities into questions of sharing with distant family in rural areas. With infrequent visits, the spouses of migrants controlled their money more tightly and shared less with extended family (Palriwala 1993: 70). Adults earning through urban wage labor did not feel the pressure to contribute financially to their families as they would have working on family land (Jesmin and Salway 2000: 692). Some families used the concept of togetherness and love to elicit help, only later to deny family members' requests "because we have our own expense to worry about" (Bear 2007: 190; Vatuk 1972: 135). The families I became closest to asked me for sympathy in their own struggles to ask for fair financial support, described the tense negotiations that happened when I was absent, and, at times, awkwardly invited me into their debates about family contributions as they happened right in front of me. When women wanted care from their families but did not receive it, they asked themselves how to make family meaningful in the absence of care.

Even if family did not provide care, it was still needed as a symbolic gateway to other resources. Though callous domestic violence was looked down on within low-income neighborhoods, other women felt unable to intervene if the broader kin network was not assisting in any way (Das and Das 2004: 56). Thus, even when women faced neglect and abuse, they still had "a stake in maintaining relations" (Das and Das 2004: 6). Other women feared that, without their families, they faced rape and serious abuse if they were to live on their own (Jesmin and Salway 2000: 702). In a setting where family goings-on, including violence, are largely public, women displayed whatever family they had to for neighbors to avoid the shame of being without family (Grover 2011; Sangari 2005). Thus, as women were careful about the way that others watched them in public, they knew that family was one of the vehicles through which they were known. Women used their neighborhood social interactions to reflect on what their family practices said about themselves.

Numerous studies show how women oscillate between foregrounding their individual self and absorbing themselves within a collective self. At times, some women asserted, it was important to forgive abuse (Das and Das 2006: 52). In swallowing the pain, women submerged their individuality within the family. They might purposefully reinterpret illness symptoms as normal bodily signs to accommodate financial stress or to prioritize other family members' health (Das, Das, and Das 2012; Das and Das 2006). In this most intimate way, shared needs became embodied, though often unequally. Women's sense of justice was not lost; it just remained unexpressed (Khare 1998: 222). Yet embedded within the need and desire to have a family-based self, women grasped their individuality tightly. Even poor women in arranged marriages challenged male authority through their moral entitlement to refuge at their parents' home (Grover 2009: 14). Men were fully aware of women's ability to make claims for themselves and sometimes nervously joked that their rights to sex and visiting their home villages were contingent on resources that their wives demanded (Ramaswami 2006: 217, 220). As women now commonly work and accumulate their own savings in secret, relations between husbands and wives have shifted, with women now less likely to accept the addition of other wives and less willing to tolerate abuse or neglect (Jesmin and Salway 2000: 695, 698; Parry 2001: 803; Rashid 2007b: 117; Roy 2003: 118).

All of these dynamics suggest that women were neither encompassed wholly by family patriarchy nor simply self-interested individuals. Women invested themselves in relationships, while making their relationships tools to build their selves. Though women were aware of the distance between their family realities and their ideals, they also remarked on why the ideals were worth hanging on to, and what was felt in relational well-being. Women's sense of themselves within family relationships shapes the distribution of resources within families and the practice of family caregiving that produces health.

UNKNOWN PUBLICS, DANGEROUS SPACES

Geeta admonished me to mind myself in public. "Stop acting like a buffoon, for one," she noted. I should lower my voice and eyes and keep to myself. In the open, whether they were on her front stoop or at the bus stop, one neither knew who others were, nor what they might be trying to do to you (Ramaswami 2006: 217; Khan 2007: 529). Even going to the bathroom out in the open was a time for caution; everyone had heard stories of women assaulted at such a time (Haider 2000: 389). Geeta's lecture urged me to mind not only my physical mobility, but mobility more generally: appearances were not always what they seemed these days. As transformative as was the mobility offered in the present, in equal volume came accompanying uncertainties. The anxiety provoked by mobility in India has been discussed mainly as a middle-class preoccupation (Bhatt, Murty, and Ramamurthy 2010; Dickey 2000; Frøystad 2003; Lukose 2009). But Geeta's comments suggest that social anxiety is more democratically distributed, including among people living in slums. People had good reason to hide their true identity: manipulating their identity could allow them more freedom or power. To navigate others' manipulations unscathed required practices of surveillance.

While caste continues to play a role in shaping marriage as much as politics, more researchers have focused on the ways that *class* organizes social relationships across caste—whether to bring people together in political claims (Appadurai 2002; Chatterjee 2004) or to foster shared protection in urban neighborhoods (Datta 2011; Ring 2006; Unnithan-Kumar 2003). But this togetherness was carefully balanced and usually short-lived. With neighbors of diverse class and caste backgrounds, it was easy for people to feel apprehensive about the quantity of their assets and their self-presentation (Das and Das 2004: 6). From anxiety sprouted the feeling of alienation and the fear of what must be lurking beneath the identities others displayed. Living within a neighborhood hardly consti- tuted belonging to that place, and often women perceived social distance between themselves and those around the corner. Fear of movement made many women's worlds even smaller (Chandola 2012a; de Zoysa et al. 1998; Ramasubban and Rishyasringa 2008).

In slums, communication networks spun much faster than those of iso- lated wealthy neighborhoods, connecting washing areas, front cots, and dense, thin-walled housing. As sites where power is publicly contested, neighborhood spaces in low-income areas carry "the danger of being over- heard, of having words misinterpreted and returning as accusations, all contribut[ing] to a sense of foreboding" (Chatterji and Mehta 2007: 82). With so many differences between neighbors, rumors quickly accelerated small family problems into dramas on a larger stage (Jesmin and Salway 2000: 694). Parents were terrified of adolescent romances that could bloom under their noses, marring their children's relationship futures (Magar 2000: 16; Marrow 2013). Women were careful to steer clear of certain neigh- borhoods. Not only could certain neighborhoods physically endanger them, but neighbors watching their movement could speculate about what wom- en's passage through such unsavory locales revealed about their family's true character (Chandola 2012a). As I went back and forth between households, women were specific with me about what I should share and what I should not—which family details, which costs, and what we did together.

The stakes of public interaction were high. As neighbors and local lead- ers reproduce caste hierarchies, flaunt class differences, send messages of religious exclusion, and demonstrate their power, they build a foundation of everyday violence (Das 2006). When daily neighborhood fractures col- lide with powerful state-engineered campaigns, everyday violence is transformed into violence of a different scale—as in the sterilization cam- paigns of the Emergency or the 1984 and 1992 communal riots in Delhi and Mumbai that left thousands dead (Das 2006: 157; Chatterji and Mehta 2007: 66). Smaller episodes of violence punctuated these out- bursts. Fights over water sometimes left people dead. The names of neigh- bors could show up in lurid criminal reports in the newspaper.

This might be a brave new world of imagining, but imagining that occurred strategically, with full awareness of all of the threats that loomed (Lukose 2009; Marrow 2013). Reputation, as a gateway to sharing daily work and engendering future marriage prospects, was a carefully conserved resource. More often than not, imagining could be lonely. Women struggled to reconcile the fraught process of how others tried to know their selves with their own assertions of what they wanted their own selves to be. For as intertwined as lives were in new urban communities, intertwinement did not guarantee intimacy.

INDIA'S NEW OPTIMISM: MIGRATION, WORK, AND CHANGING SOCIETY

As much as material poverty has remained—and in some ways increased—post-1990s economic liberalization, economists have shown that measures of social dignity have improved (Kapur et al. 2010). Shifts in politics, livelihood, and residence show multiple cases of "an accumulating sense of change" (Khare 1984: 73) amongst Dalits[11] and lower castes, urban migrants, and residents of slums. Residents of slums are mostly poor, but not equally poor; mostly lower-caste, but not entirely lower-caste; mostly less educated, but not entirely uneducated; moderately urban, but often still connected to rural home places. From the outside, diverse people get made into a population of "slumdogs"—or, alternatively, toilers or the subaltern (i.e., Pendse 1995). But economists have fractured this monolith, uncovering where people have come from and how they shape their trajectories through the urban opportunities they make for themselves. Those who have migrated to cities and live in slums may not be the countryside's poorest or most desperate. Sometimes it is those who have the capital to make the move who do (Banerjee and Kanbur 1981; Kundu 2007). As stigmatizing as the label of "slum-dweller" was, for many people, consciousness of their poverty began with their arrival to the city (Haider 2000: 43).

When I traveled with Durga and Sunita to their home villages, they pointed out to me the vast distance between their small city *jhuggīs* and their larger family homes. Their city homes could only say so much about them. Over time, many migrants living in Delhi's slums have increased their wealth, gradually obtaining better jobs as they gained access to better networks of information (Gupta and Mitra 2002). For Dalits particularly, the migration of family members has reverberated into social shifts in their rural homes, increasing the power of their families within village politics and loosening the hold of patron-client obligations (Kapur et al. 2010: 47; Witsoe 2011: 81). No longer could it be said that interdependence between caste groups (i.e., Dumont 1980; Kolenda 1967; Wiser and Wiser 1971) was the basis of the society. Status and place said as much about people as who they were gradually becoming. In other words, how much did Durga and Geeta feel like the slum-dweller that I had made them out to be?

In Ghaziapuram, I spent afternoons with women as they sewed buttons and beads onto clothing for export and screwed on the caps of hundreds and hundreds of pharmaceutical tubes. As they counted the few rupees they received in return, it seemed just another example of the decreasing wages of so much work in India, particularly after liberalization (Joshi 1999; Papola 2007). But as the months passed by, people eagerly offered to take me to their factories and schools. An eighteen-year-old girl showed off the miniature dresses and pants she had made as samples for the vocational sewing program she had joined to prepare young women to work in factories. Shaista's son proudly displayed the labels he was making in a Ghaziapuram factory and explained how he was learning the computer software that would let him design the next ones. While rightfully emphasizing the lack of advances in income, job security, or power, researchers have been challenged to illuminate how mobility is also a transformation of meaning, a meaning displayed in people's investment in their education and work.

Changes in work patterns can bring increased demands even as they also alter the social status of people who are lower-caste and poor. No longer living with their employers, domestic servants now worked part-time for several different households and rushed between their different employers' homes. But they avoided the overwhelming expectations of a full-time employer and were freer to make their own lives that defied the boundaries that their employers nostalgically recalled (Ray and Qayam 2003: 538; Dickey 2000: 469). Even if traditional caste occupations like leatherwork were not left behind, lower castes and Dalits sometimes felt that leaving behind the demeaning ideas tied to them was sufficient to feel transformed (Khare 1984: 73; see also Bear 2013).[12] In this climate, there are numerous poor and lower-caste families that put faith in education as a tool for mobility, despite the frustration of government schools and the overall costs of education (Munshi and Rosenzweig 2006; Naudet 2008). Increasingly, low-wage workers articulated how, even if they could not determine their wages and security, they could articulate the meaning of their work and what it represented about themselves.

Through politics people were expanding their access to state services. Political relationships received more attention as a new form of hierarchical patronage, in which poor people were granted services through corrupt means (Blom Hansen 2005; Weinstein 2008; Harriss 2005; Witsoe 2011). The contemporary political field stretches from formal political parties to temporary alliances, leaving in their wake "discomfort and apprehension in progressive elite circles" (Chatterjee 2004: 47). Poor urban people in contemporary India route urban governments toward serving their needs in ways unstipulated by formal urban planning (Connors 2007; Edelman and Mitra 2006; Jha, Rao, and Woolcock 2007). With the passage of the Right to Information Act in 2005, residents of slums not only negotiate for their rights through making demands, but also scrutinize the government's activities (Kabra and Wadhwa 2004). People living in slums are called the "kingmakers" of politicians, since residents of slums vote much more frequently than anyone else in cities, giving their votes and receiving urban services (Connors 2007: 96).[13] In the rural states of Bihar and Uttar Pradesh, from where many of Delhi's migrants hailed, Dalit and lower-caste people have ascended to positions of political leadership, giving the key perception that "power had changed" (Witsoe 2011: 79).

But even as these political relationships generated amenities and votes reciprocally, it was unclear how much people living in poverty could count on them. Were politicians sincere, or did they manipulate appearances for their own ends? Politicians put more effort into the appearance of providing services rather than actually *providing* them (Connors 2007: 79). The burden of discerning politicians' intentions lay with their constituencies. "We have to accept with a lot of caution now what people say, do, and mean," one Lucknow Chamar[14] explained, "for they either do not do what they say, or do so, but for their own covert purposes, or say vigorously what they actually never mean" (Khare 1984: 115). While new politics offers the potential to upset hierarchies, engaging in political relationships is felt to open the self to risk for usury.

In combination with public policies, these efforts for mobility at the household level shape how and if people overcome poverty (Krishna 2010: 112). By looking at mobility as "improvements in self-respect in daily inter-actions" (Kapur et al. 2010: 40), scholars may be able to measure more of the possibilities that this moment might offer, no matter how small. These transformations suggest that as much as poor or lower-caste people are vulnerable, they may not define themselves preeminently through their vulnerability.

PHYSICAL VULNERABILITY, PHYSICAL TRANSFORMATION

South Asian models of relatedness have emphasized a physical dimension to relationships, through substances that bind people to one another and to their environments (Carsten 2001; Daniel 1984; Marriott 1968; Östör, Fruzzetti, and Barnett 1982). In South Asia, write scholars, ancestors are made through offerings of milk (Lambert 2000), ingesting soil and water ties people in kinship to land (Daniel 1984; Lambert 2000), and the qual-ities of food being exchanged orders caste relationships (Marriott 1968). A properly cooked meal brings a cook in conversation with the divine (Aklujkar 1992) and joins two families properly in marriage (Khare 1976). Yet when it comes to the environment where many South Asians actually live now—in urban slums—all we see is an environmental abyss (Chaplin 1999; Davis 2006).

Yet the slum environment was a key tool that many families used to change their circumstances. For many families in slums, the process of building and moving between homes in slums was a never-ending task (Dupont 2005). As they moved between homes, families traded one type of security for another. Some families who could afford to stay in rented rooms in lower-middle-class neighborhoods elected to live in *jhuggīs,* small huts that are sometimes free-standing, sometimes attached to other homes. This move swapped better plumbing and piped water for no toi-lets, more polluted water, and greater risk of demolition. But it allowed families to avoid investing significantly in an urban home while demolition policies were in flux. If demolition policies were in their favor, they gambled for a plot in a resettlement colony where they anticipated greater security (Chandola 2010). If urban infrastructure improvement schemes prevailed instead of demolition, owners might opt for a different form of security. They might choose to move on from their improved environmental situation, using the profits to better their circumstances in other ways (Anand and Rademacher 2011: 1764–67).

Poor families sometimes joked about the dubiety of their wagers: What assets really mattered? In the case of homes, for instance, their accommodations often looked the same. But as they compared their homes, they asked who was better off—did it depend on their comfort in the present or the future payoffs of their real estate choices? (Ramaswami 2006: 220). While people living in poverty are frequently required to respond to chronic emergencies, these housing strategies are a way to build long-term assets (i.e., Appadurai 2002). In light of this, I waited for families to discuss their homes before initiating my own questions. After many visits, many families affirmed homes that they had disparaged in initial conversations with me, showing the stigma they had anticipated from an outsider.

In Delhi, middle-class people use gating and restrictions within their homes to segregate themselves from the poor and lower-caste people who work for them (Dickey 2000; Waldrop 2004). But through consumption, environmental segregation is made hazier. Perhaps poor people would be kept out of parks in middle-class areas and their *jhuggīs* demolished. But other aspects of physicality were not so easy to control. As one domestic employer worried, poor servants could "dress up to the standards of almost us . . . you might not be able to figure out that they are people working for somebody as servants" (Dickey 2000: 479). Since liberalization, lower-caste people improved their material lifestyle significantly as they began to use commodities that were formerly only symbols of their inclusion (Kapur et al. 2010: 39, 42). Farm laborers that used to subsist on sugar cane juice to get them through their long days were now eating more vegetables (Kapur et al. 2010). Through the use of commodities, lower castes and poor people challenged who counted as "good people" (Frøystad 2003: 167) and shed the symbolic markers of their exclusion. These physical markers opened the ability to reimagine the self, but they also posed new burdens to take part in a consumer lifestyle that was barely attainable (Han 2011).

Environmental approaches to health have stressed how physical conditions engender health: whether the tuberculosis and respiratory infections that arise from overcrowded housing (Firdaus and Ahmad 2013), the stunting that emerges in neighborhoods with a paucity of affordable nutritious foods (Hassan and Ahmad 1991), or the chronic diarrhea that results from inadequate water and sewage facilities (Karn and Harada 2002). Attention to the nuances of the physical conditions of people living in poverty presents additional questions. For the best physical conditions are not always clear, as the joking about uncertain housing strategies reveals. Changes on the plates and in the clothing fabric of people living in poverty show that, even as much as remains to be changed, smaller pieces of the environment already have.

THE "HERE" AND "THERE" OF RESEARCH: RESEARCHER AND INTERLOCUTOR POSITIONS

From the first time that I met Durga and her neighbors, they asked me about the "there" where I would share what I learned. From their experience of poverty that I saw at the center of their lives, they alluded to the frame I placed around it and the audience to whom I displayed it. The widespread interest that the reformers and researchers had in slums meant that residents of the slum where I did research were familiar with outsiders coming to collect their experiences of living there. Women knew the questions researchers asked and the glossy materials that resulted. Yet people in their community were not uniform in how they felt about whether this was right or not. On the day their slum was bulldozed, community members accosted an activist there to document the event. The day before, none of the media outlets we called thought it was newsworthy enough. Now men demanded angrily of the activist, "What is the point of doing anything now? There is nothing that will come of doing this now!" While some nodded in agreement, Ritika commented quietly, "He is not wrong. He wants to show how this is experienced to show what happens to poor people in this city." In the stern advice and chiding comments that women gave me daily, they reminded me that their lives must be considered more fully than the binary of "have or have-not" into which I often pushed them (Anand 2011; Chandola 2012a; Chandola 2012b; Ghannam 2002; Gibson-Graham 2006). Everyone wanted to get their dirty stories, but no one was interested in staying around for anything besides that—be it long-term relationship or learning anything more than they intended to.

Bent on fighting misrepresentations of the women who I knew (Khare 1995: 148), I sought to explore survival when perhaps survival's pressing needs were not the only ones pressing. In "feeling sorry" for the women with whom I did research, "guilt-ridden" condescension prevented me from really listening (Domínguez 2000: 366). However, the women with whom I did my research quickly pointed me toward my own misrepresentation of how their lives should best be understood. My field notes were turgid with my tense conversations, confused expectations, and irate frustration with women. The "politics of rapport" meant that whatever closeness we built laid on a foundation of their questioning my assumptions about them and what research was supposed to be (Jackson 2010). I follow High (2011), who suggests that, in light of the steep power differentials between anthropologists and their interlocutors, anthropologists should account centrally in their analysis for "the formative relationships made" that entail "the direct experiences of pleasure, desire, and guilt" (High 2011: 229).

I had often felt it necessary to explain my research to women in ways that explained the audience it would reach. I emphasized why their voices had not been counted: people outside the slum who made laws or worked in NGOs, the wealthy, and foreigners like me said that slum residents did not know about health, and we needed to prove them wrong! If we did, I explained eagerly, maybe we could change the ways that they were treated. But women repeatedly reframed my research in terms of *my* education, rather than the benefits of applied knowledge. Saraswati suggested that if we just explained to women that if they gave interviews, they would be helping me to get a good job, only then would they participate. It was good to do studies (*paḍhāī*), women agreed, that is what they would help with. They recontextualized my study within the real. No matter what hope I might have had for this research, there was little to no chance that anything that I produced would reshape their lives. Studies were great, but the value of abstract knowledge was questioned.

I emphasized that, unlike those who left afterward never to look back, I would remember them when I was gone. I tried to represent myself as someone motivated by what was right, and that my intense fieldwork meant that I understood the long-term reciprocity expected. Geeta corrected my self-righteous statements on my second trip there: "You're here for work. That's what brought you here. You said you would call when you went back to America after your first trip here, but you did not." Where I had tried to emphasize myself as a caring participant, Geeta required me to reference the fact that my interaction with them was research at its root, not simply motivated by individualized care. Women repeatedly held me accountable for the sentiment for them that I avowed. If I really cared, then why was I always chasing interviews? If I really cared, then why was not I willing to come visit just to watch television or roam around the city for fun? If I really cared, then why was I always focused on work? If I really believed in their medicine, then I needed to take their home remedies (*gharelū ilāj*). If I really believed in their creativity, then I needed to eat their food. And if I really honored their houses, I needed to nap in their beds and pee in the same places they did—even if I did go home to a middle-class neighborhood in the evening. If I really respected them, then I would not point out their trash heaps or cover my nose next to the drains (*nālās*). From the negative comments that I heard repeatedly about the local NGO, I realized that I could not neutrally engage with both, so I passively cut ties with the NGO and stopped attending most all of their events. To be different from other researchers, I needed to prove that I was interested in them, in our relationship, in enjoying each other's company. Not in "*jhuggī-wāllāhs*" (people living in *jhuggis*), but in *me*, Neetu, or in *me*, Geeta, or in *me*, Saraswati.

As if to follow this, my relationship with each family was drastically different and evolved dramatically during the course of my fieldwork. During fieldwork, I became very close to Saraswati, Durga, Geeta, and Neetu's families. I also spent time with the families of Padma, Shaista, Mohan, Mrinalini, Sunita, and Jyoti. I spent time with all of these women (and one man, Mohan) and their families in their homes and sometimes accompanied them elsewhere. Each of these families connected with their neighbors for interviews that I did on health and histories of the slum, including Asha and Hema. I hired Saraswati from April to October to help me conduct my interviews. Part of the evolution of these relationships was driven by practical realities. (Durga moved back to the village, and much of Mohan's family moved.)

As I negotiated the research process, I spent time with different people, trying to fill in additional perspectives, a point that tested loyalties and caused hurt on both sides. My interlocutors' inspection of my relationships also played a part. Because several of my interlocutors were quite powerful in the community (and one had allegedly treated her neighbors cruelly), I had to distance myself from them at times. Though I had hoped to reach out to include Dalits within my study, it proved difficult, as the women I was already close to commented endlessly on the danger of speaking with "those people." There were others who were targets of great disapproval within the community whom I continued to spend time with anyway. In the histories that women shared with me about their present and former neighbors, women argued for whom I should do my research with and whom I should not. Particularly after the demolition, when I traveled between distant homes, I followed women's warnings to go only to the homes of people I had known from beforehand and avoid travel at night. Finally, my relationships were guided by what women expected of me and shared with me, as well as how I related to each of them. With Geeta and with Saraswati both, we joked that we bickered like old married couples—because we did. They repeatedly demanded that I account for my promises and, in so doing, asked me to be a different type of researcher and a different type of friend. It was easiest to become close to women who let me do things alongside them in their households and were willing to critique me directly. In most all of my relationships, there were periods of closeness and periods of questioning. It is because of these different relationships that each of these people shows up differently in this book.

There were moments when people took hold of me like a microphone and said, "This is what you must tell people." Aamir ranted into my tape recorder that they were sick because the government did not clean their streets. Sunita pointed to the German funders who blindly trusted the NGO to spend their money as they said they did. Geeta's neighbor pointed to the violent murder attempt that happened within their community. But most of all, people said it with the way they welcomed me into their home—"you'll tell them in the U.S. how we took care of you." Women took pains to allow me to be normal too, rather than always stay a strange outsider. Saraswati, for one, was willing to use her metal slotted spoon to protect me. When I came to visit her in her new room for the first time after demolition, the kids on her lane swarmed around the door to see the white girl visiting. Laughing, she handed her two-year-old the cooking spoon and pushed him toward the door. "That's right," she said with a smile, "hit them! Hit them!" In moments where people told me, "say this," they assured me they knew I was always learning and documenting. I have tried to write this book with the families I worked with on my shoulder (as Durga describes later), asking what values they wanted me to show them trying to approximate, and the true struggle that it took. By hearing "this is what you must tell people," I do not remember only the positive, but remind myself to whom I have the greatest accountability (cf. Domínguez 2000: 366). And the times that I understood incorrectly, the mistakes are mine alone.

But more often than these clear moments of what they wanted me to tell were many others when I heard, and then later recorded, sordid details about neighborly and family life. When women complained to me about their husbands' inability to hold down a job, their disappointment with relatives who neglected them, their neighbors' false portrayals of themselves, did they remember I was a researcher? These moments always frightened me, because I was afraid that in sharing their private lives later in my analysis, I would reveal things that people had meant to keep secret from me or had meant for me to keep secret for them despite the caution I had taken with explaining research consent and confidentiality. Yet alongside my awkwardness, I agree with others who have interviewed South Asian women that such private interviews enabled a free criticism of family members and intimates that was not always available in daily life (Menon and Shweder 1998: 144). In women's commentary about my research, they adjudicated my claims about what it was. Though my anthropological practice was motivated by respect, and what I hoped was an "anthropology of love" (Domínguez 2000), dealing with the expectations of my interlocutors was "complex and often ambiguous," as much as it was "gritty [and] guilt-ridden" (High 2011: 230). They painted a picture for me of how research was potentially humiliating, usurious, and useless for them, built on the appearance of sincerity and promises that were easily snapped. They asserted that there was no "they"—Saraswati was different from Neetu, and Neetu was different from Durga. I was to pay attention to each of them for who she was, the decisions she made, and what brought her to this place. Though our relationships were based in research, I should do the dignity of treating them as more than research subjects and come and play with them, acknowledge the equality we shared, and remember the differences between us. What follows in these pages is a result of our interaction. As Khare reflected on his research with Untouchable women, "My memories and writing relate with and respond to *their* ways of remembering, forgiving, and forgetting within their world. We both are at the center . . . reflecting on each other and on our respective cultural locations and self-limitations" (1995: 147).

They pointed me to bigger questions than I had known to ask, questions that the contemporary landscape in India posed for slum-dwellers and government ministers alike, men and women, adults and children. They placed the exclusions that they faced alongside a constellation of other daily priorities. Though I had peered onto the small stage of the slum to understand their lives, they opened the curtains wider, to new possibilities, new questions, and new ways of understanding themselves.

BOOK OUTLINE

Can families be meaningful for women even when their demands outweigh what they provide? Chapter 1 examines how women asserted their own strength in the midst of abuse and neglect. Data from sustained observations of families, private conversations with women, and formal interviews about family care are combined in this chapter to compare women's ideals of family life with the frustration of enacting them in daily life. Being a good person, they explained, meant "living for others." At the same time, they asserted to family the care they deserved. The ability to sustain this care "through a thousand sadnesses or happinesses," as they put it, demonstrated their powerful faith and closer proximity toward a selfless ideal. Yet exercising such strength was an emotional and physical struggle that wore women down. Nearly every woman had broken ties of marriage or family. Keeping these histories secret, however, ensured that women, rather than neighbors, retained the ability to judge their moral meaning. These mental health strategies enabled women to make claims for their own health needs within their unequal family relationships. Through embodying the value of living for others, somewhat ironically women reminded themselves of their own individual strength.

In chapter 2, I examine why women were deeply suspicious of the neighborhood social networks on which they relied. Through the sordid tales they recounted, women argued that neighbors used others in their own immoral schemes of mobility. They preyed on hard-earned gains and threatened families' stability. As much as they engaged with others, all the while women carefully protected themselves. This chapter revisits public health and anthropological research that holds that low-income neighborhood relationships facilitate advocacy, social support, and resource sharing. Women's private commentary on their relationships, in conjunction with my observation of them in action, enabled me to see the varied techniques through which women retained charge of their interactions. They bolstered secrecy about their own identity, suppressed bonds, and yet still knew each other's lives intimately. Women challenged the notion that the solidarities that generate daily health endure over time. Instead, their experiences indicate that what endures beyond the social resources of everyday health promotion were independence and accountability for their own actions.

Why would residents of a slum facing impending demolition assert that they were "getting ahead" in society? Chapter 3 considers how families made sense of their own citizenship as demolition of their industrial slum ended an era of cooperation between their families and political patrons. In interviews on their migration experiences to Delhi, residents explained that previously patrons had given them formal recognition and incentives including everything from water to medical care, recognizing the importance of their labor and their expansion of the urban frontier. But as demolition approached, women offered a moral concept of citizenship that emerged as I participated in stalled community efforts to protest demolition, watched families plan for the future, and engaged women in reflection in the months afterward. Their decision to live in Delhi, house or no house, was a quest to "get ahead" (*āge baṛhānā*). Men and women recounted the physical insecurity, poverty, and loneliness they suffered in exchange for longer-term mobility for their families. While they hoped that demolition could be halted, women argued that public protest would make them vulnerable. Avoiding the dangerous networks of politicians whose nodes reached into the slum community itself required families to get ahead on their own. Though researchers have celebrated how collective advocacy enables communities to improve social conditions, this chapter suggests that families' calculations for health are motivated by complex notions of security.

Chapter 4 examines the way that women used the slum environment as a tool for personal and social redefinition. Urban planners and environmental historians have long pointed out how the unequal urban environment stacks the odds against the health of the poor. Women spent their days immersed in managing their home environment, especially because of their responsibility for domestic respectability and their caregiving obligations. From initial disgust when they first migrated, women's reactions to the slum environment slowly changed. Over time, they described its potential. In a series of semistructured interviews about home health practices and the causes of illness, women elaborated their sense that attention to the environment could build a different kind of health. Women's efforts to endure, rather than escape, the harsh climate built physical strength that made them less vulnerable to sickness. I observed the hygiene techniques and housing decisions through which, surrounded by an industrial slum, women established home microenvironments that ideologically and physically separated their families from the slum around them. Though women's transformation of the slum was limited, they used their environmental practices to communicate self-worth in the midst of social stigma. This chapter suggests that practices to manage environmental hazards and promote hygiene have deeper ramifications for self-definition.

The conclusion offers suggestions for the book's findings to be employed. I offer recommendations to adapt domestic violence and hygiene promotion programming that is extended by NGOs in many slums. Bringing together findings on neighborly and community relationships, I will recommend to policymakers that women's cooperatives, a development practice for empowerment and problem solving in low-income international communities (Galab and Rao 2003; Hossain et al. 2004; Magar 2003; Roy, Jockin, and Javed 2004), must account for the potential for abuse within these relationships. I address how community-based participatory methods frequently utilized in public health (Mullings et al. 2001; Sabo et al. 2013; Silverstein et al. 2010) and celebrated in anthropology (Appadurai 2002; Chatterjee 2004; Harriss 2005; Holston 2008) can be adapted for populations that, despite shared poverty and health risks, are highly fragmented. I offer suggestions on how health care policy could build on the health-seeking strategies commonly employed by women in slums. Finally, I use the findings of this study to propose several methodological recommendations and new themes to be followed up in further study.

1 "You Should Live for Others"

TENSELY SUSTAINING FAMILIES AND SELVES

When things became really bad between Padma and her husband, she persisted. Laying in the dark under the clanging fan to escape the midday summer heat, she told me, "He is still with 'her.' And they parade it all in front of me. He even takes his food over there sometimes to eat." It had been like this for months. It had started as an affair and, since moving closer to this other woman after demolition, things had unraveled into an unrecognizable tangle between Padma and her husband. Padma explained a kind of insecurity that she felt through her whole body. "Neither does he take me to be seen [by a doctor] nor does he look after me or my child. All day and night he hits me. Now he wants to throw me out of the house and leave because of his 'connection'—because of his other place." Her words pushed this other woman away, as much as she could. In return, he pushed her away. "He doesn't even want to see me. When he comes home from work, as soon as he takes off his work clothes, he goes to her house. He is happy with her children, he is happy in her house."

Maybe Padma's humiliation grew as the affair unfolded in front of her; maybe something at work had provoked her husband's temper.[1] Padma was not shy about showing her bruises—increasing daily in number and size—to her new neighbors, to me, and to her friends from the old *jhuggīs*.

Figure 2. Mother India. Photo by Mayank Austen Soofi.

In spite of this display, things did not change. She told me brave stories of fighting back and even of when her son tried to defend her. At times she called her previous husband just to talk; she had left him years before because of the violence. But mostly she just worried about the lack of options. There were rumors about what happened on the train tracks that could be seen directly through the small hole in their wall. "Maybe I should just go sit on the train tracks," she said repeatedly, as if tempted to do the same. Sometimes she laughed afterwards, sometimes she did not. She pulled at her stomach skin that she used to jiggle for us for laughs in the *jhuggīs*. "There is hardly anything to pull out anymore," she said. "I cannot even die from hunger when I try."

Lying there, she told me, "Deepak's father[2] used to keep me so well." Where she was now reminded her of where she had been earlier. "I left another home because I was beaten so much. . . . Then I met the kind of man who would be there in happiness and sadness. He did this for fifteen years." He took care of her when she was sick; he always made sure she had good food to eat. More than once, she had shown me the pictures from their son's fifth birthday party, with a cake and party hats, to prove that they had been something else together before this. Knowing how much he had cared for her made her even sadder that they had grown apart, she said. Occasionally, she called me to sample the special foods that she had cooked for him. In the morning as he zipped his pants and buttoned his shirt, she folded his *roṭīs* into one metal canister and filled the other to the brim with hot *sabzī* (vegetable). She massaged his body with hot oil when he was tired from standing all day at the factory. Waiting would make it better. He would get better. I thought she was crazy.

Then it was fall. They had moved to a new room and Padma was happy. For the first time in their marriage, they were fasting together to celebrate the end of Navratri.[3] When I arrived, leftover crumbs of food that they had fed to neighboring children were strewn across the floor. Padma smiled. They had been cooking since 3:30 in the morning. When her husband went outside, she mentioned with a chuckle that he had yelled to her the whole time about how all of the food should be made and what she was doing wrong. Having grown up Muslim, this was the first time she had kept the fast and, because of that, she did not know how to cook the special foods to break the fast. Once he was asleep, she laughed, she'd slap him hard for revenge. These days, there were no bruises. Right now what was real was before her: the newspapers she had freshly pasted on the walls of their new room, the children they had just fed, the holiday foods they had just shared. A fresh beginning, as much as a return to what they had had.

What did family mean to Padma so that she was willing to do so much for it? Why was it worth it for her to stick with her relationships?

FAMILY AS CARE . . . AND ALSO *MORE* THAN CARE

I was not sure how to make sense of how Padma nursed her kin relations from bruised hopelessness to a new secure beginning. I was frustrated by not understanding how many women, like Padma, repeatedly invested themselves in their families even as they claimed that their families did not give them the support they deserved. At times, it seemed to me that Padma's reaction represented her acquiescence to patriarchy, or lack of awareness that she deserved better, as many feminists have argued about women in their critique of patriarchy and domestic violence (Haider 2000; Jejeebhoy 1998; Kakar 1978; Koenig et al. 2003; Mishra and Tripathi 2011; Visaria 2000; Visaria 2008). From this perspective, having a greater sense of empowerment and autonomy to make their own decisions would help women to create better family conditions that would improve their health, and their overall well-being.

But it felt dishonest to listen to Padma under the fan and then turn to my computer to write that she misunderstood her relationship. Sure, she argued that she was not getting what she deserved from her husband. But to characterize her family as insufficient did not account for the way that time and time again Padma showed me the other side of her kinship: her imperfect yet perfect Navratri meal, her husband carrying his lunch box (tiffin) to work, and her once jiggling stomach. By emphasizing the *process* through which kinship was lived in this community (Carsten 2004: 78), I shift the question from how families struggle to provide for their members, often failing (Cohen 1998; Das and Das 2006; Jesmin and Salway 2000; Palriwala and Pillai 2008; Rashid 2007b; Uberoi 2004; Vera-Sanso 1999), to why family is still meaningful to invest in, even if it does not provide for social welfare. As important as it is to critique the altruistic ideologies of family, I fear that to ask only what people expect of kinship in an environment where the political economic circumstances make it impossible to fully provide is to risk defining kinship only for its failures. In this chapter, it is my goal to explore the local forms of kinship through which Padma and other women lived their relationships, as much as they made room for changing what to expect from them (Menon and Shweder 1998: 179–80). I have written this chapter primarily from my intimate conversations with women and my observations of their family lives. The perspectives of the men that I describe here also deserve to be explored, but my limited exposure to their interpretations would risk speculation.[4]

In this chapter, I explore family relationships through care, which glosses closely with the Hindi word, *sevā*, or service. *Sevā* has gendered variations: for women, it encompasses the work of feeding, nurturing, cleaning, and rituals of deference (Menon and Shweder 1998); for men, it implies generalized support of relatives (Cohen 1998; Vera-Sanso 1999). In this sense, *sevā* is the stuff of general social welfare, but also the basis of everyday health: how well care is done plays a role in nutrition, hygiene, the effectiveness of health care seeking, the prevention of violence, and mental health. In Ghaziapuram, however, the link was made directly. As Durga put it, "Women's health is bad because gents cannot support (*sambhālnā*) them right. Men today are not like those of before who could support women."[5] With attention (*dhyān*), Durga and Saraswati explained, women could prevent their own illness as well as that of family members. This stress on care prioritized care as a primary preventive measure: "The person who takes care for her health, her eating, there will not be any problem."[6] The health effects of care could be built up in the body to sustain oneself for periods in life with less. As Saraswati explained, proper nourishment could build up strength in the body, such as strength that was reserved from a childhood of being fed well by parents that could sustain one later.[7]

In Ghaziapuram, affirmations of relatives were voiced through descriptions of their care, echoing the value in North India of care emerging through interdependent family relationships (Cohen 1998; Markus and Kitayama 1991; Marriott and Inden 1977; Ramanujan 1989; Vatuk 1995; Wadley 2008). Geeta and Saraswati talked at length about the ways their mothers had fattened them before marriage and took care of them even in the present, Geeta's mother traveling from distant Bihar and Saraswati's mother secretly visiting her in defiance of her husband's forbiddance. They remarked on husbands who came home regularly for lunch to spend extra time with them and the tender care that their husbands had given them after childbirth (Grover 2011). They pointed to loyal children who did the hard work of cooking, cleaning, and earning money in the present and who remembered their parents in older age (Cohen 1998; Lamb 2000; Vera-Sanso 1999). These were all examples of how family members had kept them right (*kisī ko sahī rakhnā*), done service (*sevā*), and gave support (*sahārā denā/lenā*), through feeding, providing, giving a home, the tools for life, and paying attention to the health of relatives. Women pointed proudly to their families to indicate their precious social anchor in this extremely unpredictable world.

I had assumed that women would have a utilitarian approach to kinship, in which they would pick and nurture the relationships that kept them best, making their families to build their security, both bodily and materially. Yet Padma and other women challenged the logic that I had unknowingly adopted from empowerment and autonomy approaches to health, which ask women to take more dramatic approaches to family neglect than I saw in Padma: approaches like refusing to take food last, rejecting domestic violence outright, demanding their own health care, and making household decisions (Haider 2000; Jejeebhoy 1998; Kakar 1978; Koenig et al. 2003; Mishra and Tripathi 2011; Visaria 2000; Visaria 2008). Tolerating a lack of care, in this general view, is evidence that women do not believe they deserve care from their family members.

Yet many women hope the "family might become a place for care" (Das and Das 2004: 44).[8] Women in slums in Delhi swallow pain and make space for "small hurts and reconciliations" (2004: 52). When facing great sickness and risk, women seek treatment options that make their social relations endure (Das and Das 2006: 201). Often embedded within behaviors of self-denial or endurance was both a means to shape their social relationships and bring themselves peace of mind. They found ways to complain—and thus push for change—even though their requests were not to radically redefine the family (Menon and Shweder 1998: 179; Raval 2009).

It became clear that women's complex map of relationships was taken as permanent: even as they moved away from family, left husbands, scorned bad family members, they still imagined themselves embedded within family. Relationships were not broken but tended to, even if unequally. While I had interpreted her relationship as abusive and far gone, Padma felt her relationship as a "dynamic and transformative process" (Carsten 2004: 78). She focused on the social processes of feeding, massaging, home managing, remembering, and persistent staying as the basis of her relatedness (Bodenhorn 2000; Carsten 1995; Lambert 2000). Yet unlike other studies that assert relatedness as social process, Padma and other women did not describe how their relationships were created, grown, or destroyed. Despite constant changes in household membership and tense rifts between relatives, relationships were not described as broken or ended. Rather, women charted how their relationships changed over time through care (or its absence) and longing (Trawick 1992b).

Women argued for the moral imperative to live for others in the face of unequal reciprocity, violence, and the difficulty of everyday survival. In other words, as much as women argued for their desire for a good, caring family, they argued that their dedication to family even through the absence of care showed their lack of attachment to their individual needs, and thus, their higher moral power. Living for others reflected on their individual self, even as it also contributed toward a shared, collective family honor (as I explain later, in chapter 2). The ability to sustain this care "through a thousand sadnesses or happinesses," as Mrinalini put it, demonstrated their powerful faith and closer proximity toward a selfless ideal. Deciding to abide by selflessness regardless of what they could count on from others enabled women to "harness control from within" (Krause 1989; Menon 2013; Menon and Shweder 1998: 182).

Women wrestled with this principle, interpreting both their ability to care and their endurance of others' lack of care to argue for their strong selves. Perhaps part of their tension in living for others was due to the contradictory, ambiguous expectations of different kin positions (Cohen 1998; Trawick 1992b). It was certainly expected, anthropologists show, that particular kinship positions (like daughter-in-law, or widow) were more vulnerable to neglect (Cohen 1998; Das Gupta 1995; Lamb 2000; Menon and Shweder 1998; Seymour 1999) and that acting outside family wishes (like through love marriage) could break the bonds that entitled one to care (Chowdhry 2007; Derne 1995; Grover 2011). Nonetheless, vulnerability seemed to show up in all sorts of life positions, some that fit these expected kinship patterns and some that did not.

So I draw on what I was able to learn, the process of kin relations in the small everyday processes, like those with Padma lying in the dark on hot days. This scale illuminates how women's criticism of their families can be central to their investment in them, rather than a symptom of their families' impending dissolution (see also Menon and Shweder 1998: 179). My focus on everyday acts articulates how women's feelings were conflicted and their acts of affirming relationships were creative, making me hesitate to describe patterned kinship processes (contrast Carsten 1995; Lambert 2000). In a setting where families have so often been condemned for their shortcomings, it was in the everyday that I could understand the nuanced ways in which women found their imperfect families meaningful. Therefore, my analysis here is less concerned with the specificity of kin positions than with showing how women made their relationships meaningful in spite of the numerous challenges they faced in keeping them intact. My goal is less to describe the "who" of family and more the intimate question of "how." While all the women I knew explained what they should be able to expect from their families, the political-economic insecurity and the emerging new family forms in slums meant they often had to improvise on patterns that they knew of, but were not quite their reality.

I begin by arguing that though women might have wanted care from their families, they did not construct care, or love, as an assumed symbol of kinship (i.e., Bear 2007: 170; Trawick 1992b). They concentrated instead on what their continued ability to care for their families indicated about themselves. Women resolved their serious questioning about their family members' negligence by asserting their relatives' capacity for caring and by strategically trying to pull them closer. In cases when they received insufficient care, they demonstrated to themselves and their families that their care continued without attachment to what they received in return. Finally, in cases when women made individual family decisions (such as to leave a husband or make a love marriage), they reconstituted their decisions as social (Mody 2002). Somewhat ironically, as they sustained their families through fragility and violence, all the while women sustained—

and affirmed—their individual selves. This embodied struggle to "maintain the domestic" (Das, Das, and Das 2012) reveals women's efforts as social and spiritual mental health strategies that enabled them to do caregiving work that sustained their family members and aspired to create a social world that sustained them as well.

"THE BIGGEST WEAKNESS IS THAT OF THE FAMILY": WANTING, BUT NOT ASSUMING, CARE

Mrinalini and all of her children loved to get her three-year-old grandson, nicknamed Appu, to dance for them. After feigning shyness, Appu caved to their demands and eagerly spun around, tapped his foot, and then only after a few moves, he quit. His uncle (Mrinalini's son), exaggerating sympathy, asked, "Are you tired? Okay, I'll massage your legs," and playfully put on a serious expression to massage his legs in the way a daughter-in-law would to her mother-in-law. Appu's mother, Leela, smirked from where she was working. Appu hopped over to join one of Leela's younger brothers taking a bath in the opening of their room. The younger brother laughed at him as Appu poured the water over himself with glee and then he turned to soap up Appu. Leela smiled and rolled her eyes as she explained to me that Appu already had two baths today—indulgent in a place where collecting water required so much work. Appu came toward Mrinalini with a film of water over his skin and a huge smile on his face. From the other side of the room, another of Mrinalini's children tossed a towel for us to dry off Appu. In his little croaking voice, Appu stated simply, "Powder," to advise his caregivers of what he wanted. Mrinalini responded with great melodrama, "Oh, hero [movie star] wants powder—okay, we'll put powder on hero!"

Their family delighted in Appu's act, but their dramatized reactions spoke of a less endearing subtext. To Appu, the delight of taking a bath, using powder, and being massaged was limitless—and watching him act out his limitless expectations delighted his whole family as well. They did not mind giving him whatever he wanted. In truth, everyone wanted family to care for them as endlessly as Appu the hero, but they all knew that later he would face what they had, that family care most always had its limits.

As a child, Appu was entitled to a larger share of family nurturing (Seymour 1999)—whether his requests for powder or for so many buckets of water. As he grew older, like other children in low-income families (Seymour 1999), more would be expected of his contributions to care for others in the family—like Leela's sisters, now teenagers, who had taken over their mother's cooking and cleaning responsibilities; and like Leela's unmarried brother, who was now the primary income earner for the family. Women like Leela, who were married, could not ask for all the powder they wanted— instead they spent their time feeding their husband's whole family, if they were in a joint family (Menon and Shweder 1998), or maintaining their household by themselves, if they lived in a nuclear family, as was common in communities like Ghaziapuram (Haider 2000; Unnithan-Kumar 2003).

Leela also represented the broader lack of care that young daughters-in-law face: she was now recovering from TB, because her health needs had been so neglected in her husband's family (i.e., Das Gupta 1995; Ramasubban and Singh 2001). Yet many women were comforted by the fact that one day they would be in the position of Mrinalini, with grown children who take over the family responsibilities, supervising the giving of care rather than being embroiled in it all day long (Menon and Shweder 1998). After this peak of security, both men and women faced vulnerability in their older age, depending on whether their children chose to support them or not. Many older parents in low-income households simply try to continue contributing income and to appear emotionally stable as a way to ensure that they continue to receive care (Cohen 1998; Menon 2013; Vera-Sanso 1999). In this pattern well known to women like Leela and Mrinalini, beneath the umbrella of mutual care that the family represents is an understanding that the amount of care they are supposed to give and what they will receive will vary throughout the life cycle. Part of why this model is accepted is because of an understanding that by giving care over time to one's family, eventually one can expect to gain status in the family and receive more of it oneself (Lamb 2000; Menon and Shweder 1998).

All of this talk of care, however, was incongruent with recent research that increasingly questions how much families are a place of care,[9] pointing particularly to families living in urban poverty (Cohen 1998; Das and Das 2004; Das and Das 2006; Jesmin and Salway 2000; Rashid 2007b; Roy 2003; Vera-Sanso 1999). South Asian feminists have long asserted a

similar position, critiquing "the presumption that altruism is the governing principle of family relations" (Uberoi 2004: 292). While the family
form in South Asia has always been evolving, these researchers capture
how low-income urban women increasingly break off their marriages if
they do not provide or if they find themselves vulnerable to being left
(Grover 2009; Grover 2011; Jesmin and Salway 2000: 693; Parry 2001;
Rashid 2007a: 116). As women may escape physically abusive husbands,
they are often forced to leave behind children, so that sometimes women
may end up with multiple children in different places (Grover 2011). With
fewer shared assets and the growth of the wage economy, family members
engage in charged negotiation over how to define their mutual obligations
and the division of shared resources (Das and Das 2004; Jesmin and
Salway 2000; Palriwala 1993; Vera-Sanso 1999).

Ghaziapuram, like other poor urban communities, had predominantly
nuclear families. (Maitra and Schensul, 2008, report a rate of 70 percent
nuclear families in their Mumbai study.) But because of the stigmas of
leaving husbands, secondary marriage, and living without a family network (no matter how far), women were too sensitive to talk frankly about
their families. I noticed that the genealogies that they shared changed dramatically in membership and sentiment over time (see the Introduction).
Because many households were small and interactions with extended
family were often unpredictable and infrequent, it was difficult for me to
know which family relationships were meaningful and which were social
markers to the world of one's family identity.

In these new arrangements, some of the old patterns of giving and
receiving care were disrupted. In joint families, senior family members
reward caregiving daughters-in-law with more authority over time (Menon
and Shweder 1998: 180), making it unclear to whom young women in the
smaller, likely nuclear families of slums perform their caregiving work.
Since marriages are often unstable in places like Ghaziapuram, it's not
guaranteed the sacrifices that many women make early in their marriages
ever amount to later security—or if upon remarrying women are thrust
into the same type of vulnerability they faced in their first marriages, but at
a younger age. As women's everyday caregiving work is done by themselves
or in conjunction with their husbands instead of with their husbands'
extended family (Haider 2000; Unnithan-Kumar 2003), questions arise

about whether their expectations of husbands change. While men have tra-
ditionally been expected to be the economic providers for their households
(Derne 1995; Grover 2011; Thapan 2009), what happens when economic
shifts in contemporary urban India make it hard for them to do so (Das
1994; Go et al. 2003; Magar 2000)? Since love marriages often result in
women's natal families restricting their support, it is not apparent how this
affects newly married couples living in poverty, with no other deeper
resources to depend on (Grover 2009; Grover 2011). These questions were
asked more frequently by women in the *jhuggīs* because of the way that
class shaped their intimate relationships (Parson 2010) in different ways
from wealthier women in Delhi. They were more likely to be geographically
distant from their natal and affinal families, more likely to be cut off from
natal family support because of love marriage, more likely to have to contribute financially to their households, and to have husbands frustrated by
their inability to fulfill the gendered expectation to provide.

Within the collective of their kinship, women often described themselves as alone and uncared for. Other researchers have documented how
women in slums have posited, "'You cannot rely on anyone, including your
own family these days'; 'no one cares unless you have money'; and 'this is a
new era, and we have to cope on our own'" (Rashid 2007b: 117). While
many women spoke of the weakness that family care embedded in their
bodies (Ramasubban and Singh 2001; Rashid 2007b), Durga pointed back
in the other direction as she stated flatly, "The biggest weakness is that of
the family."[10] Even if women did sacrifice to keep their families together,
researchers emphasize how they held firm to their sense of what they were
owed within families (Grover 2009; Khare 1995). Like other work which
has questioned the difference between ideal and actual families (Collier,
Rosaldo, and Yanagisako 1992), this body of research centrally questions
the degree to which family members actually care for one another. Yet this
it does not fully explain why women would seek care within their families
even if they acknowledged how rarely it was that they received any.

In order to understand this paradox, women's language of care and its
absence must be more carefully scrutinized. Women did not take care's
presence for granted. Though women wanted to find care giving in their
families, they hardly assumed they would be successful. Durga suggested
that a large reason why there was a lack of care was poverty. "In Delhi

there is very little money, there is no work, so because of the lack of work the whole world gets sick in the wrong way."[11] Despite their hard work, she said, families were unable to feed and clothe their members adequately. Scholars have argued similarly, demonstrating how poverty keeps people from nourishing each other through kinship. Or, as Lawrence Cohen (1998: 247) puts it, within families poverty keeps people from having equally adequate "*chapatti* counts," referring to family members' disparate stacks of the round flat bread.

Women were not the only caregivers within families. Saraswati some-times directed her young son to "go eat with Papa," and Akshay rolled up small bits of *roṭī* for him, and directed him toward the small container he drank from. Neetu's husband asserted his caregiving sentiments more gruffly, as he looked around their neon lamp–illuminated room to his sick wife and son with a broken arm: "no one takes their medicine on time here!" (He fell into a silent smirk when I asked if he did.) Jyoti's husband's chiding was directed toward health practitioners. To her statement that her body was in chronic pain after repeated visits to a private doctor, her hus-band cut her off: "He's a worthless doctor." At other times, Neetu's eleven-year-old son advocated on her behalf. He urged his father, hungry upon returning home, to stop asking his mother for food because she was sick.

Still, women argued that they bore a disproportionate burden of medi-ating the difficulties of their families. Extrapolating from the experiences of three hundred households across multiple low-income communities in Delhi, Das, Das, and Das (2012: 1669) explain that "Women related how their care-giving functions made them much more vulnerable to misfor-tunes, small or big, since they had to depend on others to help them tide over difficult situations." Or, as Geeta explained solemnly, "Women have to endure the sadness of everything. There are the troubles of children, the trouble of the home; there is tension, tension from all things. So women have too much trouble. They are so weak (*kamzorī*) so that if that they have eaten, if they take medicine, they won't even feel the impact. Their tension is too much. That's why nothing takes, no matter what you give them"[12] (see also Cohen 1998: 234). Not only were women tired from the work of caregiving itself, they were weighed down by the fears of how they would need to rely on others—particularly those who were not so dependable.

Across South Asia, women used the English word *tension*[13] to describe the stress of supporting their families, particularly when they bore so much responsibility on their own (Ramasubban and Singh 2001: 18, 21–22; Rashid 2007b: 118; Rodrigues et al. 2003: 1801).[14] Tension was described both as an illness and as dangerously putting women at risk for other illnesses (Patel and Oomman 1999; Rodrigues et al. 2003: 1799). All of the women I talked with described how their health deteriorated after marriage from decreased food consumption, increased work demands, domestic violence, and long-term health problems related to childbirth (see also in Kanani, Latha, and Shah 1994; Magar 2000: 15). From providing for and managing the troubles of family, women felt tension, and from tension they became weak. Contrary to being a place for receiving care, many women found their families a place where the demands for giving care proved exhausting. Saraswati complained that the needs of her family were limitless. Referring to her three-year-old whom she had tried so hard to wean, Saraswati said, "They just want to drink all of you up—no wonder we feel so weak (*kamzor*) all the time." She explained to Jyoti that she had tried to stop breast-feeding her son but, in the middle of the night, he still found a way. He dug underneath her nightgown and the next thing she knew he would be pulling her breast out to nurse. Though she knew he had needs, his unceasing demands were excessive. The weakness produced by these demands was severe enough to sit stubbornly, untouched by medicine or a hearty meal.

This tension had the potential to consume women wholly. On the bus, Saraswati's three-year-old sat on my lap, slapping the back of the chair in front of him to the confusion of all of the passengers around him, including us. We finally realized he was pretending to be the bus conductor who was trying to get the bus to move. His gesture exactly mimicked that of slick conductors who would jolt the driver to continue with the click of a coin on the wall or a stern slap on the seats loud enough to be heard in the packed public buses. After playfully encouraging him with a cry of, "That's right! Let's go!" the woman beside us turned to Saraswati and asked pensively, "Isn't it funny how children watch all of their surroundings so carefully and we don't even pay attention? Why don't we do that?" To the stranger, Saraswati answered with resignation, "When you're so worried about whether there is even salt at home, then you don't pay attention to anything. You just have your own tension all the time." Still in awe at Saraswati's son's playful excitement, the passenger agreed: "You're right, children don't have any tension at all. But that's all that we know." Women argued that managing their family lives left them chronically worried and distracted (see also Han 2011; Rashid 2007b; Yarris 2011). Women felt themselves snap in anger at their children or lose track of their daily responsibilities (Rodrigues et al. 2003: 1801). Other researchers report of a woman so immersed in worrying about her future after being abused by her husband that her sari caught fire from the stove she sat before (Ramasubban and Singh 2001: 25). In this sense, the scarcity of resources—from money to energy to negotiate endless needs—meant that women associated care with tension. Neither could they give enough, nor did they receive enough in return.

Durga maintained that the invisible hand of poverty was not the sole reason for the tension that threatened families' ability to be a place for care. Family members' failure to prioritize caregiving, she argued, compounded the threats to care posed by poverty: "Here, there are too many poor people, and there are no hard workers; there are drunkards. Only when money is saved from their drinking will their children get well."[15] Nearly every woman shared with me stories of families unwilling to help. In place of care, they felt neglect (lāparvāhī). Shaista argued that family fostered relatedness only when they personally benefited. Even the people who could help chose not to. Neetu said that, at the time of the demolition, although she told her whole family what happened, not one of her six brothers had offered to help. "I am the only one who is poor," she said, highlighting the effects of her family's stinginess. Her husband had even asked her not to go back to the village to visit her family, solely because every time she returned she was so dejected.

But even still, she described family care as equally likely to be present as absent. Neetu told her personal history through a spectrum of family relationships that were as neglectful as they were nurturing. She reflected that "as much trouble as my sister and sister-in-law have given me, so much did my first husband also give me. But the biggest things are the love that my mother and father gave me." It was almost as if her relationships were balanced on a scale, telling both the risk posed by kinship and the care it potentially offered. These reflections suggest that women's desire to make family a place for care may be grounded in what has been modeled for them or as a defiant refusal to replicate what was absent to them.

There was one final dimension that challenged the notion that women assumed family would be a place for care. In this final dimension, women's statements made it clear that they also must cultivate their family as a symbolic resource, even if they did not directly benefit from its care. Women depended on others, even if they were not dependable, so they could appear grounded within family to broader society. Even when women did not need family to care for them (because by necessity they had learned how to be self-sufficient), they needed to cultivate their family as a symbolic resource that was equally important to survival (Baruah 2007: 2103; Grover 2011). According to Neetu, women still needed family for their social welfare: the difference was that their family was a symbol that enabled them to care for themselves, rather than depending on care to flow from within (Das and Das 2004; Jesmin and Salway 2000). In addition to societal approval, women's choices are constrained by financial security (Grover 2011: 123).

In South Asia, women's overall well-being is tied to their ability to integrate within families (Menon and Shweder 1998: 160–61, 165; Seymour 1999). To the degree to which they could keep their families together, women felt they could also lessen their physical hardship. Keeping the family together, as shown in other places in South Asia, was key to keeping cognition in check for the elderly (Cohen 1998) and preventing "sinking hearts," physical sensations in the chest accompanied by worry (Krause 1989: 571). But in this setting, where, as Durga said, the biggest weakness is that of the family, they did not simply integrate into their husband's already intact joint family. Here in Ghaziapuram, with family far and their dependability tenuous, women had to be more creative in their making of families and more fierce in ensuring they kept the family unit together.

While many women did leave abusive households to start new families, they knew that they could only do this for a limited period of time. Padma put it frankly. In the middle of her husband's straying to his mistress' house, she was haunted by the fact that, after leaving another man before, she had no more cards to play: "I just keep changing husbands. But there is a child, then I leave. . . . Will I just keep doing this? Now I just can't do anything else. Besides dying, there is no other path ahead." Padma's despair arose not only from her sadness about her husband's distance, but also from the fact that, if she could not make it better, she had nothing else. The older she became, the oncoming decline of her fertility, and a reputation of being a woman who leaves conspired to limit the families she could make from here (Grover 2011).

In these critiques, women argued that, although they wanted to make family a place for care, they often felt this was an unattainable possibility. Like others who have grown skeptical of the enduring nature of kin bonds (Peletz 2001; Weston 1997; Weston 2001), women in Ghaziapuram knew from their own experiences that family would not always provide. In this in-between place of wanting care but knowing the obstacles to it, I argue that through their kinship practices, women aspired to enact an ethic of caring for others. Durga explained, "The person who helps others, that is the biggest spiritual merit. The one who lives for himself, he is not a man. The one who lives for others, that person is called a good man." And then as if to reaffirm the importance of her point, she repeated, "The one who lives for others, that person is called a good man."[16]

In a setting rife with negligence and tension, this sentiment was practical, allowing women to sustain their family lives even through periods in which they did not receive care. Ultimately, however, women invested meaning in providing care in spite of the impediments to it. Women hoped to provide care without seeking reciprocity; they argued that selfless giving cultivated their soul, even if they were left without care in the present. This required women to let go of their desires to ask for care in return and their fraught emotions about giving care when they felt weak and unable. Women hoped to give care without limitations—giving care even to those who might neglect them, caring without tension that it was insufficient, and caring without intention to appear familial to others. In so doing, women derived moral power from tactics that were ascetic (i.e., Masson 1976; Pearson 1996: 10) and from suffering a subordinate status (Egnor 1980: 14). Transcending and enduring physical pain are lauded in both Hindu and Muslim traditions, representing communication with, and ultimately reward from, God based on the principle that "endurance augments the sufferer's capacities" (Pugh 1991: 29–30).

Living for others was an ascetic practice, yet it was distinct from renunciation of the world entirely, celebrated within the Hindu and Muslim traditions. Rather than developing their spiritual powers in isolated settings free of the worldly desires associated with family and home life, women were guided by what scholars have described as an ideal self "of restraint and self-sufficiency" (Cohen 1998: 236) within their households. This orientation toward renunciation does not contradict the Hindu religious prescription to immerse one's reproductive years in promoting household prosperity. Rather, asceticism in this life stage is an idealized ethos to guide it (Cohen 1998: 237; see also Khare 1984). Holding on to restraint in relationships was the greater task of spiritual refinement. In so doing, it seemed that women could "harness control from within" (Menon and Shweder 1998: 182) by serving others while controlling their emotions (Krause 1989).

Here, I turn the attention away from how women give care to what the giving of care does for *themselves*, even though the ideology of this work is self-*less*. Even as women point to how their care makes them tense and exhausted, I argue that their interpretations of how they continue to provide it promote their mental health and cultivate their self-worth. Doing this allows us to see women's lives as more than failed exchange (i.e., Lamb 2000)—relationships that take and never give. Attention to complaint enables us to understand the ambivalence that is at the heart of South Asian kinship. Regardless of class or location, discussions of kin relations in South Asia reveal "constant allusions to betrayals of trust, infidelities, and the failure to live up to the high moral ideals of kinship solidarity" (Das 2006: 10).

Yet this ambivalence often is a way that, through care, people make claims about themselves. Selfless work had the dual result of nurturing their moral self and providing indirect communication to family members to change the terms of their care. Ultimately, these two types of effects—on relationships and on self—are intertwined. While ultimately their family members' behavior was beyond their control, sincerely performing their care for family members allowed women to decide how they felt about these acts and, through self-denial, offered the potential not just to transform themselves but also their family members (Egnor 1980: 14; Menon 2002; Menon 2013; Pearson 1996: 113). For women who strived for this goal of selfless care, it demonstrated their ability to be successful as wives and mothers (Das, Das, and Das 2012; Das 1976; Derne 1995; Donner 2008; Narayan 2004) and, at the same time, to do "the protection of their families" (Pearson 1996: 131). As a woman in Benares explained, "When you master yourself . . . [it] affects those around you, especially as you direct your thoughts and hopes and prayers toward them" (Pearson 1996: 199). Durga and Neetu's complaints about families that failed to look after their own reflected on their strength to believe in family despite this fact. At the same time, their complaints censored the individualistic behavior of wayward family members—whether violence, neglect, or lack of financial support—and modeled the care of their families that they hoped family members could grow into.

Here, I demonstrate how women struggled with their ideal to live for others. While they hoped to make a place for care through their selfless efforts, it was hard to ignore their nagging feelings of injustice about the lack of reciprocity. It was necessary to protect their individual needs, and to judge whether their relationships deserved their dogged efforts. For families could idealize care or even joke about it as an endless resource, as did Appu's family as they fawned over him, but they all knew that giving and sustaining care for their families was grueling and often left them weak (Bang and Bang 1994; Kanani, Latha, and Shah 1994; Patel et al. 1994; Ramasubban and Singh 2001; Ramasubban and Rishyasringa 2008). Women awkwardly balanced between their different selves. Their worldly selves needed to be immersed in family, cultivating a social self through which they were known to the world. Their health and wealth in this world depended on their actions within their families. Their tension was a sign of their ongoing negotiation to create a place of care and find faith in relationships' potential. However, to accept how often their family was not a place of care, women stressed what was lasting—selfless action that created merit, acceptance of all circumstances, and dissolution of their self and its needs. In this move, women found meaning in their persistent ability to care, regardless of their families' responses.

CARING WITHOUT RECIPROCITY

In the middle of Padma's struggles with her husband, she described how care was given in her family, "If Deepak's father [my husband] gets sick, no matter what he does, no matter how much he hits me, I am still there. If something happens to the children, then both of us [my husband and I] will look after them. If something happens to me, then no one will notice."

Padma contrasted the warm care that embraced her husband and son when they were sick to the care that receded when the same happened to her. As women described their care, they highlighted its persistence to protest the withered efforts of family. But equally insistently, women used their care to illuminate what they perceived to be the selfish behavior of their family members. Women elaborated how the suffering they experienced at the hands of their family demonstrated their own selflessness.

Many women looked toward their family members' selflessness with admiration. Saraswati described how her mother's care persisted in spite of her father's desire to punish Saraswati for her love marriage by exiling her in the present. Saraswati explained that when she and Akshay were in financial distress because Akshay had quit his job, it was her mother who offered them money. Saraswati argued that Akshay took advantage of her mother's generosity. Having spurned an arranged marriage to a wealthy woman for a love marriage to Saraswati, Akshay felt justified in his requests, she explained. But, in these circumstances, Saraswati said, her family did not really have to give anything. It was her mother's generosity combined with her respect of custom that pushed her to fulfill his requests. The only new clothes I saw Saraswati wear—other than the one sari she bought for herself—were what her mother had given her. Saraswati complained to me that she wanted to buy gifts for her mother, but that she could not because Akshay scrutinized any money spent outside their family. Saraswati described the ways that her mother had always been there for her since her childhood, sticking with her father after their marriage even when it became apparent that he had lied about his education to be considered for the match. Saraswati indicated the risk that their continued interaction posed to her mother after her father's prohibition of it. It was doubtful what her mother stood to benefit from continuing to engage with her. When she wanted to visit her mother, she sent me alone up her mother's street with explicit directions on how to recognize the house, making efforts to cover whatever evidence might indicate our visit. She grew increasingly worried that my missteps would be a big white sign revealing her mother's activities to her father should the neighbors catch sight of me. If her father found out, she warned cautiously, and then trailed off without having to complete the threat. Saraswati found in her mother an example of care that was as resolute in nurturing as it was unmotivated by personal gain.

In Saraswati's understanding of her mother's care, however, she left unmentioned her mother's conflicted loyalties. Saraswati's mother had mentioned to me her misgivings about her husband's choice of a match for Saraswati's younger sister—he was dumb and ugly, she said outright, no match for her daughter's intelligence and beauty. After Saraswati's younger sister ran away from that husband about a month later and showed up alone at the Delhi railway station, I no longer heard of visits from her mother. Saraswati represented her mother's care as boundless and compassionate to best approximate a model for herself. But she downplayed the mixed feelings that might be embedded in her mother's care, the frustration she might have felt toward Saraswati's father's choices or in mediating Akshay's unending requests for money, which were quite common in slums and frequently led to violence (Grover 2011; Magar 2000). By elaborating her mother as a selfless protector (Trawick 1992b: 169), Saraswati retained her claims to her care, but also made her mother approximate the ideal of one who lives for others, erasing her mother's doubts and needs that represented her individual self.

The obstacles to giving care were many. As much as many of Sunita's neighbors scorned her family decisions (see chapter 2), they still commented sympathetically on how her son repeatedly rebuffed their relationship. When I visited Sunita in her new *jhuggī* in the drawn-out days at the end of summer, she stumbled bleary-eyed from a nap to sit down on her front stoop. Recently she had a lot of pain in her legs: it had started at her foot then traveled to her knee and hip. With it, the pain in her back had returned. "I would get medicine for it, but when there is no money, what can I do?" she asked me rhetorically. She was flustered because her twenty-year-old son had hit a cement wall on his motorcycle and fallen off it a few days ago, scraping himself up and damaging the expensive vehicle. And this morning when he left, she said, he had left his phone behind, not eaten the *rotī* she made for him, not taken his medicine, and asked for two thousand rupees. "Where is that money supposed to come from?" she asked. He had just left his job. "And why was he roaming around at midnight?" she wondered with annoyance. "That's when he got into the accident—in Rajesh Nagar [a distant neighborhood], of all places. I don't know. He called me in the middle of the night. Tell me, can I come to get him in the middle of the night? How am I supposed to do that? Today he said he was going to Noida [an East Delhi neighborhood forty minutes away] to try to get some kind of computer work there. Who knows?" She paused her fretting and returned back to her body, where she started. "You know, this boy is the cause of my illness. Because of him, there's tension, and because of tension, there's illness. I would not be like this if it were not for him."

Sunita narrated her pains to emphasize the suffering that she incurred in the process of her continued care. He was asking her for money that she did not have to give, when at twenty—and as the sole provider—he should be providing for her. But in this economy, it was hard for men to provide, leaving many of them idly "passing time" or "waiting" in unemployment (Gooptu 2007; Jeffrey 2010). She did not express an outright expectation that he give to her, but instead focused on the poverty they shared—there was no pot of money from which they could draw. She described him as carefree and unattached, despite the fact that they had no money at home, leaving his phone so that he could roam freely without her contacting him. As she mentioned her doubts about the far-off locations where he wandered, she questioned the supposed aims of these journeys, guessing that in fact they had nothing to do with providing the resources they needed. In her narrative, she was at home, waiting for him, worrying about him and their shared sustenance. He was interested in his individual adventures.

Sunita mentioned that she was also hurt—literally—by the way that he cast off the nurturance that she could provide. Sunita articulated how her care was tied to his well-being, feeding him and ensuring he took his medication, even as he pushed these away before he went off to work. But she described her care as continuing despite his rejection. Even if he traveled in places where she could not help him (as he did again in another accident a month later), she imagined that she might be able to help. In her narrative, the fraught undertaking of caring for him left her drained, settling into her legs and back. Sunita had reacted to her son's refusal to accept her care by embodying it as painful tension. By naming her son as the cause of tension without naming his neglect outright, she highlighted the care she continued providing for him despite his insolence. From next door, Geeta whispered to me that Sunita was exaggerating the story to elicit pity from anyone who would listen. Sunita's representation of her continued care was not aimed directly at her son, but instead was aimed at affirming her abilities as a mother, which were constantly under attack.

At times, however, women demonstrated their stubborn care to their delinquent kin through the way they embodied family tension (Wikan 1987: 359). Saraswati's aunt Urmila greeted us with a fake smile when we met her at her small store, a shack that remained in the middle of the demolished slum. Slowly, she unraveled her awkwardness. That morning she had readied her children for school quickly and made food for her husband. But he was angry and refused to eat it. In this anger, she did not want to eat anything either. She knew that her husband would eat food outside instead of at home. In the aftermath of her husband's anger and violent rejection of her nurturance, Urmila's appetite disappeared. In fact, it had been several days since she had eaten anything. Saraswati nodded in sympathy. She pronounced that "Men are the cause of 80 percent of women's illness." For both of them, their appetites would evaporate at the onset of tension with their husbands. At meal times, women served everyone but themselves. Over time, the effects became cumulative—Saraswati, her aunt, and Padma all gradually lost weight. Riddled with tension, Saraswati explained, she was unable to give her body what it needed for health. By giving her body the right attention, she knew she could be healthy. But distracted by the tension caused by her husband, she did not eat the right foods, she did not eat at the right time, she did not attend properly to symptoms of illness—hers or anyone else's (Snell-Rood 2015).

Women commented on how their appetites had faded of their own accord, unlike the deliberate appetite suppression of fasts directed toward auspicious or purifying ends (Pearson 1996). By stressing how their bodies were beyond their control, they highlighted how their bodies acted of a different will, thus diminishing the tie between their personal interests and their bodies. To a certain extent, the bodily separation that they emphasized showed their detachment from the physical world. Like Gandhi's hunger strikes and renouncers' refusals of food, the disappearance of women's appetites halted normal action. To keep on eating as their husbands did would have indicated life as normal. But every time their appetite disappeared, the absence of routine physical needs removed them from the realm of routine daily life. Their bodies' refusal to be normal highlighted husbands' mistakes, even if they never admitted to fault. In its place, women's continued care of others was a stark reminder to indicate husbands' embarrassing lacks. Appearing powerless in front of neglect can paradoxically enable a woman to "achieve power through the strength of her passivity" (Ewing 1991: 144).

At other times, women's silent protests faded and they began actively to search out doctors. Saraswati sought out a doctor in the lane behind hers, then in another adjacent neighborhood, and then, frustrated with that doctor, she hiked further to a recommended doctor in a lower-middle-class area. Akshay began accusing Saraswati of spending all of their money extravagantly on her imagined illnesses, tracking doctors from all over the place. Though it was fine for her to express her feelings and thoughts through the body (Kostick et al. 2010: 542; Krause 1989: 569; Pugh 1991: 26), Akshay argued that she did this too much, dismissing her complaints as self-indulgent (Chua 2012: 225; Menon and Shweder 1998: 164–65; Wilce 1995: 932), morally weak (Krause 1989: 569), and self-centered (Krause 1989: 570). Saraswati argued back that she had to seek out care for herself because he did not take her physical needs seriously. Her experience was not unlike that of many other women in slums whose health needs were dismissed by family members (Das, Das, and Das 2012; Das and Das 2006; Ramasubban and Rishyasringa 2008). Sometimes the medicine worked, but mostly it did not, she said to me in private conversations. She followed Geeta's earlier line of argument: under such constant stress, her weakness had accumulated to a point that no treatment could cure it. Despite what Saraswati said about the control she could enact over her health through her expertise (see chapter 4), in practice she alternated between anger about her health and then cynical resignation. Meanwhile, I felt sympathetic when Akshay complained that Saraswati's frustration kept her from settling on any regime at all—when would she really take medicine consistently? As she refused the medicine from one doctor after another, Saraswati demonstrated that the tension at the root of her illness could not be simply dismissed.

In earlier examples, Saraswati's detached, diminished appetite had made the point of her persistent care obliquely. But at other times, Saraswati used her body as a badge to openly critique Akshay's neglect and reaffirm her self. Coming in from filling water, Saraswati changed out of her soaked clothes to put on her husband's pants, the only dry clothes around. She pulled the waistband out to show her diminished body from its once plump state to both him and me. "When I married you," she said with comic anger, "I could not even fit in these pants—and now look!" Saraswati's intentional displays of her sickness had the dual effects of critiquing her husband's lacks and foregrounding the persistent care that she left in their place. Speaking through their bodies (Chaturvedi et al. 1993; Husain and Tomenson 1997; Nichter 1981; Trollope-Kumar 2001) was one way that women communicated the intensity of their care to their families. In this way, their families could know all they received, but also the moral fiber of women so determined to give (and so demanded to give) that it literally hurt. By emphasizing her bodily suffering as a condition so serious it was beyond the control of her or doctors, her persistence was illuminated in deeper relief, to show the strong soul embedded within her weak body. He left her with tension, but she continued serving her family food, finding medicine for herself because others did not, and hauling water with her stick-thin frame. Her persistent caring, unmoved by physical discomfort, was permanent. Her refusal to acknowledge her health seemed to show her detachment, or *vairāgya*, as she remained "indifferent to illness, pain, loneliness, sensual temptation, material goods, uncertainty, fear, and even insults" (Khandelwal 2004: 26). For Hindus, detachment toward earthly life increased their powers, showed their moral high ground, and brought them closer to God. Saraswati used her continued caring to show that her husband's actions could not thwart her own ethic of nurturing family life.

Women were unhappy with their family members' rejections of their care, suffering not just emotional hurt, but violence, lack of material support, and failed health. Yet here I focus not just on their critique of their family members, but also on how women responded with their sustained ability to care, which articulated their own strength. Women held their care in relief to their suffering to indicate their detachment from physical pain and dedication to the ideal of selfless care. By showing their suffering in ways that emphasized bodily separation—a body shrunk away from a waistband, a stomach uninterested in food—they marked their bodies as sacrifices for their families, rather than conditions they had chosen or ones that could be healed. Women idealized a care that was selfless and enduring, like Saraswati's description of her mother who gave despite the risks, with no chance for reciprocity. But even while admiring others' care, it was also possible to understand how giving care might just as well result in crises of faith. For though women asserted their ability to continue to care, they were not always sure that their families were worthy of receiving that care.

CONJURING MEMORIES OF CARE TO SUSTAIN RELATIONSHIPS

It was Padma's back-and-forth with her husband that confused me the most. Her reactions to him extended across a spectrum—from anger, to frustration, literal hurt, apathetic resignation, and warm attachment. Through the spectrum, Padma's attachment seemed to wax and wane. Even as she expressed her anger or frustration, she also deliberately tried to bring closer family members who had grown distant. Repeatedly, she returned to what they shared in relationship, how they were able to care for each other. She used the history of her relationship to anticipate what could be expected, imagine what potential might be held, and accept that relationships had good times paired with bad. The fact of relationship was taken for granted, so few people described their relationships as permanently broken or grown from nothing. Yet the process of sustaining relationships through numerous social, economic, and emotional obstacles was a struggle. Additionally, because people's family lives were intrinsic to their very personhood, when relationships seemed to falter, people were left with grave doubts and worry. Women's faith in their relationships demonstrated the hope they had for them to transform from a less caring present. As much as women sought to transform relationships, they avoided ultimatums that framed their relationships teleologically. Even as women oscillated in their feelings about their relationships, how did they persistently pull them back together while their relatives pushed them apart?

Saraswati could not understand what had happened to her husband these days, she told me over and over again. When he had asked her for salt on his food and Saraswati had added some with a spoon, he accused her of being a foreigner (*angrez*), too good to use her fingers like Indians did. He threw his metal plate filled with food at her. This was the time that she had been spending a lot of time with me. It seemed he feared that her loyalties were shifting. He accused her of being too friendly to a male neighbor for whom she had hauled water since he had no family to help and punished her with a slap. They fought over money he thought she had hidden from her work. She did not understand why Akshay kept constant surveillance of her daily behavior. From the time of their love marriage, when they had looked after one another despite rejection from both of their families, it had faded to this.[17]

There were days when Saraswati told me she was ready to leave Akshay after his months of unemployment and greedy grabs at her salary, and then she stayed. One day, after listing the places where he had hit her, explaining her frustration at him, exhausting the options of where else she could stay, and urgently exploring the logistical matters of leaving her husband, Saraswati suddenly paused. She suggested that we go to Bir Baba's grave (*dargāh*). It was in a dusty part of the city where the multilane highway thrust ordered lines amongst large auto showrooms, fancy new office buildings, large sandy patches and pockets of *jhuggī*s. She had come three years earlier, asking for a husband. Within the month she had found Akshay. Since then, she had been trying to get him to return with her. But whenever she asked, he said he did not want to go. When she explained all this to the caretakers of the tomb, they were silent but they nodded in understanding. Saraswati said that Akshay did not need to worship God as she did. He only needed to honor (*mānnā*) her words, to consider her perspective. In her current moment of frustration, she recalled her past journey to pray here. Though I had concentrated on the literal hurt, frustration, and practical considerations of leaving, her thoughts now seemed anchored. She no longer asked why Akshay had hit her, or what she should do, but instead how he could be pulled back closer. Now she gathered strength to pull him back in by asking him to honor her words. Her desire was tempered, asking for him to affirm their relationship through listening rather than asking for his care. This was enough for now.

In the months that followed, Akshay continued to pull away. When Akshay's violence continually resurfaced, Saraswati recalled how it mirrored the violence his mother had inflicted on her when they stayed with his family in the village for a few periods of time. She could not think about it without tearing up. There in the village, she told her former neighbor Jyoti and me, they made her work all the time—she had to cook for everyone, do all the cleaning, and do the water buffalo work of never-ending milking, cleaning, and the dung collection and patty making. "I worked all day and no one would ask anything after me, just about the work, and cursed me that it was done wrong," she said. There, with his family nearby, Akshay beat Saraswati so hard with a piece of bamboo on her shins that it could no longer bleed. She indicated the two black scars right on the bone. Though she could not even move, Saraswati said, no one had asked after her. All of this occurred, she said, when she was carrying their future grandson. She felt that around his family, he felt emboldened in a terrifying way that evaporated his capacity for caring.

Back in Delhi, she had a feeling that her relationships with Akshay's extended family haunted her in the present. As with her suspicion at the saint's tomb beforehand, she mentioned that, since they had been married, she felt that Akshay had dramatically changed. His violence was far from the increased intimacy with which they had begun their relationship, like many contemporary relationships (Derne 1995; Seymour 1999: 174). Her origin story to their relationship painted them as starting in Delhi to get ahead, escaping families and community scrutiny. But now he, like so many other men entering love marriages in low-income communities (Grover 2011), was enforcing gender rules that she thought she had avoided.

Eventually, she told me that she was convinced that her mother-in-law had paid to have magic done on Akshay so that he would no longer respect her, eventually dissolving their marriage.[18] These days, he threatened to leave her, saying that his parents wanted to arrange a second wedding to someone who was wealthier. Saraswati was not surprised when her in-laws made her work so hard; it was expected that mothers-in-law extract hard labor from their daughters-in-law (Das Gupta 1995) and abuse them verbally (Jeffery, Jeffery, and Lyon 1989). But I suspected that her feeling that they were driving the wedge between her and Akshay pushed her diatribes about the treatment by her mother-in-law to such hostility. (She was so enraged that Jyoti called me later, concerned, to make sure that Saraswati would not actually enact revenge on her mother-in-law.) Saraswati paired their abuse of her with her physical endurance. She described how she fulfilled her family obligations for care—from household work, to feeding, to bearing sons—with full awareness that she was not only being neglected, but that his family was actually trying to break her and the family she and Akshay had grown. Saraswati affirmed how her endurance contributed toward making their family a place for care and used memories of Akshay's past care to distance him from the violence he embodied when with his parents.

Saraswati paired her persistent frustration with continued efforts to reclaim Akshay. She secretly sought to exorcise their influence—literally—by appealing to three different specialists to undo the magic her mother-in-law had inflicted. She enlisted our work together as a front to let her travel all over Delhi to get her work done. At the healers' different offices, she explained that she had been having problems with her husband for a long time: "There is a lot of fighting, a lot of hitting, and it has not always been this way." Now, she explained to them, her husband was talking about going to the village and then making another marriage from there; even more, his family was really bad toward her. Healers suggested different techniques, but they also required expensive rituals that made Saraswati suspicious of their motivations. So she left the work undone. She was no less convinced that he was controlled from afar, simply less convinced of healers' skills to ameliorate the problem. By seeking out healers, Saraswati suggested that Akshay's behavior was anomalous, outside of the spectrum of personhood that she knew of him. She declared that his behavior in the present could be reformed, restoring Akshay to the man she had married.

Saraswati persistently brought up how much Akshay loved their son. Even at the height of tension between Akshay and Saraswati, the only thing that would calm her three-year-old's terrified squeals from a bath was when she passed him wrapped in a towel into his father's arms. Akshay carefully and quietly dried him and their son was transformed. Akshay's capacity to nurture Saraswati in the past and his gentle care for their son in the present were evidence to her that he could be the same way to her. The few times she contemplated leaving, she decided not to when she mentioned how much Akshay loved their son. In September, a month and a half before I left, she asked me to stay over for Karva Chauth, the twenty-four-hour Hindu fast women make for their husbands' long lives. Akshay had left mysteriously for the village and now was not answering his phone, even though she called him repeatedly.[19] As much as I emphasized to her how Akshay was not caring for her now in an effort to protest his treatment of her, she went ahead with the ritual. In all of these cases, Saraswati identified the discrete forces that pulled away at Akshay: his jealousy of her increased independence as she started working, his mother's embodied influence through magic, and his growing suspicion that he could "do better" and remarry. Saraswati's various efforts were aimed at re-investing Akshay within their family personhood. She wanted him to honor her words so that she could be understood. As she prayed at the Bir Baba temple, Karva Chauth, and visited healers to exorcise his mother's influence, she tried to restore holism within their relationship.

These pointed efforts were punctuated with daily doubts that indicated Saraswati's awareness of her individual self. As she repeatedly considered the possibility of leaving, she recalled her own needs, her desire for safety, and questioned the benefits of her efforts. It was all perfectly encapsulated by Saraswati after a fight with Akshay over contributions and demands on shared finances. They had both just recovered from weeks of severe illness, and debated the recent purchases each of them had made on their medicines, food, and clothes. Saraswati asked me to buy her a suitcase. Laughing, Akshay said flippantly, "She's going to Haridwar."[20] "What, are you becoming a *sādhū?*" I asked. She smiled and affirmed that she was ready to join the ranks of ascetics who renounce their worldly ties—from wealth to family—and wander to develop their spiritual power. By constructing the *sādhū* path as escape, Saraswati reversed the widespread belief that the spiritual work of the *sādhū* is most difficult and revered. For Saraswati, to leave the world of family was to renounce the true test of faith—disregarding her individual needs constantly in service of keeping her family together. Saraswati located the true dissolved individuality of the renouncer within the task of sustaining her family. Becoming a *sādhū*, implied Saraswati, would be vacation.

By tracing women's anguished process to affect their relationships, I demonstrate that women saw their relationships as neither solely failed nor entirely nurtured. They understood their relationships to be always changing, in some ways that were beyond their control—like the influence of extended family or the tension of poverty—and in other ways that were not. Here, the struggle of living for others was keeping faith in their relationships. Akshay had been, and could be again, a caring husband with the capacity to listen to Saraswati. As an extension of her own familial personhood, Saraswati was optimistic that he had the capacity to again recognize what they shared. Women balanced their critique of family members' behavior with actions to actively bring family members closer or more passively wait for them to change (see also Han 2011).

Women's agonizing assessment of how to transform their relatives' behavior was exhausting. At times they broke, exploding in anger or violence at stubborn relatives who never relented in pushing them away. In these ways, women did not accept their family members' behavior at face value, but situated it in terms of their expectations of what it could be. While they sought to pull their family members more closely to their family responsibilities, women asserted their familial selves. In affirming their capacity to act, they recognized their individual selves. But in keeping faith in their relationships, women asserted their selflessness, living for others even if it was at the expense of their selves.

MAKING WHOLENESS THROUGH THE BREAKS

It took me a long time to realize how many times family relationships could not be sustained. I gradually learned that nearly every family had stories in which they had made significant choices to change their households to lessen conflict. Along with their husbands and children, Geeta and Mrinalini left abusive brothers-in-law to start their own households. Saraswati left an alcoholic father to live in Delhi on her own. Durga, Padma, and Neetu all left behind marriages that had been arranged by their parents and were bad or abusive; some of them also left children who were not allowed to accompany them. Along with their children and husbands, Shaista, Jyoti, and Sunita left extended family households after unstable employment led to family falling-outs, inducing their current chronic financial insecurity with even less kin to hold onto. Geeta and Durga were moderately estranged from some of their children. That left only one family without a break in their family story—Mohan's—and after I left, it seemed that his son had split off from their household permanently.

Although there is plenty of evidence that households change over the course of the life cycle (Kolenda 1968; Uberoi 2004), the silence in which these transitions were shrouded was striking (Derne 1995; Grover 2011). When Saraswati had argued "no one will tell you the truth about their families,"[21] she spoke to the gap between women's eagerness to talk about family and the painful decisions hidden in their family histories. Secretive and ambiguous in the personal histories they shared with neighbors, family, and myself, women often left controversial questions open—how and if husbands were left, the children they may have been forced to leave behind, and what reliance they might have on neighbors because of family difficulties. Their silence spoke to women's fear that their neighbors would misinterpret them (see chapter 2), but also to their difficulty in admitting how living for others sometimes exacted too many costs.

I was drawn to account for how women made these choices. Indeed, as I saw Saraswati, Neetu, and Padma consider their relationships' insufficiencies over several months to the degree that considered the logistics of leaving, it seemed they were practically weighing how they benefited from relationships with how they were harmed by them. I had guessed that their complaints about the insufficiencies of their relationships were evidence that they would leave them behind to make better ones. In the end, I realized that it was impossible to answer this question (see also Raval 2009: 506). The reasons that family members gave for leaving—from abuse, to insufficient financial support, to cruel remarks—were also often there in the present. My preoccupation with what finally caused leaving led me to imagine more fractures than women saw themselves. Rather, as decisive as they acknowledged leaving was, they affirmed the continuity of their kinship. Women embedded themselves in family even as they made extreme changes to the way they lived their kinship—from whom they lived with to how they interacted with them. Instead of seeing what they might be hiding in their silence, it was more important to listen to how they modified the meaning of family during the course of adjusting their relationships.

I had been in Delhi for about a month when Durga insisted that I come with her to her Punjabi village to meet her family. In the *jhuggīs*, Durga usually sat alone on her cot, depending on her neighbors and me to massage her when she ached all over. But despite what seemed to be occasional loneliness, Durga was deliberate in pointing out the importance of her family when she went to the village. Over the course of those three days, we visited two of her three sons and their wives, her grandsons, her sisters-in-law at her affinal home (*sasurāl*), her sisters at her natal home (*maike*), and even two of her youngest daughters-in-law's (*bahus*) brothers. All had mutually exchanged joking accusations that the other had not made enough effort to visit more. She related warmly to her family, exchanging stories about how they had looked after each other, braiding her grandson's long hair every morning into its protected Sikh topknot, and comparing dental decay with her older, smaller sister. She had searched endlessly for the right gift to bring her favorite grandson, a four-year-old, scouring the market in Delhi and the rest stops on our trip for the candy-covered fennel that he loved. He chewed it halfway and then spit it out midbite. Durga barked at him in fake disapproval and then looked at me and laughed, "He's so bad (*itnā shaitān*)!" She then turned back to him to resume her pose of disapproval, her arm held as if she would slap him. When he indeed gave her his child's punch, she broke into an endless cackle of delight. For every visit that Durga and I made, her grandson stayed with us, eagerly perched on her lap as we bumped over the country roads. As we set off on the bus to Delhi after the visit, Durga laughed at how she had to trick her grandson in order for us to escape. She had convinced him that we were getting him a treat. She chuckled when she saw his face as he realized he had been fooled. It was sad, she pointed out, but that was the only way he would let us go! As the bus pulled away, she turned to me and said, "Now you see what a big family I have." Then she paused and smiled, asking me to confirm: "Is it big?" It was, I answered. "And people in Delhi say that I do not have anyone. Now you know."

As the bus reached the highway, she continued in a different tone. Right after mentioning her family pride, she continued, "All they do is take, take, and never give." As much warmth as Durga felt for them, she had mentioned to me that part of the motivation for this visit was to empty out her village bank account that her sons were not shy to draw from. When we had gone to the bank with her youngest son, she asked me for my purse and stuffed in the large stacks of bills that she had withdrawn before handing it back to me. I wondered whether this was meant as performance in front of her son, to indicate her diminished trust in him, or merely the convenient size of my bag. Not wanting anything to do with it, I immediately handed the purse back over to her and told her to keep it until we returned. She had paid for her youngest son's failed trip to work abroad, thousands of rupees per visit on gifts and on her sons' clothing, and they gave her nothing in return. Even after her youngest son's previous trip abroad, he was still unhappy, she said, and that is why he was asking me now about how to migrate to the United States for work.

Durga pointed out that it was not poverty that prevented them from giving in return. For all of these reasons, she declared, she lived in Delhi, in her own house. Durga observed, "Today you must help yourself. Everyone knows what today's children are like. If I have money, they will help me. If I don't, then even the children from my own stomach won't help me." Sometimes mothers are in the structural position where their vulnerability or desire to protect kin forces them to give (Cohen 1998; Vera-Sanso 1999). But though Durga needed their help for some things, when it came to financial support she did not. In the years since she had left, she had become quite successful. In the aftermath of demolition, she could rest with more security than most. She patted her bosom where she kept her money and smiled: "This is the Punjab National Bank."[22] Durga was well endowed, but she kept on with bonds that made her insecure because she did not want a life without family, no matter how little help her family gave her.

Back in the *jhuggīs* it was true that women whispered about her not having a family. Some women said it was a shame that her sons were so unreliable, but what could she expect after leaving them at such a young age? Durga told me that she had left her husband some thirty or so years ago, when her youngest son was four. Just as Saraswati and Padma had used their injuries to indicate what they had endured, so did Durga. In her kitchen, she pointed to scars to indicate chronic abuse driven by alcoholism and mentioned how her husband had told her that she was so ugly that he would not look at her. Durga was like other women who left who could not bring their children with them. Durga said that she came to Faridabad, an industrial hub nearby Delhi, where she lived with her parents and developed her midwifery skills. This was all that she mentioned of her leaving.

Through silence women obscured questions of agency that public questioning exacted. Durga mentioned her husband's actions that had caused her suffering, leaving her own agency in leaving vague. Though Durga had been forced to leave her children behind, for Durga, this move had not meant extrication from family, only redefinition of her involvement. Her continued investment in her sons' lives, even to the extent that they could prey on her, conveyed that her actions were for others. By commenting persistently on their family ties, women contended that they had always lived for others and discounted neighbors' suspicions that they had left of their own accord.

Though some of her neighbors held firm to her leaving, Durga held firm to herself as a mother. In the present, as she talked to me, Durga used kinship terms to refer to her now late husband as "your uncle" to indicate an intact relationship. (Though I was never clear on the exact history, like Padma, she had continued to occasionally be in touch with her husband after she had left for Delhi.) She carried on with regular visits to her village relatives, including in her affinal home (*sasurāl*), and kept track of her grandsons' exploits from afar. As a well-renowned area midwife, Durga had other means to attest to her kin credentials. Through her work, she often modeled caregiving that kin had shirked. She instructed women on proper caregiving within the family, often conveying messages that others could not. She pointed out to pregnant women experiencing bleeding that their husbands needed to temper their eager desire for sex throughout the pregnancy. She sensed the subtleties of daughters-in-law's physical conditions by suggesting, "Have a few more *roṭīs*, you look weak." Indirectly critiquing family politics of care, she added to their mothers-in-law, "If you want your daughter-in-law to give you a strong son, you better start giving her a glass of milk every day, not just tea." Others did not deign so openly to judge others' household distribution of food, but because her general advice was sought, she took broader liberties in the topics she covered. Durga warmly received the title of "ma" that Padma and others gave her, indicating the number of local children she had delivered. So even as she stayed protected from predation in her Delhi home, Durga remained firmly within her family and those of others.

In all of these ways, Durga sustained her family and her identity as entrenched within family, even though she was far from her kin. Durga had backed away from her family for her own protection, guarding her bank account, establishing her own home, and cautiously considering her youngest son's impending requests for funds. She felt that giving in endlessly to her sons' requests did not constitute selfless giving, but could only be foolish placation. She argued that her limits on giving were not a refusal to share. Rather, because their desires were insatiable, her giving never brought them any closer to their happiness. (It was never clear to me if she thought that they felt justified in their requests because of her long-ago leaving.) Durga's practice of family highlighted the dangerous desires intimately within the family. Unlike the desires of neighbors, Durga did not draw strict boundaries to protect herself from her sons. Her boundaries were more fluid, indulging some of their requests and not others, engaging enduring love enacted through tempered caring. As frustrated as Durga felt with her sons, she seemed drawn toward the pleasure of being with her grandson. I was not sure if the attention she lavished on him (over and above her other grandsons) was an attempt to experience her own sons' childhoods that she had missed in moving to Delhi. The fact that she continued to give in spite of their predation was a clear sign of how she persisted in living for others from afar.

Though Durga was flattered by the title of "ma" given to her locally, she did not consider her relationships through her midwifery practice to constitute an equal, alternative family. Even still, to a certain extent, Durga moved closer to her ideal of selfless care amongst her clients. Perhaps because her self was not invested in these relationships, Durga could exercise her true freedom to articulate how relationships really should be without investment in her personal stake. It was true that neighbors sometimes mentioned she was on her own to imply her tainted reputation. Durga's repeated mention of her "big family" disputed these rumors and represented the family that she needed because, as Neetu said, society would not let her live on her own. But regardless of the rumors about Durga, her reputation for her caring work was far greater. It mattered less that the people receiving her care were nonkin than the fact that she so reliably gave care. To the people to whom she was known, Durga's living for others was most enduring beyond her family. Durga had pointed to what people remembered (chapter 2) as the true portrait of their character. Perhaps she meant that it was only outside of family that one could give truly without interest for one's self.

I was often struck by the fact that as extensive as women's families were—like Durga's "big family"—and as surrounded as they were by hard-working neighbors and their children, women seemed alone. On countless visits to Shaista's family, they pulled out an album barely held together at the corners to show me or neighbors pictures of their far-flung family members. Brandishing carnivalesque photos, Shaista's husband Aamir divulged the exciting life of his brother in Uttar Pradesh, who, as a karate black belt, organized competitions in front of huge crowds in which he and others would be run over by motorcycles and trucks. With warmer tones, Shaista pointed to pictures of her relatives, cousins who were engineers in Delhi and South India, her sister living in Karachi, and her older sister who was a principal of a school in their Uttar Pradesh town. Shaista remembered them all fondly, and sometimes grew silent and looked off into the distance before she walked away suddenly from the conversations she engaged in. To explain, her twenty-two-year-old son Adil pointed to the one framed picture in their house, that of Shaista's brother, that stood on the TV. He excused her by explaining that she was crying; she missed him. Before they came to the *jhuggīs*, Shaista's brother had financed Adil's education in a private school. In a time when they had little money, Adil explained, he came to school in sandals, instead of the regulation black shoes. After being berated, Adil was so embarrassed that he stopped going to school. Shaista's brother (Adil's uncle, *māmā*) eventually found out and was incensed. He bought Adil a nice pair of shoes and swiftly returned Adil to school, having taken away his excuses. Not long after that, Shaista's husband fought with his father so intensely that they came to Delhi (see chapter 2). These days, Adil admitted, they hardly visited, and he had been a child when he had last seen some of their family.

The few visits in the interim had been strange. When Shaista's youngest sister last came to visit, Adil said, Shaista treated her with the unbounded affection she embodied when she opened their photo album. Her son Adil had taken them all over the place—to the Red Fort in Old Delhi, shopping in the maze of markets at Chandni Chowk, everywhere! Then they asked when they would go to Shaista's house. Shaista immediately suggested with excitement, "Why not now?" "She did not know," Adil explained to me now in front of Shaista, "that it would be strange if they did that. She was just thinking that this is my little sister; why not?"

But Adil knew that they could not take his mother's middle-class family members to the *jhuggīs*. He pulled his mother aside and said that they could not do it. He explained to me, "our house did not have a bathroom or water, it was a not nice house, and it was right in the middle of all of the *jhuggīs*. They would think it was really strange, just like it was strange to you the first time you went there." So he turned to them and lied, "Actually, our house is three hours away by train so it will be too hard for you to get there." After insisting a few times, her family finally relented in their request. Adil noted it had been hard to deny the awkwardness. In a later visit, Shaista's brother had summoned Adil to come visit him in his hotel room in the Crowne Plaza. Adil laughed as he explained that, to avoid the humiliating request to be hosted at their home, he had managed to disappear under the pretext of using the bathroom. Eventually, through some network of information, Shaista's brother's family appeared at their home in the *jhuggīs*. Neetu, whose *jhuggī* was opposite theirs, recalled the story independently and explained how sad it had been. The women of the family had come with their *dupaṭṭās* (scarves) placed squarely over their noses, their gesture insisting that the *jhuggīs* must smell. Shaista and Adil had understood their initial impression, but explained to me that as offensive as the *jhuggīs* might have been, gradually it had become home to them, and they realized that some of the people were good. Left unasked was why their family could not share the same understanding.

"But how are you poor and they are not?" I asked Shaista, trying to connect the dots. "Because uncle would not work from the very beginning!" she said with indignation, "and he used to beat me all the time and pull my hair." "If he did not work from the beginning," I asked, "then why did your parents arrange the marriage to him?" Both she and Adil were silent. Then I saw the hint of a devious smile on the corner of their mouths. I suddenly exclaimed in realization, "Oh, you married of your own accord, just like an American!" Adil chuckled, saying he had wondered when I would finally understand this silence. Adil explained that he knew his mother's love marriage had been one of the reasons that her family had withdrawn their support (see also Grover 2009; Grover 2011). Shaista was aware that in her family's narrative, she was the one who had threatened their family through her independent choice. Yet now, as she professed the continued importance of her family, she indicated all of the ways that she had held their family together. It was she who had remembered them and kept them in her family, even as they seemed to drop her. Through pictures, Shaista and her family enthusiastically told a story that showed their genealogy, linking them to "the sense of a past and a future in the present that such continuity of family would give them" (Bear 2007: 265).

In her moments of disappointment, however, she contended that their circumstances had in fact always been unequal. From her initial narrative that her poverty was caused by her irresponsible, but chosen, husband, she now posited that her unequal fortune had deeper origins independent of her own choices. She explained that her mother had died when she was a newborn, and her father's second wife had always been partial to Shaista's younger sister over her. She was the only child who had not been allowed to finish her education. Articulating this part of her history, Shaista pointed away from her marriage—and the independent, desiring self this implied—and asserted that individuals had always been recognized within what should have been a whole family. In this way, she diminished the unstated accusation that her marriage fractured the family. In fact, it had been fractured all along. That she still nurtured these relationships through this original inequality, even if only through narration, indicated how selfless her continued dedication to family was.

Shaista placed less emphasis on where many people felt her selfless dedication to family shone through most clearly: in her sons. Her five sons' admiration and support of her was clear. Though residents rarely had kind words for the family practices of their neighbors, it was remarkable how many families looked with admiration toward Shaista's relationship with her sons.[23] Without prompting, they set out food and utensils, washed dishes, helped her with cooking, and kept an eye on the time to know when they could begin collecting water.[24] Once, when Adil's younger brother ignored his mother's instructions, I saw Adil slap him. Adil reinstantiated his mother's authority, underlining the cohesion that she had long established. From coming to the *jhuggīs* with so little, she had two sons in leadership positions at a local factory and the other three now studying in private schools. In comparison to the harsh battles of discipline that I saw enacted in other households, Shaista commanded respect even from her diminished height and often preoccupied, melancholic moods.

In spite of the fact that she and her sons had made their family an enormously successful place for care, Shaista seemed haunted by her extended family, who appeared commonly in conversation despite how rarely she saw them. Her most common remembrances were completely disconnected from her accusations that she could not rely on them for help.

Shaista said that her family would surely give the best interviews on the health questions I was asking because they were educated. She too would give an interview, she asserted in response to my request, but not in front of her sister when she was finally visited. She mentioned how hard it was to go to her father's funeral a year ago because she felt ashamed of her poverty. What was the point in going, she remarked, if she knew they would say bad things about her? And though she had raised her sons to say *namaste* politely in greeting, her brother's daughters were not the same. She implied that they must think her unworthy of a *namaste*. As eager as she had been then to share what made her proud of them, now it was Shaista, making *roṭīs* after a long day of work, who said occasionally, "If you don't have money, no one is your relative, but when you have money, everyone calls you their relative—they visit, they're happy to see you, everything."

The degree to which this feeling of rejection shook Shaista was evident in its reverberations in all of her interactions, even beyond the family. One of the first times I visited them in their new room after demolition, she welcomed me warmly. After an hour of conversation and our mutual assurances that we would remember each other even after I left in five months, she paused to ask me if I was just selfish (*khudghraz*). After having extracted my work from them, would I fail to recognize them?[25] As I listened to her conversations with neighbors, repeatedly she commented to them that their wealth must have prevented them from visiting. (Often these neighbors were of the exact same class.) Having been promised the warmth of family before and seen how it faded with others' awareness of her class, Shaista envisioned further opportunities for rejection.

Shaista's eager display of her educated family showed how much she respected education and class. She was concerned with demonstrating they were not just "of the *jhuggīs*" but valued education in ways that others here did not (Bear 2007). They were not the same, and her family, as they stood in the pictures, proved so. But at the same time, her repeated comments about class critiqued the insincerity of others' sentiments of attachment. The other women of this chapter were bold in arguing what they could and could not count on in their relatives. Shaista minced no words when critiquing her husband's shortcomings, but when it came to her extended family, she remained more vulnerable. It seemed she feared further signs of her exclusion from her family, despite the efforts that she extended within her own home indicating otherwise. By continuing to remember her family fondly and extending invitations without hesitation (even if Adil wanted to protect her from the potential pain that followed), Shaista let go of her doubts and reimagined her family's sincerity.

Though it was Adil who always called me to extend his family's invitations to visit, in my last month of fieldwork I heard Shaista grab the phone from him urgently to order me to clear my schedule: her older sister, a school principal, was coming to town with her daughter, a graduate student just like me. I would understand them because they were educated, she said eagerly. In the long day I spent with them, I had never seen Shaista smile so much. Her sister and niece seemed to sit as comfortably in their room as anyone else, despite the bathroom Shaista's family shared with a floor full of neighbors and a space no larger than their former *jhuggī*. They enthusiastically exchanged gifts brought for each one of each other's family members, told stories, and ate so much that we all had to nap afterwards. Behind all that I was sure floated tensions and difficulties. But here in this moment, it seemed less important that Shaista had struggled on her own for so many years in the *jhuggīs* without the help of her family. Here, it was possible to have family despite how different they were, and to stay close even if Shaista felt betrayed in some ways. As she considered the critique that her family likely leveled against her individual choices, Shaista had steadily countered with her critiques of her family's own individualized splintering: preserving their own class, giving only to receive reciprocal benefit, and being fickle in their affection. To sustain her hope in her family in spite of these critiques demonstrated that, for Shaista, the meaning of being embedded in family was greater than any benefits it accrued.

The work and sentiment with which women sustained their relationships demonstrated they were making something much more meaningful than what they got in return. Durga and Shaista's stories reveal that, underneath the predominance of family ideology, women frequently made decisions that were motivated by their individual needs. They answered the critiques of their families and neighbors by elaborating the shortcomings of other family members that had initiated their decisions and questioned the sanctity of the family whole they were accused of breaking. At the same time, both of them found ways to keep their families together in spite of the series of cracks in which they may have played a part. Durga financially supported her sons from afar and stayed connected to the family group that she had long ago chosen to leave for her own safety. Shaista remembered her relationships even at a distance, highlighting her similarities when presenting her family to others, even though she was conscious of the judgment she faced from within. For both, they invented new forms of interaction that allowed them to be immersed within family, while still protected from it (see also Raval 2009). It was possible to give and live for others without having others take your life. Durga had felt betrayed by predation, and Shaista by rejection. With Durga's ample funds and Shaista's loyal sons, neither of them needed all the family members they sought to sustain themselves. Nonetheless, they sustained their families to sustain parts of themselves. And they also sustained their families with the hope that perhaps one day their families would reciprocate what they had modeled for them so persistently. For both Durga and Shaista knew what difficult work they had done to gain the pleasure that they had with their families.

THE WORK OF SUSTENANCE

With as much as women shared with me over time about their families, I often felt frustrated with their continued attempts to sustain their families. When women's resolute certainty to guard their own security faded into efforts to wait for their families to improve, my own exasperated feelings found echoes in my conversations with academics and public health advocates who feared that, when it came to their families, the women I knew in the slum "did not know what was good for them." In our disappointment, all of us assumed that women needed to be able to ask for more, to learn what they were entitled to. And when it seemed that their families could not hear them, the right action was to leave them behind. Sustaining families, in this view, was nonaction, if not women's passive acceptance of poisonous relationships. And women's gestures of self-denial seemed evidence that they accepted their diminished status—that abuse was acceptable, that they deserved to eat last, that others owed them nothing. It was as if we took Durga's biting commentary that "the biggest weakness is that of the family" as the only commentary on the family.

Yet we need to account for women's starkly divergent, strongly worded summations of kinship—as tension-causing, nurturing, harmful, worthless, abusive, loving, worthwhile, and distant—as a whole mosaic, rather than as disparate parts. By placing women's conflicting perspectives side by side, a different portrait emerges that resists defining kinship only through women's hopes that it be nurturing. Although women consistently argued that they wanted care from their family relationships, they felt that family persisted even if care was absent. Instead the coherence of women's feelings about family is found in their expectations of *their own* kinship practice. In looking toward themselves, they articulated the ideal to live for their families without attachment to their own individual needs. Surely they had such needs and they deserved to have them fulfilled, but women realized the limitations in asking and waiting for more. Although some researchers have emphasized how women cling to their families to secure their social welfare, here, women's attachment to family in the absence of care demonstrates how women make their families meaningful for deeper reasons that affirm their lasting inner well-being in addition to their immediate needs.

To guide them as a model for their ideals, women gave examples of family members who continued to care for them despite obstacles or lack of personal benefit. In their own families, women remarked that the suffering they experienced as a result of their family members' shortcomings (to provide or to be peaceful) was evidence of their own persistent ability to give. At the same time, they backhandedly protested their family's negligence by demonstrating their continued dedication toward family, even at their own expense. If they were willing to ignore their own individual physical needs for the collective, they suggested, so too should their family members also control their individual desires to live for others. While women's declarations of their weakness are evidence of sexism's weakening effects, they also must be considered in light of spiritual values that ask whether physical vulnerability is evidence of moral endurance. To split the mental and physical health of women living in poverty can obscure the resources they cultivate for well-being, to ignore that what disabled them had the power to embolden them (Khare 1995: 148). Unlike public health approaches, relational well-being stressed caregiving within relationships as the outcome to be measured and health status as a manifestation of that outcome.

Though women saw themselves as firmly rooted in family relationships, they described how their relationships shifted over time due to the influence of outside people, the tension of poverty, and the emotions of their family members. Women like Saraswati and Padma felt that living for their families required them to withstand the good and bad alike, patiently enduring at times and actively intervening to expel bad influence at other times. Women wavered between emphasizing their family members' capacity to care and at other times doubting whether their family members had grown too distant and individualized to reenvelop them within the family fold. While women concentrated on recreating a family whole, even through tepid reformatory steps, they described themselves as acting individuals whose prayers, massages, feeding, and staying demonstrated their determination. This morality was embedded in everyday life, but it was deeply reflective and fraught (cf. Zigon 2009: 260). Women struggled to survive within their families, defining their autonomous needs for health care, sustenance, and freedom from violence that gender equity advocates and researchers articulated. Yet, in addition, women stressed the survival of their family as a whole as its own unit that needed caregiving and protection.

There were, however, times when women decided that family relationships were beyond recovery. In these cases, women refused others' accusations that they had willfully abandoned family through recasting their circumstances as unlivable conditions created by their families. Instead of constructing themselves as living apart from family, their stories, photos, and continued involvement commented on different techniques of making family beyond ritual, interaction, and shared social welfare. Women's purposeful display of their family demonstrated their family as a comment on their status and their gender (Bear 2007). But even more so, women longed for the pleasure of relationships that their individualized decisions had potentially forbidden—in Durga's case, contact with her sons and grandchildren; in Shaista's case, interaction with her siblings. Both women argued that even their families' predation and negligence could not deter what they wanted: to be in family, even if it had to be on their own terms. In so doing, they cultivated a social resource that had little to do with their health security—resulting in no caregiving or improved livelihood. Instead, being in family provided gendered meanings of security.

It seemed no coincidence that the morning when things seemed to have finally turned around for Padma and her husband was the morning that they fed the neighborhood children together. This act was not unique to them, but a routine way that Hindus accrue religious merit (Khare 1992: 208). Her husband explained that children are like gods—*kumārīs*—so feeding them in the same way they fed the idol of the goddess Durga at the temple, they are also worshipping the goddess Durga. Padma came over to tie a red string on my wrist and smear a red *tikka* on my forehead to mark the performance of the religious act. She muttered to me that her husband had been on her case all morning about tying the string in the wrong way. It was her path here that spoke to the larger significance of this moment. Her ribs still hurt a little, even though the bruises had faded. Her neighbor still ran into their new room to intervene in their fights. But it was that she had sustained her family, and that today their hands gave the food together—that was what was important. That was what had sustained her. And if she had to slap him in his sleep to show she was right, so be it.

2 Let the Dirtiness Go

MANAGING RELATIONS WITH NEIGHBORS TO PROTECT
THE SELF

Durga often seemed to me to sit at the social center of her ten-thousand-person community of *jhuggīs* in Delhi. As a local midwife, dealer of pharmaceutical and Ayurvedic medicines, and known fertility expert, there were few times when Durga was not being sought. Neighbors leaned through the shutters of the store in her front room to buy the foodstuffs that crowded its sagging shelves. When she was cooking or uninspired to get up, in her carefully arranged small three-room home, Durga hollered to the closest person to hand over the goods from behind the counter and deposit their money in the plastic basket under the portrait of Lakshmi, the goddess of wealth. On sunny winter days, you could find Durga on her fold-up cot right in front of the *jhuggī*. Crowds of female neighbors often gathered around her cot. Their conversation turned like a contoured landscape, dipping into valleys of quiet gossip and peaking into jagged spikes of laughter at Durga's crass sexual comments. Inevitably, Durga looked around her to notice that the crowd pushed the bounds of comfort for her cot, and she swiftly barked: "Do you think you can fit the whole world on my cot?! You better have five hundred rupees to pay me back when it breaks!" So many crowded intimacies seemed evidence of Durga's hopeless intertwinement with her neighbors and they with her.

Figure 3. Sense of Place. Photo by Mayank Austen Soofi.

But on the day of the slum's demolition, Durga argued that, as much as she engaged with her neighbors, all the while she had been carefully drawing boundaries to protect herself. That afternoon, in her old neighbor Neetu's new rented room, Durga and Neetu had it out about how much they hated their former neighbors. They recounted stories in which a local woman used her sexual relationship with a local policeman to become an area leader (*pradhān*); and how another neighbor financed her family's move out of the slum with her prostitution. "You did not know that, did you?" Durga asked me, as if taunting me. "All that time you thought you could just be friendly with everyone, sit wherever you want, say hi to whomever you want. But you don't know people here like we do," she said. "That is why I am not sad today," she continued. Durga waved her hand and said forcefully, "Let all of the filth (*gandagī*) go. Let it all wash away. I am happy—this is not a sad day." A few hours after her *jhuggī* had been bulldozed, her suit soiled by her neighbors' tears, Durga sat and celebrated the fact that now it was all gone.

If someone like Durga was so clearly intertwined with neighbors, why did she celebrate their separation as a process of purification?

"YOU DON'T KNOW PEOPLE HERE LIKE WE DO": NEIGHBORS AS SOCIAL SUPPORT OR *GANDAGĪ*?

Both before and after Durga's cleansing, time and time again I saw women distance themselves from the neighborly relationships in which they appeared to be so deeply embedded. Were these women in denial about the fact that they relied on their neighbors every day—or was I seeing neighborly interdependence that was simply not there? In the past few decades, as Durga was building these very relationships, international public health, epidemiological, and social scientific researchers were examining how these relationships might be vital to community health, particularly within low-income communities with few other resources. Studies tracing the health of large cohorts over time found that mortality and morbidity were positively affected by social support, social cohesion, and social integration (Berkman and Syme 1979; Berkman et al. 2000; House, Landis, and Umberson 1988; Kim, Subramanian, and Kawachi 2008; Knox and Uvnas-Moberg 1998). These same social measures were associated with decreased stress and depression (Israel et al. 2002; Lin and Dean 1984; Manuel et al. 2012) and improved mental health (Almedom 2005; De Silva et al. 2005). The relationships Durga had characterized as *gandagī*—those at the neighborhood level—promoted trust and shared norms that facilitate cooperation, stability, and safety (Kawachi et al. 1997; Putnam 1993; Sampson 1999). Researchers demonstrated how, particularly for women in low-income urban communities, social networks play an essential role in mutual care in the absence of economic resources (Gonzalez de la Rocha 1994; Marris 1962; Mullings 2005; Mullings and Wali 2001; Sampson 1999; Stack 1974). Furthermore, these relationships offered protection from stigma and a sense of belonging (Fullilove 2004; Mullings and Wali 2001).

In South Asia, neighborhood relationships have assumed more salience as urbanization has increased and caste relationships have evolved. Economic researchers highlighted how neighborhood social relationships are essential for poor rural migrants to obtain jobs (Mitra 2004; Singh 1976). In contrast to the more rigid social codes of rural South Asia that prescribe interaction between groups, urban neighborhoods—and slums in particular—are characterized by immense social diversity within close quarters. Anthropologists and social theorists argued that neighborhood relationships bridged this diversity and helped to manage conflict (Datta 2011; Nandy 1995; Ring 2006). In slums, where family sizes are considerably smaller than in rural areas, women like Durga spent considerably more time with her neighbors than in rural settings. They worked cooperatively for water collection and child care, as well as shared information on health resources (Chandola 2012a; Singh 1977; Unnithan-Kumar 2003). Neighbors could help slum residents to obtain ration cards—the key to receiving numerous state services, as well as a resettlement plot in the event of demolition (Chandola 2010; Srivastava 2012). In some cases, neighborhood relationships in slums have been the basis for collective grassroots organizing for improved urban amenities and more secure claims to housing rights (Appadurai 2002; Chatterjee 2004; Harriss 2005).

But as much evidence shows people living in slums to be embedded in neighborly relationships, Durga's accusation of social filth was justified. For women in contemporary urban South Asia, social interaction provokes more specific, bristling questions. For middle-class women and poor women alike, being in public to pursue work, daily errands, or education meant being at risk for harassment and slander (Ali 2010; Chandola 2010; Chandola 2012a; de Neve 2011; Fernandes 2006; Ganguly-Scrase and Scrase 2008; Khan 2007; Kumar 2001; Lukose 2009; Marrow 2013; Saavala 2010). Respectability was significant, impacting not only how others saw their families (Chandola 2010; Derne 1995; Khan 2007; Marrow 2013), but also, for unmarried women, their long-term marriage prospects. Interacting with women who were seen as sexually or socially loose would potentially make women more vulnerable to violence in the open areas where they traveled (Chandola 2010: 156; Chandola 2012a). Poisonous rumors could result in ostracization (Jesmin and Salway 2000: 694). In response, in slums, many women chose to isolate themselves from neighborhood networks rather than bear the social consequences of public scrutiny (Haider 2000). Daily insult had the capacity to build over time to eventual explosion, given the right political circumstances.

Ethnographic examinations of the aftermath of communal violence in Delhi and Mumbai in 1984 and 1992 have asserted that everyday life in Indian slums is structured through tense interactions between neighbors that lay the foundation for violent events (Chatterji and Mehta 2007; Das 2006; see also Tarlo 2003 on the Emergency in Delhi). All of this indicated that those contours of conversation around Durga's cot had finer topographic features than I had understood.

So then how did Durga do it—how did she get help for the things that her achy knees prevented her from while not getting stuck in the dirt? Or, in other words, could women get what they needed in a social setting where neighborly assistance is vital yet not endanger themselves in the process? In this chapter, I show Durga's social techniques as a moral process through which she tried to make herself through her own action (Foucault 1981; Laidlaw 2002). Women suggested that, in an urban setting crisscrossed by social distinctions of caste, class, religion, regional background, and power, the identity and intentions of their neighbors were always unclear—whether they had known them for twenty-five years, as they had in this neighborhood, or whether they had known them for a week or a month, as they did with their new neighbors after demolition. They explained that behind the outside appearance that their neighbors presented to the world were insides that contained their true intentions. Women argued for the importance of constructing a particular appearance for self-protection, but they pointed out that others' appearances could disguise unfounded moral claims or dangerous desires to subvert others for their own interest.

In order to protect themselves, women suggested that they must know the insides of others to judge risk and build boundaries to fortify themselves. Thus despite the deep, enduring engagement produced by their intimately shared lives and daily interdependencies, women's persistent cultivation of boundaries to protect themselves made the bonds between neighbors endure only tentatively. As women evaluated each other's insides, they articulated a theory of right action that gave their neighbors and themselves the agency to make morally sound choices. From equal disadvantage, they pointed out, women's differences in the present emerged from their individual moral decisions. Though I had heard Durga's sentiments in the midst of demolition, it became clear in the months afterward that the threats to which she spoke were not extraordinary like demolition, but supremely ordinary.

By counterposing women's narratives about themselves with their daily neighborly interactions, I demonstrate women's contention that within their deep and frequently abusive social engagement, they maintained their individuality. They held this individuality as a key part of their inner well-being. In their repeated quests to know others' insides and protect their own, women asserted the moral accountability they had toward themselves, the need to consistently cultivate their own selves, and the significance of the actions that they choose in everyday life to shape their insides. In this way, women's ephemeral relationships challenge the tendency to examine community relationships only in terms of their outcomes: the benefits and dangers they pose to health. I argue that the proof is in the *gandagī* too, that the difficult process of negotiating these relationships had their own effects, enabling autonomy, cultivating safety, and avoiding stigma. When I look back at the negotiation, Durga's intertwinement was less tangled than it first seemed. Durga's hands reached out to her neighbors—but her hands were not as open as they initially appeared.

PLAYING WITH APPEARANCES

> The distinctions between the holy man and the bum are
> subtle. (Khandelwal 2004: 160)

Nothing was ever as it seemed. Lying on her cot on a winter day, Durga patted her big stomach and said to me and to whomever else was in earshot, "Five children have come from this! I am sixty years old, an old lady (*būḍhī*)." She pulled up her long shirt (*kurtā*) and patted her belly in front of everyone. One much younger neighbor slickly followed with a few grim jokes that agreed with how fat Durga was. Then Durga sternly ordered me to lay down even as she roughly pulled me down herself onto the cot with her, wrestling my head into her bosom. "Oh, she's thinking that I am her boyfriend!" she said to the small audience. "Give me a kiss like I am your boyfriend!" She laid my arm out over her, to further dramatize me advancing on my imagined boyfriend. Padma, on the side, curved her hand over her stomach as if it were expanding gradually, smiled and cackled, "That's what happens next!" The other women laughed. Trying to dispel the sexual connotations of their joke, I said with panic but little thought, "No, that's not what happens!" Padma replied, "Oh no, that's what happens in India, in America, everywhere," continuing to make the gesture as everyone surrounding us howled in more laughter. Later in the day, Geeta warned me to be careful about playing around with Durga and Padma in public places. They were not good people, they talked about dirty things, and, she implied, it was not such a good idea for me to be seen with them.

There was both pleasure and danger in playing with the question of what truth lay inside the appearances they so carefully constructed. They positioned my own self-constructed appearance as one more instance of what everyone in this neighborhood did. Durga physically exposed herself as respected mother and grandmother whose body was a sign of her honorable familial contributions (i.e., Lamb 2000). Jiggling her belly, she could not be further from the neighborhood rumors that she in fact had a boyfriend—and some less-than-grandmotherly exploits that went with those rumors. She, however, implied that beneath this motherly appearance was more of the same: the tired, hard-worked reproductive system of a dedicated mother. (On another occasion, she called it an "old bag" that did not work anymore.) For the past few months I had exerted my own respectable outside in a setting where my white skin referenced, among other things, the scantily clad white showgirls popularized in recent Bollywood movies. I explained that I had a boyfriend far away in the United States, in part to be honest and in part to show that I too had aspirations for a committed, heteronormative future distant from the white skin they were familiar with. In the present, I wore Indian clothes, mostly avoided direct eye contact with men, and feigned innocence about all sexual matters whenever possible. Durga answered by wrapping me with her own allegations of what lay beneath my surface. She expanded the scope of the imagination beyond where we sat now to where I might be with my boyfriend—and the ways that I might not be so far from Durga's alleged exploits and the busy belly she now displayed. In India, in America, so said Padma, it was always the same. They knew about me, they implied mischievously, regardless of what they knew I was actively putting on for them.

Women told me that, particularly in Delhi, you could never know who people "really were" (Srivastava 2012). Saraswati told me how here in Delhi she had helped a man who had come to her door and explained that he had had nothing, not even food or family. She told me that she had helped him out because she felt bad for him. Then she came to find out later that he was lying. In fact, he had much more than he admitted, but having never seen him before, she had no way of verifying who he said he was. Women like Saraswati drew attention to the specific uncertainty of the urban context while their stories echoed religious folklore about the unreliability of exteriors to judge others' characters.

In many Hindu narratives, there was a similar sentiment that was explained through stories in which "lowly entities are always turning out to be something more than they appear" (Shweder et al. 1997: 148). These legends showed that essentially all people were equal and their circumstances should not be judged: inside their raggedy clothes was a valuable spirit. Yet alongside the optimistic assertion of a stranger's potentially kind inside was another set of warning tales, that of the false guru. In these narratives, the false guru promises viewing (*darshan*) of God but really knows nothing of God; he feigns spiritual purity while stealing the money of his followers and breaking his public vows of self-control (Khandelwal 2004; Narayan 1989). In both versions of the narrative, it was clear that engaging with someone on any level brought into question who the person really was.

As for the responsibility of discerning the true identity of potentially fake gurus, the burden of discrimination fell on the disciple to tell the difference in who people were (Khandelwal 2004: 142). This was neither straightforward nor easy. For disciples, first of all, "the relationship between interior and exterior is multiple and shifting." Strange behavior—like drinking, for instance—could indicate detachment from earthly distinctions and desires as a real guru should have, or it could indicate attachment to earthy desires as a false guru would have (Khandelwal 2004: 172). What, wondered women during the course of everyday life, was the difference?

Second, "the interior may be deliberately hidden by the exterior" (Khandelwal 2004: 172). Gurus could act out greatness, just as advertisers transform products, as one guru warned. "The more advertising you do, the greater a thing becomes," even if it started off as "nothing much"

(Narayan 1989: 133). Even disciples could be indicted in maintaining false fronts, pretending to see a God that they do not in order to avoid appearing a fool (Narayan 1989: 152). These difficulties were "combined with the lack of institutional controls" over religious authority and instruction to make "fertile soil for deception" (Khandelwal 2004: 172). To fail to discriminate risked falling prey to a false guru who could cause harm (through trying to take money or exert control), cast a path away from God, and spin unlucky ones into his "webs of deceit" (Narayan 1989: 152). In the end, to save face, you would have to become a collaborator in spreading the lies of his powers.

The folkloric archive makes clear that there has long been tension about who is who and that the stakes of investing stock in someone are high. Even though women rarely drew explicitly on these folkloric narratives, their emphasis on the distinction between inside and outside made use of this broader cultural imperative to grant trust to strangers tentatively. As Sunita put it, "Here, people will say one thing, but they're different. What is inside [*andar*] people can be different from the outside." Their inclination toward distrust was furthered in their particular social context. As I mentioned in the introduction, the contemporary moment in India poses new uncertainties about who is who—opportunities for mobility were as much a vehicle of potential personal transformation as they were vehicles to only *simulate* changed status (Osella and Osella 1999; Srivastava 2010; Srivastava 2012). People were aware that as much hype as there was about mobility in contemporary India, there were as many people who remained stuck where they were, unable to fulfill the dreams they were sold (Das 1994; Fernandes 2006; Jeffrey 2010). City life, offering more freedom from community knowledge of kinship and caste histories, provoked more need to verify which was which. With Durga's children living in distant Punjab, who knew whether she was the giving mother she said she was? With my boyfriend in America and my apartment a bus ride away, who knew if I was the respectable woman I claimed to be? Now, in more pressing ways, it seemed pertinent to ask the difference between the outside that people boldly advertised and the inside they might be hiding.

The extreme diversity of the slum produced many identity markers that slum residents had vast expertise in discerning the meaning of. In factories and on the streets, residents debated and joked about their regional, religious, class, and caste differences (Datta 2011: 755; Ramaswami 2006). As residents classified others, they made sense of who others were, but also, by contrast, they had to define who they themselves were. Aamir's son Adil looked down from his third-floor perch to identify the origin of neighbors passing by. Though everyone was wearing relatively cheap clothing purchased locally, as he examined the style of shirt, sari material, body shape, and hairstyle of passers-by, he identified Bihari, Bengali, and Rajasthani[1] without hesitation. Geeta and her neighbors, extending their toe rings, explained to me that the number and type of toe rings of their neighbors revealed their regional origins. Yet people did not look upon all regional differences kindly (Datta 2011: 755–56). So behaviors deemed to be too loud (as Bengalis were stereotyped to be) or too gender-segregated (like Rajasthanis were deemed to be) were disciplined in order to retain regional and caste identity (Chandola 2010: 159–61; see also Osella and Osella 1999).

Who was poor and who was rich were never apparent to me—but only because I did not know the signs. Women judged a neighbor's resources by the size of their *jhuggī*, the foods they ate, the clothing their children wore, if they were renters or owners, their home appliances (TV, cooler, fridge), the income that could be estimated from their occupation, the amount of gold they wore, and the girth of their waists. But still, they searched for hidden clues. Was the jewelry real or fake? Did teenage children go out with their friends to restaurants? Did they send their children to private lessons[2] or to schools, as was the growing trend amongst mobile slum residents (i.e., Alderman, Orazem, and Paterno 1996; Tooley and Dixon 2007)? And, if so, in wealthier Roop Nagar or poorer Suraj Nagar? Skin color, name, and job were used to assess caste (Naudet 2008; Osella and Osella 1999). Family histories and character were also weighed. How many times had she been married? Why don't we see her elder daughter anymore? Did she ever plan on returning that money, or was it her plan to keep it all along? Whatever knowledge they gained was used to then weigh the claims that neighbors made about themselves.

Durga passively used others' sense of her wealth to cement her respectability—essential for both a single woman and a midwife in need of local business. People secretly calculated how much she must make from each baby she delivered in her midwifery duties. After all, women told me repeatedly, she lavishly buttered her *rotīs*[3] with clarified butter (*ghī*), used water buffalo milk nostalgically to recall her native Punjab instead of cheaper bagged cow's milk, wore new outfits, and hung that thick gold chain that must have been real on her neck. When I came back from a trip with Durga to the village, Sunita and Geeta both asked me, "So how big was her house?" When I tried to elude the question with vagueness, uncomfortable with "informing" on class status, their questions became more pointed: "She said that she has three rooms and one room on the roof. Is that true or not?" They speculated that she was exaggerating her wealth to people in the *jhuggīs* to claim status whose benefits were not hers to collect on. (To answer their question, it was true.)

But neighbors sometimes called Durga clever (*tez*) because of the way she concealed things to achieve her purposes. Once when I was sitting with Durga and her boyfriend, he pulled playfully at that very gold chain. "This is real—look how rich she is. All gold!" he said, joking. Durga looked back at me, then shyly at him and then said with a huge smile, "No, it's fake." In total confusion, I asked for clarification. "It's real; it's real!" her boyfriend urged as she hit him to silence him. Later when he had left, she told me that she gave him everything, from gifts to food every day. He earned a *lākh*[4] a month, had a car, and no longer even lived in the *jhuggīs*—and gave her nothing. I suspected that he had a good idea of what Durga really earned; she did not really think that she could fool him, but more enjoyed the spectacle of fooling me. However, his vehement claim to correct her only served to remind Durga what he had at stake in supporting the notion that she was "really" wealthy. As she retrospectively turned the truth telling in his direction, she transformed the details of class into tokens to negotiate what each should expect from the other. Technically the debate was over the quality of the gold—real or fake—but really it pointed to something else real or fake: the identities they claimed for themselves and the quality of the affection that bound them. Was Durga a woman living in the *jhuggīs*, earning her own income and entitled to some material generosity from her boyfriend? Or, in his representation, was she a rich woman who spent freely?[5]

Although Durga relied on her status to be seen as a respectable healer, there were times that her clients used this against her. When she told one family the overall costs of their fertility treatment, the mother-in-law of the client in need of treatment paused. They were in a bad place these days, she said; they really were poor, her son was not getting much work recently. Durga insisted that she was in a rough place too, she had just lost her home to demolition and she was giving them the price that she gave to people whom she had known for a long time. After they left, Durga mocked the woman's voice. "We're poor (*ham gharīb hain*)," she whined, "It's a lie! They own four nice homes (*koṭhīs*)!" In the *jhuggīs*, Durga's status made it difficult for her to demand the income she deserved and to ask those with whom she was in relationship to take her needs—and what she was owed—seriously. Poverty and wealth were both practical and symbolic resources whose meanings were not stable (Osella and Osella 1999; Srivastava 2012: 83). As solid as the gold of Durga's necklace seemed to her neighbors, with the dramatic decrease of her business after demolition, she ended up returning to the village for a lack of other options.

In this setting, even characteristics like caste and religion that seemed stable could be manipulated. For instance, Padma was born Muslim but because she married a Hindu man, she put the red powder *sindūr* in the part in her hair and a small felt circle *bindī* on her forehead, both marking her status as a married Hindu woman.[6] Yet when I went with Padma to visit the Muslim world of her family ten minutes up the road, she washed the red out of her part and, as soon as she crossed the boundary of her neighborhood, took off her stick-on *bindī*. She smiled at me to acknowledge her cleverness, and gave her young son the *bindī* to put in his pocket. After demolition, she made some adaptations. She explained, "People in the *jhuggīs* knew about my family, but people here don't know yet, so why explain?" In a mostly Hindu area, it made sense to obscure the signs of her stigmatized Muslim origins.

Similarly, Saraswati avoided the stigma of her Bihari background (Rasu 2007)—and the caste of her family, which she never told me. When asked, she always gave the caste of the man she had chosen to marry, a *Rājpūt* from Uttar Pradesh, in place of that of her natal family.[7] Yet when visiting her husband's family in the village, she explained to me, she knew they muttered disparagingly behind her back that she was Bihari. Durga's, Saraswati's, and Padma's intentionally molded stories reveal their desires for respectable origins (Bear 2007: 187) but also have the practical purposes of avoiding stigma and being paid or respected as they felt they deserved. While these moments of self-fashioning demonstrate the flexibility of their identity, they also show the limits of identity transformation (Chandola 2010; Das 1994; Srivastava 2010). They could change, but only so much. Neighborly interaction, as Datta puts it (2011: 758), is built "upon reworked social hierarchies."

Some women responded to scrutiny by reducing anything that could draw attention, pulling themselves closer to a simpler norm. When I brought back a shawl for Geeta after some travels, she admired it before tucking it under her covers and explaining, "How will I wear this? Other people will ask where it is from." Even though we were seen together, she felt it was important to hide whatever was exchanged through our relationship. I knew she worried about the danger of inciting jealousy (*jelan*) in others (Dean 2013)—both the *jelan* that would be incited by something new and perhaps that of friendship with a foreigner. For her part, Geeta urged me not to share with others the picture of myself in a strapless bridesmaid's dress that I had used to illustrate American weddings. She understood; but if other people saw it, they would interpret all the skin I had shown in the wrong way—and then men would treat me differently (i.e., Khan 2007: 1530; Lukose 2009). In both cases, revealing one's possessions or private life could be read in ways they should not be—there was no way to know how others might read what details you made known.

Husbands helped their wives in self-policing too—though it was not always clear how helpful their wives thought this was. Neetu's husband stopped her in her tracks as she returned from sweeping the washing area they shared with a number of single Bengali men, all splitting the rent to save money. He pointed out the absence of her scarf, *dupaṭṭā*, over the front of her tunic, as he barked, "Have you become cheap?" The dupatta obscured attention to her breasts, but also literally protected her honor, *izzat*—and posed the question that she was literally now without it, *beizzat*. He nodded his head toward the crowd of men in the area she just cleaned, lounging around in underclothes, to indicate the fact that she had an audience. He demanded the protection of her *dupaṭṭā* in his presence and absence to insure she was not misunderstood.

Beyond practicality, it was fun to mock the game of appearances that everyone played, but pretended they did not. In the street, Saraswati handed me her son to carry and when people would look at us cockeyed and ask, Saraswati would answer without hesitation, "He's *her* son! She's *my* sister! What's strange about that?!" She loved to make appearances that challenged belief, pretending to ignore the blatant hole in our story—our strikingly different physical appearances—to create a façade so confident that strangers were wary of challenging it further. Geeta was forever irritated with Sunita because of her cunning manipulations for power, but even still her reliance on her put them in regular interaction. She knew how in interviews I tried hard to appear empathetic to Sunita's complaints when, in reality, I too had begun to doubt Sunita's claims as hypocritical. Sitting next to Sunita but with her face out of Sunita's line of sight, Geeta puffed out her cheeks and rolled her eyes to indicate what she really thought of Sunita's thoughts. Much to Geeta's delight, I struggled to maintain my face with Geeta's antics in my peripheral vision. Geeta's thinly concealed disrespect demonstrated how little effort she put into maintaining her appearance of support for Sunita. (In contrast, her husband could not even disguise his disdain for Sunita. He avoided her entirely, even though their *jhuggīs* faced each other for years.) At other times, such play was used to trick family members. As Neetu's son remained engrossed in playing with the MP3 player that he always found in my bag, his dad slyly gestured to me to notice his wife Neetu more closely. Underneath the cloud of smoke from his *bīṛī* (small cigarette), Neetu leaned behind the bed to take her own drag from a *bīṛī* held in her extended, hidden fingers. They confirmed their conspiracy to me with winks and wry smiles before returning to their stance as smoking husband and respectable wife. Playing around with appearances made clear how much effort went into their daily maintenance. But it also indicated how different parts could be tried on, either to see how far we could fool people or to get our work done without losing a bit of self-respect.

Women needed to hold on to multiple refractions of their identities because they all could be real in particular contexts. Durga was wealthy compared to some, poor compared to others. Padma's Hindu and Muslim parts were both necessary for her to honor her new family and her old. However, what mattered more than simply knowing their neighbors' caste, religion, class, and family were their intentions in presenting themselves in certain ways. People resented Durga's denial of her wealth when they felt she used it to charge unfairly for her services and claimed the inadequacy of protesting demolition when she likely had better housing options than others to follow. But when women mentioned Durga's sons in the village, who were rumored to rely on her financially, they revalued the poverty that she sometimes presented and considered how much of her wealth she had shared with them, since they had not fulfilled their financial responsibilities.

While some scholars emphasize the tenuous unity produced within slum neighborhoods (Datta 2007; Datta 2011: 224; Roberts 2008), here, behind cohabitation was continued questioning. In all situations, as women wondered what motives might be hiding behind neighbors' representation of themselves, they asked the significance of their neighbors' manipulations for themselves. Might Sunita try to appear a victim because she was waiting for you to offer help? Might Durga spread a rumor that threatened your reputation because it was good for her business? No matter what, it was never taken for granted that people were as they appeared.

Constant speculation ensured that the tricky neighbor would fool no one. Although aspirations for mobility provoked identity fashioning throughout liberalized urban India (Dean 2013; Fernandes 2006; Jeffrey 2010; Osella and Osella 1999; Srivastava 2010), the extreme intimacy of people in the slum forced women into habitual consideration of their neighbors' motivations, whether they wanted to or not (Boo 2012; Chandola 2010; Chandola 2012a; Chatterji and Mehta 2007; Jesmin and Salway 2000: 694–95). For women who washed clothes in the same spaces, heard one another's conversations, and saw each other's every move, how did they manage the uncertainty that their neighbors posed? In spaces that formed the stage of enacting everyday appearance and exacting questioning of neighbors' true interiors, women asserted the extreme risks that interaction with their neighbors posed, no matter how careful they were.

LURKING DANGER: THE IMMORAL USE OF APPEARANCES

On the day of demolition, Durga had told me what she had repeated to me many times before: "You don't know people like we do. You cannot just sit with anyone." There were multiple levels of knowing. The most general was that which was shared in Ghaziapuram, before demolition, where there was a basic accounting for who each person was. In their new improvised home in a small hut after demolition, now Geeta's husband interrupted his morning routine of making *jalebī* dough with slow yawn after yawn. Already two things had been stolen from his *jalebī* cart that he parked outside their house after each day of vending the sticky sweets to workers in the industrial area. It was hard to sleep knowing that more could be stolen. Where they lived before, he explained, everyone knew each other so it was safe outside. But here, neither did they know people nor did people look out for each other in the same way. Geeta spoke to a deeper degree of knowing, one that looked inside people rather than looked out for them. After demolition, Geeta gave me her ultimate evidence for the point that she, Saraswati, and Durga made to me separately, holding up a small square of an article cut from the newspaper. The article explained, and she renarrated, that in the neighborhood chaos of moving belongings on the day before demolition, a man had worked with his friends to try to kill his wife. They had struck her on the nearby railroad tracks and left her for dead. The rumor was that they were hoping to extort money from her. "Remember the man we talked to two weeks earlier," she asked to spark my recognition. It turned out that I had talked to him several times. She explained to me, "This is why I don't sit down anywhere and why I tell you to not talk to everybody; not everybody is safe." To Geeta, there was no question of whether her neighbors provoked danger. It was just a matter of whether you would learn in time to protect yourself or find out later—in perhaps more compromised circumstances.

To know neighbors required extensive knowledge that I did not have. In the first few months of my fieldwork, I bounced between conversations with many different women of the slum, sitting with them outside while they worked and being dragged inside as they showed off their *jhuggīs* to me. When I returned to Durga's house, she would be fed up with my naïveté, having catalogued all of the women I had visited as well as her corresponding level of approval for each of them. Durga made clear her objection to my efforts to know the neighborhood democratically. Some people were okay; some were not. But I neither knew the difference, nor had any idea of what danger might loom. When I told her it was wrong to refuse interaction with people I did not know, she asserted that it was wrong to interact with people whose true character I did not know. Knowing character was asymptotic. As you learned, you reached closer to understanding a person's character, but no matter how much you knew, as Saraswati put it, "You could not trust anyone around here."

Many signs of risk could be explained away as illness or bad luck when, in actuality, women explained, they indicated their vulnerability. Few women talked to me at length about *nazar*, the evil eye, or magic, except to mention its avoidance. But the frequency with which it came up in matters of sharing food or intimate spaces with neighbors made me suspect that it may have a larger presence (see also Dean 2013). Saraswati warned me not to follow up with one family that I had interviewed. She had since found out they were Bhangi (a Dalit caste) and reasoned they could put poison in our drinks in order to do magic that would control us. When I responded by critiquing her caste prejudice, she defended her reasoning. It was not their caste; it was the magic that they would try to do. Neetu similarly suspected her neighbors of doing magic on her food. She complained to me that she could not stand living near Bengali people because they were dirty and bad. About two months ago, they gave a sweet to her son, and since then, he had been having problems in his stomach. She knew that he had done magic (*jādū*). Likewise, when I became sick after eating food that Durga had made but had asked Padma to serve me, Durga cited Padma's evil eye (*nazar*) as one possible cause. In all of these cases, the people accused of inflicting magic had stigmatized identities—being Bhangi (an untouchable caste), Bengali (sometimes conflated with illegal immigration), or Muslim (even if not presently so) (see also Ring 2006). Because of the feeling that such threats loomed, women were cautious not to eat in public or to leave the curtain open so that others could not see into their homes when they ate. People with bad intentions could use them powerfully through innocent-seeming vessels (Khandelwal 2004: 145–46).

There was an underlying fear that interacting with the wrong person meant that one could be controlled against one's will or have one's things taken away. While this has been mentioned in a variety of accounts as evil eye (*nazar*) or the fear of magic (*jādū*), here I consider it seriously. Partway through my fieldwork, I wanted to accompany Geeta to her village. When

I casually mentioned it to Saraswati and Akshay, they reacted strongly. Akshay said abruptly, "I am just going to tell you my opinion, but you should not go." The two of them looked at each other as if to confirm their shared understanding, and Saraswati turned to me gravely and said, "Everyone in the neighborhood knows that Geeta wants you to marry her brother." When I probed after her question, she hesitantly explained, "Sunita told everyone that when she, you, and Geeta had gone to visit Geeta's youngest brother, her sister-in-law [older brother's wife] had made a joke, calling you sister-in-law (*bhābhī*) instead of sister (*dīdī*)" (thus implying that I was married to the youngest brother). When Sunita had returned, she had recounted this to all of her neighbors. Saraswati said that Geeta's silence on this matter was evidence that she also must support a plan to marry me to her youngest brother. I dismissed her fears by explaining, "She knows my plans to marry my boyfriend and she knows that I am not going to get married here—she would not do that."

"Everyone wants to get married to a foreigner," they explained. "And once you're there in her village [in Bihar], you'll be so far away that they can do anything they want to you." Again, I scoffed at their warning: "What?! They cannot just get me married like that!" "They can do this," Saraswati said, as she pulled my arm behind me to imitate forced submission to their control, and insisted:

> It happens here. You don't know that it happens here, but it does. They can pull you back and make you do the *pheras* [the bride and groom's circling of a ritual fire in a Hindu wedding] and then you'll be married. Then what will you do? You'll be all alone there. And you haven't seen what we saw in the neighborhood. We saw what happened with her daughter, how they made her work so hard and yelled at her so much that she ran away. And when the police came in the middle of the night with her daughter, she said that she would rather stay in jail than return—that's why her family arranged her marriage so quickly. If she treats her own family that way, how will she treat you? All of this stuff happened right in front of us. This kind of thing happens in Bihar. You've heard this now, you can decide on your own. But you should know.

Saraswati painted a particular confluence of factors that intersected to create the presence of danger. In Geeta's sister-in-law's comment about my becoming the wife of Geeta's brother, she saw a dangerous aim. What I saw as a joke Saraswati read as a genuine intention for this marriage to take place—regardless of what I wanted or did. Her description of me in a far-off Bihari village—important because of the stigma of backwardness and lawlessness that was attributed to her home state of Bihar (Rasu 2007)—where I would be married literally by force highlighted my lack of agency.

Saraswati discounted the closeness of my relationship with Geeta, a closeness that I reasoned disproved the alleged intentions. All it showed, in her mind, was that Geeta had successfully duped me. In the way that false gurus fool their overeager and insufficiently cynical disciples, I, a foreigner eager for friendship and adventure, did not have the built-in suspicion that was needed to discern the truth (Narayan 1989: 155, 158). Because she had seen how Geeta treated her family—assumed to be the best predictor of one's true character—she knew what was "really inside," to use Sunita's phrase, Geeta's personality. She was incapable of the trusting relationship I claimed we had. Thus, Saraswati referred to a conspiracy of Geeta and her sister-in-law's intentions to have me married, by force, if necessary. To Saraswati, Geeta's intentions could not be challenged. However, they could be avoided.

In their warnings, women outlined the imminent risk that others' secret, dangerous desires might pose to their own selves. Through magic—whether intentional or not—neighbors' unknown desires could have disastrous consequences. As the warnings here clearly state, women's sense of danger was sometimes guided by caste, regional, and religious stigma. Fear, in these cases, was also a vehicle to justify further separation from those deemed undesirable. But to strictly classify fears here is impossible. Power, magic, poisoning, caste contamination, and religious danger are all related, even as they are not all exactly the same. To honor the common theme, I highlight how women saw dangerous, secretive desire as the uniting theme across the threats they described. In all cases, neighbors hid their desires for control or power behind appearances of political responsibility or neighborly interaction. Researchers have been hesitant to engage seriously the claims of interlocutors who warn of looming social threat in their neighbors (Das and Das 2006: 203; de Zoysa et al. 1998: 2106; Haider 2000: 42). But in other places, and in other times that are not so distant—from the 1984 riots in Delhi, to the 1992 Babri Masjid riots in Mumbai, and the Emergency in 1976 in Delhi—such dangerous desires have, in conjunction with government machinations and violent events, manifested themselves in massive violence (Chatterji and Mehta 2007; Das 2006; Tarlo 2003). Politics brought this small-scale everyday tension to another, more harmful level.

NEIGHBORHOOD INTERACTION AND THE UNAVOIDABLE DANGER OF POLITICS

The difference between inside and outside had deep political stakes. Of the many appearances that their neighbors might put forth, both men and women argued it was the expanded opportunities for political power that were most commonly exploited. In slum communities, it was not hard to be considered a local leader, called *pradhān*. But it was widely felt that the people who took advantage of the wider democratic field did so for personal gain. By itself, this was not consequential, but there was a dangerous nexus between higher-level politicians, police, and local leaders (*pradhāns*) that produced an atmosphere of thuggery (*guṇḍāgirī*), which was not merely the fantasy of the movies, but in people's firsthand experiences (Blom Hansen 2005; Das 2006; Weinstein 2008). Because *pradhāns* mediated access to everything from water to land and official documents, it was impossible to avoid them (Anand 2011; Anand and Rademacher 2011; Srivastava 2011; Weinstein 2008). The question was how to know and manage interaction with them that this posed.

Some people became *pradhāns* through leadership they enacted on one occasion. For instance, Hema told me that after leading area residents to lobby their politicians to protest previous demolition notices and stepping up after a fire in the trash collectors' (*kabāṛī*) camp, "then people starting calling me a *pradhān*." But, as much as *pradhāns* like her might exercise leadership improving "access to services and helping constituents manage risk," a cross-slum study on Delhi *pradhāns* found they were also quite concerned with managing their images. They "made much of their accomplishments" and laid "claim to a democratic mandate" even when, "to hear their constituents tell it, [they] had acquired their power largely through coercion" (Jha, Rao, and Woolcock 2007: 12). These days, the political openings made it feel as though everyone wanted power because "this way he proves to himself and to his people that he now can be socially what he could not be before" (Khare 1984: 115; see also Witsoe 2011: 79). Through gaining local power, *pradhāns* effected personal transformation.

With no elections to choose *pradhāns*, they had their own ways of making power. In their neighborhood before demolition, Akshay said, "whoever had police power, whoever had a contact with thugs (*gūnḍe*), he made himself a leader by his own choice (*apni marzī se pradhān bante the*)." The more they showed their power and the more they threatened people, the more their power grew. By always standing ready to start a fight with other residents, Akshay suggested, *pradhāns* forced conflict with neighbors to demonstrate their dominance over others. In the industrial area, explained Akshay, the land belonged to companies and the government. But "whoever had power could claim the land for themselves. People could say, 'I am feeding a thousand or two thousand policemen' and claim it in that way, but really it was not theirs." Akshay highlighted the performative process through which *pradhāns* came to be powerful. *Pradhāns* may put on the appearance that they were interested in the common good, but as residents recalled the process through which they came to power, they revealed less altruistic intentions behind their self-important surfaces (Srivastava 2011).

By itself, coming to power by such means was not dangerous, even if it was extreme play with appearances. To a certain extent, the proliferation of *pradhāns* was amusing, as if no one could prevent himself or herself from the excitement of seeking power, even power that was self-proclaimed. As Hema, the former *pradhān*, explained to me, "Some are Congress [party] *pradhāns*, some are other parties' *pradhāns*, some are *pradhāns* from your home place (*desh*). . . . Now there are so many *pradhāns* here. In every house there is a *pradhān*! So who is going to listen?"[8] Yet within the sea of *pradhāns* with no audience, she alluded to the ties that *pradhāns* kept. If these *pradhāns* were all beholden to someone else, then residents must interrogate not just the insides of the *pradhān* whose help they sought, but the substance of the *pradhān's* larger alliances. *Pradhāns* affiliated with particular political parties required the recipients of their services to hold the same affiliation, demonstrating "that *pradhāns* play a central role in the quid pro quo between slum dwellers and elected politicians, where blocks of votes and manpower at rallies are exchanged for services and protection" (Jha, Rao, and Woolcock 2005: 18).

Yet, on the local level, *pradhāns'* precise ties to the broader nexus of political power were never clearly drawn (see also Srivastava 2011). They wanted to show the authority of the state, while at the same time use a neighborly etiquette to conceal this connection (Srivastava 2012: 89). The same woman continued, "You cannot tell which person a *pradhān* has taken water from and whom he has taken money from. Election-*vāllāh* [official], MLA-*vāllāh* [Delhi legislative member]—they all say eat my two *pūrīs*."9 We don't know from whom we are taking chai and food." The technique of feeding was often a way that leaders secured allegiance and built a relationship. As Akshay had mentioned, *pradhāns* might feed policemen to secure their claims to land and power. Policemen, everyone knew, were corrupt, as demonstrated by the number of cases in which policemen have raped women who have challenged their charges or by the number of threats to those who have filed Right to Information Act requests (Dhar 2011; Jha, Rao, and Woolcock 2007: 15; Polgreen 2011). Those who gained power through alliances with police connected themselves to police brutality and corruption.

Political genealogies, like *pradhāns'* intentions, were part of the inside that *pradhāns'* eager promises were meant to conceal. Seeking alliance with or asking favors from local *pradhāns* was dangerous because of the anonymous allegiances to which one became unwittingly embroiled in the process. Through alliances and performance, aspiring *pradhāns* found the tools to realize their preoccupation with building their own power. Like false gurus who used their austerities to inflict suffering (Khandelwal 2004: 146), the most dangerous aspect of *pradhāns* was their desire for power.

Knowing none of this, when demolition notices were posted in the neighborhood in January 2009, I suggested that we take action and followed the advice of a friend of mine, Pushpa, who was an activist in a neighborhood of residents who had been displaced from other Delhi slums. When I asked Sunita if she wanted to help me survey the slum, since Pushpa had suggested this would help locals to make a political claim, Sunita declined. She explained that she had done a previous survey for the Congress party not long ago; people had recognized her from that. And then she told me a grisly story about violent thugs (*gūndās*) who she heard had, in the middle of the night, visited someone else who was politically active. She feared that asserting her stance against demolition would single her out to the powers that be in the same way as those targeted earlier. Later, when I wanted to invite Pushpa's group down to the neighborhood, Durga warned Pushpa on my phone that my involvement in organizing locally was dangerous. She explained that I came to and from the neighborhood on my own. What could they do to protect me? She alluded not to a specific history of a *pradhān* she knew well. Instead, she was concerned with what appearance I displayed—as willing to challenge demolition and asking others to feel the same.[10] She suspected that the conflict between my publicly stated idealistic aims and the dangerous desires of those in support of demolition would lead to no good end. She also offered that no one else would be willing to expose themselves so openly. "If you want to raise your fist, then raise your fist," she warned. "But if you raise your fist, you will raise it alone."

An activist who came later to help residents push their claim in court said that nothing had ever happened to him in his many years of protesting. But he also advised, "This is how it is: the more people stand together, the less other people can say anything to them." Still, there was a feeling that people with bad intentions would find a way to get their work done. People in this part of Delhi often cited the dominant rural caste of Gujjars to state their case. In recent years, as their villages in Haryana and Uttar Pradesh were subsumed within Delhi's metropolitan area, Gujjars had made significant financial gains and grown in political dominance as well (see also Chandola 2010: 102–3). Though I had seen many residents' amicable relations with their Gujjar neighbors, the repeated stories about the danger of crossing Gujjars resonated with other lurking dangers that people mentioned, particularly after demolition, when people moved into neighborhoods where Gujjars had ownership of rental properties. Residents of this slum said that they did not respect the law and had the police in their hands. Saraswati told the story of a Gujjar who hit one of her neighbors in the head so badly it began bleeding. When the police were called, the Gujjar storekeeper said the person had spilled chai on her forehead even though the marks clearly indicated a fight. The police did nothing, Saraswati alleged, because, behind closed doors, they had been paid off for silence.

The far-reaching scale of violence mounted by the collective of *pradhāns*, policemen, and politicians demonstrated most poignantly the high-risk stakes of local politics. Through their links to other powers—whether unknown or blatantly advertised—*pradhāns* amassed resources for themselves while securing resources for those in their networks. People speculated that politicians and their local *pradhāns* purposefully started fires in *jhuggīs* to create a niche in which they could swoop down as super-heroes (Pushpa Pandey, pers. comm., April 6, 2009). They cut off water supply to those who failed to support them (Cyril Robin, pers. comm., June 25, 2009). With local *pradhāns* as representatives of political parties or informers to the local police (Srivastava 2011; Weinstein 2008), many of Delhi's slum residents—particularly illegal Bangladeshi migrants—found themselves constantly vulnerable (Ramachandran 2004).[11] *Pradhāns* brought all of this political dirtiness close to home. Their machinations for power and their capacity to monitor residents in all kinds of ways—including surveys (Srivastava 2012: 91; Srivastava 2011)—made slum residents feel that their daily moves in small local lanes were always potentially tied to larger-scale consequences.

As noted in the previous section, women had emphasized the way that their neighbors might build their power through magic and the evil eye. This section has shown how these desires are connected to a larger political network that can amplify the force of their danger. Women charged that *pradhāns*, like any other malicious neighbors, were interested in self-promotion despite the veneer of public service that they showed to the community. But, unlike malicious neighbors whose character could be carefully observed, the true alliances of *pradhāns* were extremely difficult to know. Women and men alike suggested the hazards of developing allegiance to local *pradhāns*, lest one reveal one's own political sentiments in a menacing public sphere or indebt oneself to a web of unknown, snow-balling alliances. Yet even in spite of all this danger, some women were unwilling simply to accept the unchecked desires of their neighbors.

CHALLENGING NEIGHBORS' APPEARANCES: "I KNOW WHERE YOU CAME FROM"

Durga had responded initially to the dirtiness (*gandagī*) of neighbors' immoral character by celebrating how demolition had cleared away her shared coexistence with them. But people felt it was their imperative to cut through the dirtiness much before the sweeping removal that came with demolition. In doing so, not only did they challenge the false fronts of their neighbors, but they also asserted the capacity that their neighbors had in action. Ultimately such conversations redefined the moral terms that women tried to set with particular appearances, in spite of whatever vulnerability challenging others' authority might pose. Living together over the years, women explained that they knew each other's histories and were often sympathetic to each other's circumstances. In the beginning, these stories implied, they all had to put up with similar poverty and hardship. Nonetheless, many of their neighbors had neglected their capacity for positive action, in favor of just appearing better than others. Here, I focus on how residents continually challenged the appearances of one of their neighbors, Sunita. Sunita's story appears almost legendary, but other researchers (Boo 2012; Srivastava 2011) have documented similar rises to power of women in other South Asian slums. Although women repeatedly pointed out how Sunita's local power was dangerous, their warnings were always paired with residents' insistent revelation of her background. After being told so many versions of these stories, I do not advocate here for one "true" account. My concern here is with how women challenged the claims of their neighbors based on what they knew about them—and therefore how they manipulated the moral stakes of interaction.

Long after her neighbors interacted with her on a daily basis, Sunita persistently appeared in women's conversations as an object of disgust. She had been one of my first informants and was well reputed for her common complaints to outsiders or to whomever would listen. After her husband's death, she said, there was an ever-present shortage of money. Tears welled up in her eyes when she described to me and others how she was not sure how she could make ends meet. But when I expressed my sympathy with her condition to her neighbors, they instantly corrected my impression with annoyance at my gullibility. To women who told her story, Sunita's representation of herself was an outright lie used to obtain power.[12] While I still am unsure of how deserving Sunita might have been of sympathy, I was struck by the way that after demolition, almost all the families I worked with seemed determined to "set the record straight," since I had spent so much time with Sunita. Women explained to me that people were afraid to cross her because of the way that she, as a local *pradhān,* was connected to local politicians, the police, and the local NGO. She was a gatekeeper who would ensure that any outsiders to the community—from activists to researchers like myself—would go through her. To them, her appearance was convincing and effectively built trust and relationships. They did not know Sunita's inside like locals did.

Behind this neat appearance, she was "of her own making."[13] This, however, was said without the admiring tone implied in the American phrase to be "self-made." Instead, it implied that her authority was self-endowed, as Akshay had described the performative element of *pradhān* power. Mrinalini described to me how, when Sunita first came to live in the neighborhood with her husband and children, she moved into a *jhuggī* right opposite hers. She came to the city with her plain cotton sari as her only possession. "That's how poor she was," Mrinalini said with pity. "When she washed her clothes, she put part of it in the water to wash it, then held it up to let part of it dry and then put it back on. She did not have anything else." When they came, Mrinalini remembered, Sunita was awful to her sickly husband. She did not wash his clothes or cook for him. He wiped up feces with one hand and in the other would be the one *roṭī* (flatbread) that she gave him. She said that he secretly turned to them to ask for another *roṭī*. He was in such a poor condition that eventually he went to the nearby temple, where he subsisted for several years off more food than he received at home.

A little bit later, Sunita became friends with Dilip and moved into his *jhuggī* with him. Not long after that, multiple women told me, she also became involved with a local policeman, who was the key to solidifying her power. Her husband returned not much later with a huge tumor on his neck—she gestured with her hand and an expression of sympathy to show how big it was. But even then, she would not do anything for him— not give him food, not even do his laundry. "What could we do," Mrinalini reflected. "If we had said anything, then she would have come to us later. We could not do anything." Akshay told me that unlike Sunita's recollection that her husband had died of cancer, she had killed him. "She never went to visit him in the hospital, she did not even go to his cremation! She said his body stunk [*badbū iske sharīr se ā rahī hai*] and left him to others." He and his aunt attended the cremation, though even Sunita's son did not go to fulfill his role.[14] "She wanted him to die so she could continue her relationship with the policeman," said Mrinalini. "Not long after that, she got her policeman, and after that, everyone became afraid of her." "She does this," Neetu remarked as she gestured a slap that stood for sex, "because of what she gets from it. Other women do [sex] from difficult circumstances [*mazbūrī*], but look at all she got," she explained as she elaborated how these men had paid for both Sunita's daughter's wedding and property in two different areas. In addition, women argued that she had wrested control of the local women's group and demanded salary, even when no one else was paid.

What women emphasized were the warped intentions guiding Sunita's rise to power. She obtained power by renouncing her family connections— neglecting her first husband, and then neglecting her second. She made these people into kin through marriage or living together and then shirked her responsibilities. Mrinalini and Akshay used vivid images to describe Sunita's neglect: a husband with a *rotī* in one hand and feces in the other who was better off living off charity at a temple; her disgust at—rather than care of—his cancer; her absence at the cremation that should have marked his peaceful passage from this world. This they juxtaposed with the way that she reached out to men who could provide money and power—first Dilip for his money, then her policeman for his connections— and left others to do her work for her, like attending the cremation of her husband. Sunita, they argued, only wanted a relationship if it connected her to power. If it did not, she would leave the person behind. They argued that she had made herself powerful and cited their fear as evidence. Yet because she had squandered the respectable care of her family and her body in the process, they did not recognize her power as legitimate. They might be scared of her potential for destruction, but they would never respect her authority. Mrinalini grounded the present in the actions of the past: "I saw where she had come from, what she looked like when she had first come here, and now look at her, thinking she is in charge of everyone. I saw her in those rags when she came here, and she cannot say anything to me." From equal, difficult beginnings struggling in Delhi with hardly anything, Sunita now pretended that she was superior. Mrinalini asserted a corrupt foundation on which Sunita's powerful appearance now rested precariously.

As much as women said that Sunita's power was real, they followed the background they gave on her with accounts of how they exposed her for what she really was. Neetu explained to me that Sunita no longer bothered her because of a fight over a pipe with Aamir, the neighbor who lived opposite her in the old *jhuggīs*. She explained:

> He was a renter and I had my own *jhuggī*. We had put a pipe down so that the bathing and washing water would flow out to the drain (*nālā*) over across the way. Aamir did not think it should be there and he got mad once and went to Sunita and told her about the pipe, thinking he was important. She came over in a huff and asked, "What's going on here?" I just stared at her and said, "What, this isn't my *jhuggī*? He's a renter and he's telling me what I can do and what I cannot do? You tell me what's the matter with doing this, you eunuch!" I've lived here for a long time. And after that day, she never bothered me again. I am good, I can be respectful (*immandarī*) but I can be bad (*burī*) too when I need to.

Mrinalini told a similar story. She explained that one day in front of her home, Sunita's son Sagar hurt a neighborhood child with his motorcycle and then just barked at him to get up. Mrinalini's oldest son called him out on it and there was a physical fight. Next thing she knew, Sunita was at Mrinalini's doorstep threatening her. Mrinalini stood her ground. She would not take it; she cursed at her and told her, "Go on, bring your policeman, I am not afraid, I know where you came from." And from that time onward, Sunita never threatened her.

Sunita used the fluid atmosphere in contemporary Delhi to make herself a *pradhān*, positioning herself powerfully within NGO activities, drawing in the outsiders (including me) in search of narratives of poverty into her account of the community, and utilizing the absence of nearby kin networks to create her own history of her family relationships that positioned her as giving. But waving the flag of Sunita's true character, Neetu and Mrinalini used their knowledge of her climb to power to challenge the identity that she made for herself. Though many were frightened of Sunita, both singled out themselves for being emboldened to challenge Sunita's power. Neither of them described any other community leader with the same vitriol. Mrinalini challenged Sunita's false claim to power by demanding that she outwardly claim the link to power that she obscured: the policeman that she slept with. In so doing, she discredited her power. Neetu instead pointed out her own claims to authority—her own tenure in the community and ownership of her home entitled her to use her home in the way she wanted. Sunita's efforts to extend her domain of control were rebuffed. They knew that such efforts would not dismantle Sunita's surface power. However, by insisting on telling her background in such a way that emphasized her humble beginnings, her neglect, and the ease with which they had crumbled her edifice, all of these women deflated the moral power of Sunita's public complaints and refused to accept her hollow authority. And in telling this story, they also differentiated themselves from Sunita's corruption. Women's competing narratives about their neighbors and themselves fought to redefine the moral hierarchy suggested by appearances.

In this neighborhood, women scrutinized with the greatest of detail the need that others described. Sometimes they scrutinized in collaboration with their husbands. After a visit from Padma in which she bemoaned the pattern of abuse her husband had fallen into, Jyoti's husband echoed Jyoti's own reservations. He clapped his hands together and put one to each side as he explained that every story has two sides. "After all," he noted as he told the other side of Padma's story, "it's not just him who drinks; she drinks too." There were few resources to share—from the assistance one could offer to time and sympathy—and women were forced to account for them carefully (Ring 2006: 86). Beyond this, what was the significance of such elaborate accounts of their neighbors' flexible identities?

With Sunita as the most extreme example, women argued that their neighbors manipulated their identities to achieve certain ends. The chief evidence used to discredit her was that she had sacrificed kinship—paramount for women's identity (McHugh 1989; Menon and Shweder 1998; Seymour 1999)—for utilitarian gain. They clung to the history they had gathered on their neighbors because they could use it to protect themselves. By correcting what was put on public record, women pushed toward women's individual accountability for their lives, not discriminating between the private domain of the family and the public domain of Sunita's power. Mrinalini or Neetu would never lead a community-wide revolt against Sunita, but they could challenge the wrongful authority that accumulated into the dirtiness against which Durga spoke. Though Sunita and other *pradhāns'* outside appearances may convey power, their neighbors offered their more valuable awareness of their inside character. In this way, women restrained the mobility that others made for themselves, allowing them surface power, but hollowing out their moral claims to scaffold it. Mrinalini's grave assertion of "I know where you came from" inserted Sunita into a common past of struggling, one in which she, like anyone else, had the capacity to take morally responsible action.

BUILDING BORDERS BETWEEN NEIGHBORS AND SELF

Sunita was the most extreme example of reprehensible action. With the amount that women knew about each other, there were few women they knew of who conclusively proved no risk. After all, this was the place that Saraswati said, "You could trust no one." But this hardly meant that everyone wanted to be a *pradhān* in the way that Sunita did, as much as it might feel that way. And not only that, they hardly lived in isolation. If you could not sit with just anyone, then how did women decide with whom to sit? And how did they sit with them so that they protected themselves? Although I had started my research wanting to know what relationships meant, Durga had celebrated the dispersal of neighborhood relationships and had distanced herself from anyone she had been engaged with. This was not unheard of. Public health researchers have shown cross-culturally how low-income women may deliberately isolate themselves from social networks, motivated by the need to distinguish themselves from a stigmatized group or to insulate themselves from social demands and perceived bad influences (Browne-Yung, Ziersch, and Baum 2013: 14; Caughy, O'Campo, and Muntaner 2003; Furstenberg 1993; Mitchell and LaGory 2002; Schulz and Lempert 2004; Wasylishyn and Johnson 1998). I realized it made more sense to see how women's negotiations about their neighborly relations, no matter how fragmented, may be efforts to protect themselves. How might their efforts of self-protection say something not just about their relationships to others, but their sense of themselves?

Everyone knew who each other was in the neighborhood, but there were select patterns that arose when I began watching when and how women would greet one another. As women put it, they only "sat together" with select others. Over time, groups shifted, but the bones of many groups persisted for decades. I could sit outside Mrinalini's home with her, but when she later passed in front of Sunita's house while I was there, neither of us would even glance at the other. As I walked with Geeta, Neetu would not even look my way, much less emit her usual radiant greetings. I learned from their silences that I too was to do the same. They knew I was there; I knew they were there. Women had small groups of neighbors with whom they sat and talked, and perhaps helped each other in their daily work. Within that group would be pairs of women who shared more. But as long as I sat with women of another group, they would not acknowledge me at that time as "their own." The fictive ties of kinship that have been documented within South Asia (Datta 2011; Lambert 2000) had their limits.

The lines were overlapped and nuanced according to particular histories, and trust varied over time. At the end of my research, when I decided to invite all the families together for a farewell party, these complex webs of relationships made it a logistical nightmare. I talked with Mrinalini about it. "I cannot have the party at my house because my friend and flatmate won't allow it; I cannot have it at the NGO because Padma, Saraswati, Neetu, and Mrinalini see it as Sunita's domain. If I have it at Sunita's *jhuggī*, only Shaista, Geeta, and Mohan will come. Only Sunita would come to Mohan's because the few people who know him think that he's arrogant because he's upper-caste. Hardly anyone knows who Jyoti or Saraswati are because they are loners, so they won't come. Sunita and Geeta would not come to your (Mrinalini's) place. Very few people would come to Padma's because they don't like her. Durga's not here anymore, and no one could find Neetu's far-off house. I guess I'll have it at Shaista's." Mrinalini smiled and laughed, "You finally get it!" Knowing about each other did not equate to having a relationship, and neither did sitting together mean comfort with sharing intimate spaces. At this level of relationship, women made choices about whom they would welcome into their daily lives. They asked themselves if they knew enough about them, what threats they might pose, if they had basic respect for these women's inside character.[15]

As much as the lines of sitting together had been drawn, I had guessed that they would easily move to accommodate new members. As usual, I was wrong. When Saraswati was in a deep low a few months after demolition, I brought her along to meet Neetu, whose silliness and warmth I thought would lighten her mood. (Now they lived in different neighborhoods.) I was surprised at how easily Saraswati poured her heart out about her mother-in-law and her husband's threats to leave her, revealing information that many women from the slum would think inappropriate to share with anyone but those they knew best. Neetu shared her own family difficulties, giggling about how she caught her husband as his friends were trying to ensnare him in their indiscretions with a prostitute. But when I dropped Saraswati off at home and asked her if she enjoyed Neetu's company, she was quiet. A few weeks later, after we returned from interviewing Neetu, who had shared her difficult life story, Saraswati said flatly, "She's a liar. I think she just made all of that up." When I talked to Neetu the next time, she told me, "Saraswati just thinks she is above everyone else." Then she glibly slipped in, "I know that she is on her second marriage, even though she doesn't tell anyone."

Neither of the women knew much about the other because of Saraswati's short tenure in the slum they had both lived in and the distance that had separated their two *jhuggīs*. Neetu's suspicion of Saraswati was bred by the fact that few people knew anything about her besides her supposed tendency to hide key parts of her history. Both of them shared intimate details that they would not have shared in public: Saraswati shared family troubles in the present; Neetu revealed a painful past and recent embarrassment. For neither of them, sharing these experiences as they briefly sat together failed to build anything lasting between them, nor did they feel they had wrongly exposed themselves.

Rather, they protected themselves by not allowing the other to matter to them. They said what they wanted to—Saraswati clearing her mind, Neetu sharing a good story—while closing the door to one another, doubting the truth of what the other said, and therefore discrediting the other's potential judgment. I suspected that Saraswati's distancing was also a product of her jealousy of Neetu, who, after demolition, had shifted to comparatively nicer accommodations in a lower-middle-class neighborhood. Saraswati had asked Neetu to put her in touch with her landlady and perhaps help her negotiate a different price. She was unhappy with her comparatively more slum-like room in a much denser neighborhood.

By denigrating Neetu's character and asserting her autonomy, Saraswati specified that the help that she sought from Neetu was not aspiration to become like her, but a simple temporary connection for something she needed. They might enjoy each other's company momentarily, but they certainly did not need it. These negotiations were the first layer of protection—deciding who would and would not be part of one's daily interactions.

But there was another level, so that even in everyday intimacies that bound people to one another in alliance, women still reinforced boundaries that protected themselves. Geeta had built her daily routine through the ways that she could guard her self. As she warned me why I should be careful about whom I sat with, she explained to me, "That's why I either stay right in front of my house or stay inside." In front of her house or inside, she remained in control of her social relationships and reduced the scrutiny of others. She said that she decided not to work in the factory, because at home she could have more control. At home, she kept a few pieces to work on stored away—shirts and skirt orders from the factory to which she added small touches for a few rupees—on which she could work whenever she wanted without having to worry about what others would say.

But I tried to dispute the social isolation that she argued she had built for herself, free of others' wishes, judgments, and needs. I pointed to the immediate neighbors that she helped. It was almost daily that she invited her neighbor's daughters over for a small snack, helped brush their hair, played games with them, told their mother to change them out of dirty clothes, checked up on Dilip's health, and made sure he had enough food when Sunita was visiting family. She had even taken care of her overburdened neighbor's younger daughter for a several-month period, feeding her and taking her wherever she went. I argued that even *she* would miss her neighbor's children after demolition—what would they do without her? She laughed. "I help people," she said, "I feed their children, but I mostly stay here. Even now, whenever I feed my neighbors' children, they feel jealousy (*jalan*). But I keep doing what I do. And I stay here." For Geeta, even as she opened the boundaries of herself by offering care, she made sure that these bonds did not lead to attachment or the expectation of mutual reciprocity. Through her imagery of staying close to the home or inside of it,

Geeta centered her aims on herself, reducing interdependencies that could compromise her and offering help only when she wanted to.

Other women enacted the same processes of self-protection within much more intertwined lives with their neighbors. Padma and Durga, whose *jhuggīs* were side-by-side, relied on each other to help fill the gaps in everyday needs left by their kin. Padma could often be found sitting on the front stoop of Durga's house, asking Durga to touch her arms and confirm her fever, sometimes finishing off the leftover lentils and rice—it always had a generous amount of *ghī* (clarified butter). Though Padma fed her husband generously, it was not clear that she always saved enough for herself. The few times that she appeared in something other than her ragged polyester nightgown, it was often in a suit gifted from Durga. When Padma's husband sometimes beat her in their old slum, Durga stepped in when others would not. When the Delhi municipal water tanker came, Padma collected Durga's big empty cans along with her own and pushed her way through the crowd to fill up the cans of two households. Durga stayed in her *jhuggī* floating above the current of people running frantically past her front door to claim their water before the tanker emptied out. Durga counted on Padma's more able knees and arms to collect her water. Padma and Durga's relationship— whatever it was—compensated for the fact that Padma's husband's salary never seemed to stretch far enough and that Durga had no nearby children or in-laws to help her with heavy labor.

On the morning before demolition, Padma and her family were the first to pack their things and leave. When the truck was set to go, Padma ran into Durga's *jhuggī* and, grabbing Durga, buried her face in Durga's chest and sobbed. Durga patted her and, in cadenced reassurance, told her not to cry, it would be okay. All day, people reflected sentimentally on Padma's emotional display toward Durga as they thought through their own connections with their neighbors. As for Durga, as soon as Padma left, she commented to her boyfriend and to me with disgust, "Did you smell the alcohol on her breath? She's been drinking all morning." As I sat floored by the awkward twist to what seemed a display of solidarity, Durga continued brazenly about how Padma had always been an alcoholic.

In her extensive relationship with Padma, Durga gave assistance most women would have thought threatening—intervening in her family matters, indirectly commenting on family neglect by sharing her resources.

After Durga later left Delhi, Padma repeatedly asked me to call Durga on her behalf and recalled how much she missed Durga. Padma, reviled by so many, needed Durga not just for her material assistance, but also because she had no other alliance to call her own. In her vulnerability, she appreciated Durga's affectionate care. Durga presided over a web of alliances—her clients and their connections, a young man from the slum who gave her rides everywhere, a reputation that commanded respect. Durga's comparably higher wealth and connections beyond the neighborhood gave her more social resources for health than Padma (Mullings 2005; O'Daniel 2011; Poortinga 2006a; Poortinga 2006b). While Padma portrayed a relationship rich and deep, Durga pulled away to distance herself.

Gradually, after demolition and Durga's subsequent move back to the village, Padma's intense longing for Durga faded to a critical perspective. The way they had interacted no longer made her nostalgic, but turned more toward herself instead. In describing her health over the long term, Padma mentioned that several years back she had a miscarriage while she was hauling water. She reminded me, "You knew how many people I had to haul water for, right?" After blood appeared, she went to Durga to remove whatever remained in her womb (*safāī*). Durga took five hundred rupees. "Can you imagine that?!" she asked in disbelief. "After all the things that I did to help Durga, she still took five hundred rupees? She was cunning (*cālū*)." While Durga had detached herself from Padma by openly demonstrating that she was independent of Padma, Padma did the opposite. Padma embraced the terms of their relationship: the regularity with which she hauled water for Durga (as well as her family) and the fact that it would be natural to get Durga's help for her miscarriage. Yet now she realized that Durga's true character was different than she had thought—she was cunning and wanted to use an appearance of affection to get her work done through Padma. Reinterpreting Durga in this way, Padma let go of her warm feelings for her.

Those women who were very close to each other on a day-to-day basis differentiated between what that they did for each other and attachment. In both of these relationships, women highlighted the flawed inner character of their neighbors: Padma's alcoholism, Durga's cunning lack of generosity. Being involved with their neighbors was a necessity, but women asserted that in the midst of their shared everyday life, their own character remained uncorrupted. Although Durga had denied any reliance on Padma, Padma argued that their relationship indicated her own goodness—giving until it literally hurt. In the end, women distanced themselves from their daily engagement and saw in each other a reflection on their individual selves: Padma's generosity, Durga's stoic independence. By keeping their relationship ambivalent, they could make demands based on reciprocity but build nothing permanent. While Carol Stack (1974) has argued that interdependence between neighborhood friends can make people kin, in this community, though women were interdependent, women were not interested in acknowledging such interdependence, much less using it as the basis to build enduring relations with their neighbors. Instead, their women used their neighbors to highlight how their character was different and unique. When neighbors veered closer to interpreting their daily shared experiences as interdependence, women assertively challenged what they saw as dangerous intrusion.

In their everyday intimacy, women did grow close to one another. In the months following demolition, as I visited women independently, it became clear that women did miss one another and commented that the increased sickness after demolition was because they no longer could look after one another (cf. Fullilove 2004; Wallace and Wallace 1998). When I took Neetu to visit Durga for the first time in her new room a month after demolition, Neetu erupted into excitement. Old neighbors sat in the chairs lining the wall. In the middle, Neetu sat with a satisfied smile and said how nice it was to sit in the middle of everyone. Durga laughed and said that people just keep coming—there are always at least three people in the room at any point in time. "It would be nice," Durga said, "if your family could get a room in this neighborhood." Neetu grinned as she looked around the room and considered the possibility. As the months passed on, though, Neetu's reflections on those relationships changed. "People there were not good," she said to me once dismissively, as she talked about people from the slum. "But I thought that you missed it," I said, confused. "Yeah, I miss being around people," she reflected, "but that's it."

When I listened carefully to what women missed, it was not the neighborhood, or "community," as a cohesive group. As Neetu put it to Mrinalini when she visited, "I used to love sitting out there with everyone. But after that, I went back inside my house. No one meant anything to me [*Mujhe kisī se matlab nahīn thā*]." With the neighbors that they grew close to, women developed tender fondness. They complained about unreliable families, they passed on old possessions, offered intimate opinions, and loaned money at critical times. While being intensely socially involved, women exerted effort to keep their selves detached from the neighbors they became close to. Neetu, Geeta, Durga, Padma, and Mrinalini enjoyed the company of their neighbors, but in the end, they went back to their homes, both literal and figurative, in terms of their selves. Their husbands were often less forgiving. As Jyoti's husband declared, "We don't meet with anyone—don't go to their houses, don't talk. The more people talk, the more dangerous they are."

I interpret their words through the ideal of detachment in Hinduism that enables indifference to social distinctions and worldly distinctions more generally (Khandelwal 2004: 44), thus acknowledging humanity's essential equality and inclusion with God. But here I borrow from Khandelwal's gendered approach to detachment that emphasizes how detachment is practiced within the world. Detachment for renouncers who continue to engage in the world of distinctions they have left behind requires the knowledge of "how to negotiate social relationships so as to maintain . . . integrity without harming others" (2004: 71). Female renouncers realize that if they do not tread carefully within their social relationships, they risk being attached to people and developing desire about the outcome of their relationships, both of which can dissolve their vows of separation.

In this not-so-distant industrial Delhi neighborhood, women's well-elaborated distinctions between each other seem far from detachment, as they classify their neighbors into those with whom they do or do not interact (and to what degree), and scrutinize their neighbors' more lurid histories and personal choices. They offered their actions and personal stories to one another, but again and again, women refused to ask for sustained relations or affection. Women's repeated efforts to "not mean anything" or to "wash out the dirtiness" of their neighbors' more sordid stories could also be seen as efforts to decide when and how to act in ways that protected their ideals for the self. They were forced daily to decide between when to distance themselves and when to intervene (Khandelwal 2004: 68)—and in both social negotiations, women stepped back toward themselves.

WOMEN'S INSIDE SELVES

When Durga and I made plans for me to accompany her to the village, she told me not to tell others. I asked why. "Because they will feel envious (*jalan*)," she said, citing the dangerous force of jealousy that one needed to protect oneself from (for more on this, see chapter 3) (Dean 2013). She pulled out her gold necklace, and said, "People are jealous because I earn more, because I have money. But I work hard, I earn my own money!" As she looked out, she looked back in, asserting the self that she needed to hide at times, but asserting the value of what she hid. As I told her that people will find out, her tone changed: "So what, let them find out when they do." Women knew it was a necessity to reflect on how their appearances would be understood as they sat on the cots in front of their homes, with jiggling bellies laid out, as well as on streets, with faces drawn tightly into stern expressions. This was, however, one side of the boundary, looking out to maintain how others knew you to minimize risk and manage interactions. On the other side of the boundary was the intimate self that was being protected from magic, from jealousy, from power-hungry *pradhāns*, overzealous expectations, and interloping neighbors. Was all of their looking outward framed by looking back in? As Geeta and Mrinalini described themselves going back into their homes, what did they see?

A few months later, Durga sat with me and Saraswati in her new room and complained that I made her miss a perfectly good movie on TV with the interviews I had demanded on concepts of health and the body. There was just no point to staying here in Delhi, she explained in the midst of the dry April heat, which seemed not only to bake the air but also to emphasize her loneliness after demolition even more. Perhaps, in spite of her insecurity about where to live, her frustration at being disrupted, or perhaps because of all of these things, she began to talk about God on her shoulder. God (*Bhagvān*), Durga said, is always with us on our shoulder. "He is not on our right shoulder because we use that hand to do everything, to work, to eat, to steal. God will not be involved in that. God is always sitting on the other shoulder, the left one, because we cannot do anything with our left hand.[16] Even when we close the curtain to our rooms and no one can see us,"[17] she explained, "God can still see us and knows what is happening in our house. That's why you should never think anything bad about anyone—you should not be jealous, you should not hope that bad things happen to people, because all of that goes inside of you." Durga's curtain was similar to the appearance that she constructed through which others could know her. Behind it, in her home—or her true self—were her actions. Behind the curtain, her actions constituted her self, what she did with her hands, and the intentions behind her thoughts. There was no true identity to be found out, as to whether Durga was rich or poor, or had a big or small house in the village. What mattered was what she did.

Through introspection,[18] Durga pointed to time and accountability beyond this particular moment. She asserted that to do rightfully would be felt in accumulated merit in the next lifetime: "As we did action (*karm*), in that way we will get fruits. What we will do now, later we will get. This is why it is said, 'Do not do anyone wrong! Do not say anything bad!'"[19] Durga explained that her accountability to God was measured when her soul would be placed in another body after she died. But, in referencing God's view of her at all times, she envisioned that action was done with God by her side and enacted in this world, in her home, with her hands.

In this way, Durga contextualized current situations by taking the long view of women's actions. On one visit to Durga, I commented that I worried about Neetu because her husband had been beating her. She was quiet for a little bit and then barked, "But did I not tell you that before? She married an old man, and a Muslim too; that's what happens. It's not like I told her to go ahead, but she made her own decision. And what about her first husband?" When I answered with the reasoning that Neetu had given me—that he had run off—she barked, "No he did not! He's in the village; he's just sitting there. He did not run anywhere. Tell me one thing that Neetu doesn't have. She has a fridge, a TV, a cooler—there isn't one thing that she doesn't have. She sleeps late, takes her bath, and then doesn't make food until one or two and then she sleeps again. And still she cries all the time! She has a good husband who brings home lots of money. The rest of us have to earn for ourselves. I get up early, do all my work; I don't get to live like her."

Durga argued that Neetu's mistakes had led to her current struggles. By assigning blame to Neetu for both leaving her husband and choosing a bad one against Durga's advice, Durga retold Neetu's story as one in which Neetu was not a suffering victim but an actor who had the capacity for right action and for realizing the potential of the life she lived. (Durga's story, ironically, was not that different, since she also had left her husband and became moderately estranged from her sons in the village.) Though Durga had initially described Neetu's husband critically, in the end she suggested that his ability to provide was a resource that few others, including herself, enjoyed. Durga held their lives side-by-side in comparison. Durga argued that Neetu chose an easy life, filled with the certainty of money and daily relaxation, with the full realization that her husband might not be ideal in other ways. But Durga pointed toward the intention of her action, suggesting that she suffered because she had chosen wealth over other factors. Arguing that she, in contrast, faced the pressure of providing alone for herself, Durga did not have the energy—or the sympathy—to listen to Neetu's supposed "cries." Durga argued that Neetu had squandered good action for self-interested action and, in this moment, bore the fruits of such actions.

Still, even as she critiqued Neetu's current crying, Durga was insisting on the capacity for action that she had in this moment. Emphasizing that she "did not get to live like" Neetu, Durga pointed to Neetu's action *not* to recognize the comfort that her circumstances gave her. Because at other moments Durga had encouraged Neetu to leave her husband, it is apparent that here Durga was emphasizing the capacity of action rather than condoning violence. Durga emphasized the powerful capacity of intention behind action, whether a person sat in a room that did not compare to that which the government had just demolished, as Durga now did, or whether facing domestic violence like Neetu. As women emphasized the necessity to protect their selves from dangerous others, they meant protecting their own ability to act as they saw fit, not as subject to or manipulated by others' dangerous desires. "If someone shows bad character, then move away from him!" Durga repeated this for emphasis before concluding that "Our lives have only so many days."[20] The brief temptations of engaging with bad characters were contrasted to what lasted over the long term.

Regardless of how effectively her neighbors might be able to make their outsides appear powerful in the present, Durga emphasized that eventually the self behind the curtain, watched always by God, would be known by all. For those who are bad, she explained, "After his death, it will be said that he was a very bad man; it's good [that he's dead]! It will be said twenty-five times. But if he was a good man, the whole world will cry: 'Why did you die, brother? Why did you go? We are sad.' The good are remembered; the bad are also remembered. But for the good, the world cries, even God cries. For the bad, the world just says bad things."[21] In the end, what was inside people would be known to all, even if no one could tell who they were in the present. But Durga's attention to action indicated disciplined looking inward in daily life. Ultimately women, with God on their shoulder, must govern the space behind the curtain where they manage their selves by protecting them from risk and engaging in thoughtful action. As private as this space was, Durga emphasized that ultimately the character of this self would be known to all.

THE NECESSITY OF DRAWING THE CURTAIN

Having arrived in Ghaziapuram with bright ideas of community social support and grassroots activism, I wanted very badly to find the community resources that could seed change. The gossip, the constant speculation, the carefully planned social maneuvers all felt like such a waste of energy to me. What did any of these differences between neighbors matter, if in the end everyone in the *jhuggīs* faced the same barriers to health? If they all had to run after every rupee, all saw their *jhuggīs* bulldozed, and all felt the results in their weakened bodies?

By and large, researchers and reformers have stressed the social conditions that people living in slums share. These shared conditions are what enable people living in poor urban communities to collectively advocate for better conditions, to promote health among community members, to provide each other social support, and to join collectives for self-governance and saving. When it comes to differentiating people living in slums, their differences have been explored at the community level through access to services, environmental conditions, community attitudes about gender, and demographic variations. All of these factors make a difference in shaping overall health. What people think of each other—both the good and the *gandagī*—is usually not seen as important.

Yet when women aired the dirty laundry of community life, they indicated more fine-grained dimensions of inequality than was usually stipulated by a social determinants of health perspective. Because slum life required dependence on powerful figures to receive everything from water to political identification (Anand 2011; Jha, Rao, and Woolcock 2007; Srivastava 2012; Weinstein 2008), women had to negotiate local hierarchies as they went about procuring the basic necessities of their everyday life. Neither was there equal access to the public health programs that were supposed to help the community as a whole. Some women felt empowered by women's collectives, others felt excluded. And women had every reason to be concerned about how others understood their own differences. In a setting where Muslims remembered communal riots from years earlier and Biharis were seen as more backward than other migrants, Padma and Saraswati foregrounded parts of their identity that made for less stigmatized appearances and allowed them the respect that they felt entitled to. Beyond the rich-poor binary, these were political, organizational, ethnic, and religious inequalities that women had to negotiate to protect their basic security.

Yet women's intense discussion of who their neighbors were complicated these differences. They made me wonder whether I could ever really put the people I knew into tables that would sort their differences—what *did* they really earn, and if Padma was born Muslim and now kind of Hindu, then where did she go? Here, knowing caste, class, regional origin, and family history were not straightforward but required intense scrutiny of one's neighbors (Chandola 2010; Datta 2011), and, even then, it was always felt that the full truth was yet to be uncovered.

In a setting ripe with possibilities for mobility, women argued that many people immorally exploited contemporary opportunities for their own gain. Appearances were a tool through which some area residents sought to solidify power or gain sympathy that was undeserved. But, by asserting their knowledge of neighbors' histories, women challenged the power that their neighbors sought, emptying their moral claims and limiting their power. In pointing to the corrupt paths that some women had taken, women asserted the range of actions that they could have taken from a common origin point. Though the circumstances of contemporary India posed obstacles to the mobility of all of them (Fernandes 2006; Jeffrey 2010; Marrow 2013; Srivastava 2012), women asserted the moral obligations that mobility still entailed.

In their daily lives, women were intimately involved with their neighbors, whose hands reached through the shutters into Durga's store and whose bottoms threatened the integrity of Durga's cot. All women had intricate maps of involvement, avoiding some women altogether, allowing certain women into their daily "sitting together," and employing others in mutual help. Discerning what they felt were neighbors' inner characters allowed women to better protect themselves from neighbors' potential danger. Community-level social support was not merely a matter of helping out those like you in a deprived setting. Extending oneself in relationship meant entering in a complex web of reciprocity and alliance that would shape who would provide help in the future. However, women maintained that, regardless of the degree of their engagement, they remained detached from their neighbors. Even when their neighbors' desires were far from the ambition of more dangerous community figures, women resisted needing their neighbors, fearing that attachment could threaten their own independence to act. Instead, their neighbors helped reflect women's own selves as generous, persistent, and honest. While researchers have been tempted to acknowledge these intimate ties as community, it is important to recognize that, regardless of the local tools to manage diversity (Datta 2011; Nandy 1995; Ring 2006), women prioritized their abilities to manage their selves amidst such complex sociality. The complex relationships described here show the limits of evaluating community social support through observed actions and context-free measures of perception. Instead, analytical space must be given to women's important ideas of separation and independence that provide alternative meanings. If survival alone was the goal of Durga and her neighbors, they would have accepted help from anyone.

Behind the curtain of appearance and engagement that women drew, they examined their own capacity for action. Practical daily decisions about their social interaction were based in the awareness of longer personal histories and larger, otherworldly consequences. While women relied on appearances for existence within the world, they pointed to the long-term salience of their actions. Women asserted that their actions were their responsibility alone, with God as a presence to watch them. Women honored their selves as a private space and noted that the boundaries that they marked from their neighbors allowed their sovereignty over their selves. As a space free of distinctions, this inner character would ultimately be known not just to them and to God, but to everyone. In a context in which public rumor (Chandola 2012a; Das and Addlakha 2001; Jesmin and Salway 2000) and social stigma (Haider 2000; Roy 2011) forcefully shaped the identity of women living in slums, women's focus on defining their selves formed a counterreality. By preventing themselves from immersion in these relationships, women reserved a space to affirm themselves.

In the evenings, Durga usually pulled her cot inside from the walkway and, much later, shut the doors to her shop. By day, she was a social center in this universe and, by night, she quietly retreated to her back room and watched her favorite serials on TV. She often welcomed in the older son of a nearby family to sleep in the front room or was called out to deliver a baby in wee hours. Even when she shut the doors to make space that was just her own, it seemed impossible for Durga to keep her neighbors from coming in through the cracks. But Durga did not need complete solitude to make a peaceful place for herself. As long as she protected her ability to think and act with her own hands, that was enough.

3 "Getting Ahead" as Moral Citizenship in the Face of Demolition

On February 4, 2009, slum residents finally began to believe that the government would demolish their settlement the next day. Although a demolition notice had been posted three weeks earlier, residents had reacted with disbelief, ambivalence, and uncertainty. Minutes after the demolition notice was posted, residents had torn it down from *jhuggī* walls and crumpled it. Residents said they could not believe that this demolition notice would have any different outcome from those of the others before. As evidence, people showed me notices from the last five years promising demolitions that never came and said, almost bored, "It won't happen—not at least until after the election. The politicians need our votes." This was a historical truth. They had built this city from a jungle; the factories needed their skills. Politicians, knowing this, had always said, "Let them live" (*Unko rahene do*). The residents' work and their worldly view of themselves made them *of* the city, if not its founders. Yet, despite the place they held in the city, the looming demolition was a reminder about the fragility of their rights as urban citizens.

In the days following the demolition notice, people outwardly appeared to be apathetic about demolition. Yet their circular conversations about their future and how to proceed showed more tortured emotion. Residents

Figure 4. World-Class Dreams. Photo by Mayank Austen Soofi.

exuberantly cheered politicians who showed up at rallies night after night vowing protection, only to declare those same politicians' uselessness the following mornings. Residents charged that the politicians wanted to appear powerful but that they were no longer sincere in actually keeping their promises. Neither did people want to band together with neighbors who were more concerned for their own welfare than with the collective. Residents' certainty of their physical, political, and social place in the city slowly melted into the mournful cry of "What can be done? (*Kyā kare?*)" Against the backdrop of political and media disputes over their future, residents had already answered their own question concretely. They quietly began searching for new accommodations, arranging to send kin to distant locales, and posing for pictures with soon-to-be former neighbors.

Then finally, demolition day was here. Policemen arrived several days in advance to scout the logistics for the bulldozing. The electric lines fell in the late afternoon of February 4. A municipal worker had shimmied up electricity poles to pluck the electricity wires that would not be used after that day. People stood watching him in earnest and, as if in a choreographed move, they turned to their own homes and scaled them to pull off pieces of their roofing materials to sell as scraps. By late evening, the main artery road was clogged with a ragtag army of vehicles piled high with the makings of home that residents had accumulated over twenty-five years. As the lights of the slum went out, with them went the ten thousand residents of the slum to new homes in rented rooms in surrounding neighborhoods, to the homes of nearby family, and, for some, all the way back to the village.

It was no longer clear what rights they had to basic security and whom they could rely on to access them. The bold pronouncement of "let them live" had wilted with time. So the question lingered—"*kyā kare*"—what could be done? Could they still get ahead somehow?

POPULATION, PATRONAGE, AND *PRADHĀNS:* RELATIONSHIPS AND THE STUFF OF SURVIVAL

This chapter explores how women and their families made sense of their mobility while the basic social conditions of survival shifted all around them. Homes, water, and food form the basis of what scholars and advocates have deemed to be the social entitlements and forms of basic protection that constitute the right to survival (Farmer 2005; Gupta 2012; Jacobs 2011) and one of the most crucial sites of citizenship (Appadurai 2000: 24). Social relationships with politicians, the state, and business had facilitated these protections—underhandedly in some cases, but in others, directly. Yet over the years these relationships had become unrecognizable.

In a setting where recent court orders had decreed the clearing of public lands that would likely displace three million of Delhi's *jhuggī* residents, the demolition of Ghaziapuram was one piece of a larger inexorable political shift. Since India's economy liberalized in the early 1990s, initiating the greatest ever expansion of the country's economy, the place of the poor in broader society has shifted dramatically. When India was founded in 1947, the question was not if the poor would get ahead, but how the government would support them in doing so. Leaders disagreed on the means of development, but the ends of development were clear: fighting

poverty and hunger. The means that emerged from this initial debate—
including improving the savings rate, establishing an industrial base,
upgrading the skill base, and advancing agriculture from stagnation—
gradually were solidified into institutions that lasted for decades, some
even into the present (Bose 1997: 54).

A climate of deregulation in the 1970s shifted both economic and development policy in India and internationally. In the decades that followed,
global economic leaders pushed to unravel business regulation, increase
the flexibility of labor, scale back the welfare state, and increase international trade. In 1991, India formally liberalized its economy, marking the
decline of state control of business and development in India, and the
beginning of what some see as the intensified growth of class stratification.
The wave of growth excluded the poor, and the public health spending that
addressed their needs crumbled (Gupta and Sivaramakrishnan 2010;
Gupta 2005). The urban poor in particular stimulated the fear among
middle-class people who benefited from liberalization. Might they incite
class warfare (Gupta and Sivaramakrishnan 2010)? Why would they not
simply return to where they came from, if all they had in Delhi was slums
(Baviskar 2006)? From being an essential part of the nation's plan to
progress, now what was given to the poor, as well as the place of the poor
in overall society, was completely redefined.

Unlike other places, in India, these efforts of scaling back were accompanied by a wave of large welfare programs to attenuate unemployment
and malnutrition amongst the poor. In concert with this was a dramatic
rise in a professional NGO class charged with tending to the needs of the
poor (Gupta 2012; Gupta and Sivaramakrishnan 2010). Scholars and
activists have been skeptical of these trends. They claim that NGOs, often
bolstered by state interests and global development, dilute the radicalism
of human rights concepts they hail (Appadurai 2002; Harriss 2010;
Luthra 2003; Nagar and Santin Collective Writers 2006; Sharma 2010).
When scholars have examined the actual operations of state-run welfare
programs, they have found that their benefits are haphazardly distributed
(Gupta 2012) and driven by "calculations of political expediency" to serve
the poor in ways beneficial to politicians (Anand and Rademacher 2011:
1757–58; Chatterjee 2004: 40). Programs to benefit the population end up
being governed by patronage.

Responding to increasingly unengaged states and subverted NGO agendas, researchers have combatted their malaise by examining the practices of social change that have emerged from the bottom up. In South Asia, some community groups have used the language of human rights to bypass the exclusion of the state and create an alternative moral discourse to lobby for services (Appadurai 2002; Chatterjee 2004). Citizen groups in Delhi have provided alternative censuses to correct the Delhi Development Authority's documentation of illegality with information on how citizens are eligible for relocation (Ghertner 2010). Researchers have noted that "problem solving" rather than democracy (Harriss 2010: 92) is often the goal of many advocacy groups whose solutions bypass demolition, extend water to particular groups, or improve the operation of local ration stores (see also Appadurai 2002; Chatterjee 2004). Strategically balancing relationships with local big men, elected politicians, and social workers to obtain water is a way that people living in slums "constitute themselves as citizens and subjects of the city" (Anand 2011: 546). In all of these examples, a form of citizenship is remade—cobbled together through restored entitlements, reclaiming the right to create knowledge about one's legitimacy and a collective (if undemocratic and nonuniversal) process. If the social relationships with the state, developers, and political patrons were now unreliable, then people living in poverty would instead devise "new ways in which they can choose how they should be governed" (Chatterjee 2004: 77).

But what about when people do not choose how they should be governed? What can they do when it is not clear who is governing? What about when they do not get what they want or need from those in power? In this chapter, I show why, from the community level, it is difficult to count on those in power, and why social advocacy is not always such a clear path to security. Nonetheless, other forms of belonging were used to build a bridge to security that relied less upon the help of unreliable politicians, a fickle state, and even neighbors who shared parts of one's struggle. People alternated between articulating how the social conditions of survival were mediated by powerful patrons and the state, on the one hand, and, on the other, social conditions of survival that they, repeatedly and with struggle, had to make for themselves. Residents, like many of the advocates who speak on behalf of the poor (Farmer 2005), hoped to awaken the conscience of those in power as they waited for politicians to show up on their behalf. Others, fed up with the undeveloped consciences of those in power, chose actions in their own hands. They concentrated on other forms of mobility that did not rely on others to grant rights.

In the nine months of my research that followed demolition, conversations between me and residents of the *jhuggīs* gave way to deep reflections about their lives and their place in Delhi. As residents reflected on their past, present, and future in Delhi, they traced their belonging to this city. It was here that they had transformed themselves through their migration experiences. They emphasized how their individual journeys to build new lives for themselves and their families in the city had been the process through which Delhi, and global India as well, had been built. Residents knew that political tides had turned against the urban poor, but their conception of themselves as the city's builders was the clue to the enigma of slum residents' political ambivalence. For as much exclusion as they faced in demolition and in their daily experiences of poverty, they thought of themselves through their own personal ventures to get ahead (*āge barhānā*), a process through which they emphasized their personal transformation, their societal contributions, and their struggles to get ahead in a moral fashion.

I explore the citizenship that residents of this slum offered—one that pictured the essential contribution they made (i.e., Fuchs 2005: 114)—to counter the exclusive citizenship they faced in the present that labeled them as encroachers to be removed and masses to be tamed (Baviskar 2003; Dupont 2011; Fernandes 2006; Ghertner 2010). Critics of modern governance and urban planning argue that, despite the valuable contribution that poor people make through their work, in exchange they end up displaced and marginalized by politicians and the middle classes. Citizenship, as the right to space, livelihood, and representation mediated through interaction with state actors, is a failed enterprise for poor people despite how hard they try. When scholars conceptualize citizenship as an exchange (even a failed one) between responsible poor working citizens and powerful states, they can unintentionally repeat some of the shortcomings of hierarchical patron-client models before them. In both models, there is little room for mobility or transformation of the actors—whether planners, the state, the middle class, or the urban poor. And as powerful as is the structural vio-

lence of contemporary urban planning and neoliberal governance, by situ-
ating research from the view of the powerful planner, the views of the urban
poor are reduced to a homogenous, feeble agency within a monolithic structure of the powerful.

In this chapter, I describe how women's ambivalence to looming demolition demonstrates their sense of their diversity, their nuanced reaction to
the powerful, their deep investment in their individual transformations, a
complex notion of their agency (invested in action, but suspicious of desire),
and a feeling of societal inclusion that made demolition seem unlikely. As
optimistic as was the goal of getting ahead, women in particular marked
their mobility in complex ways—not simply how much money they had,
but also how they saw themselves, and what changes they had experienced
throughout their own lifetime (i.e., Fuchs 2005). Many had moved in and
out of poverty already (i.e., Krishna 2010). Getting *ahead* was not a straight
path forward, women urged, despite the vision that their husbands often
articulated. Using an emic view of citizenship, I seek not to discount the
vast structural violence facing Delhi's urban poor, but instead, in introducing this complexity, I hope to raise different political questions.

Women's histories of their experience in Delhi emphasize their inclusion in the city and their moral struggles to get ahead in the right way. I
argue that residents offered a type of citizenship that was not dependent
on others' recognition alone, be it of government, patrons, or employers.
In a setting where power was arranged in "nested hierarchies" (Gupta
2012: 29) and complex imaginaries of power that blur the lines between
NGOs, state entities, and local leaders (Pinto 2004; Sharma 2010), it was
practical to take this stance. In order to hold onto their hope of mobility,
women had to both suspend their reliance on these hierarchies and imagine themselves beyond the poverty they were continually thrust into. They
offered the continuity of their ability to get ahead morally, whether their
work and contribution were recognized by the powerful. As residents
defined their contribution to society and sometimes rejected political society, they elaborated citizenship as an ethical concept enacted through
their daily practices of work, family, and urban life.

With their sincere political selves and with hardly any technological
resources, residents created vital international links for India and built
the city that they were now being pushed out of—and they persisted even

when locked out of the resources that were rightfully theirs. Even in a climate where aspirations for change were shared by others, women in particular found that they had to discipline family members who forgot that aspirations for mobility required endurance. Residents' adherence to sincerity meant that they had fostered a strong belief in merit and rejected others' baseless claims to power. Surrounded by people interested in the pursuit of their own power through the channels of state, business, and development institutions, slum residents' endeavors simply to get ahead on their own terms was a strikingly radical way of defining their citizenship. In so doing, their definition challenged the terms of how people living in poverty experience the social conditions at the root of their health.

"THIS PLACE WAS A JUNGLE": MIGRANTS' BEGINNINGS IN DELHI

"Before this," Asha explained, "there was nothing! It was just rocks—there was nothing!" When they came, people told me, there was jungle all along the horizon, with only a few *jhuggīs* in their midst. "And there was no one here either," Asha continued. "There were hardly any crowds."[1] In the months after demolition, I heard residents repeatedly talk about how this area had transformed during their time here. I began talking both in formal taped interviews and informal conversations with both male and female residents about their migration to Delhi and their beginnings there. Their narratives echo those of both poor migrants beginning their urban lives in urban South Asia (Sharma 2000; Tindall 1992) and of those forcibly resettled to the city's peripheries (Jervis Read 2012; Tarlo 2003: 131).

In Ghaziapuram, as in many slum neighborhoods, the majority of the families had migrated from rural villages or smaller towns starting in the late 1970s and continuing through the late 1990s. "We came here because of difficulty. Because in the village, there is not much money," Jyoti said, holding back her two rowdy toddlers. "Here we earn and eat. Our stomachs are full. In the village, there is not much wealth. Not much is grown in the fields either." But she did not like Delhi. Neither was the water good, nor were the vegetables and bread. "I mean—in the village, there is water and there is food. Everything is good."[2] In this ambivalent situation, Jyoti, like others, had to choose between a village life with land security but lack of income, and an urban life with land insecurity but the potential for employment (i.e., Gupta and Sivaramakrishnan 2010).

Nonetheless, their paths to Delhi were diverse. Some, like Neetu and Saraswati, came to Delhi as children with their families and spent their formative years shuttling back and forth between Delhi and their villages. Men like Akshay came for work opportunities in their teens, and others came after they were married. However, while residents came at different points of their lives and at different moments in Delhi's development over a twenty-year period, in all of their stories, residents emphasized how they built a place in this city—both literally, through the settlements they established, and through their work, which connected them to the larger outside world. Their migration narratives emphasized how their self-transformation in Delhi was tied to how they transformed the urban landscape. Told in an exclusionary present, their narratives emphasize the continuous sentiment of wanting to get ahead, even as my observations in the present showed more conflicted ideals. They had come here, people told me, because there was no work at home. But, as sincere as their ambition was, before they could even work, they needed to establish space in which they could live.

As they told their stories now, we sat in rooms that were tucked amidst the huge *jhuggī* cluster of Shikhar Colony or the expanded urban villages of Suraj Nagar or Chandpuri, with their winding mazes of streets that required attention to every turn to not get lost. In this industrial zone, companies used high walls to mark off their plots that contained groaning monstrous-looking industrial machines, shiny glass buildings for publishing, or large brick factories that made clothing for export or pharmaceuticals. Forming a fringe on the defined lines of these industrial buildings were informally constructed roadside restaurants (*dhābās*) and small stores for the laborers that made the industrial area run. The roads were filled with large goods-carrying trucks which waddled slowly along, water tankers, and cars of commuting middle-class managers. People explained the landscape of the past by recalling the ghosts of places that were now crowded.

Asha, one of the first migrants to Ghaziapuram, emphasized how quickly it all had changed: "Now they have come this way, in just five years. What happened, happened then. Before that there was nothing."[3]

The now bustling lower-middle-class colonies of Roop Nagar and Sarita Vihar were not even there. The urban villages of Suraj Nagar and Chandpuri, surrounded by agricultural fields, were a fifth the size they were now. Dirt roads connected the few factories that were there at that time. "The road was so big then," said Dilip to explain the sparsely settled landscape. Now, indirectly referring to the *jhuggīs*, factories, and roadside stalls crowded in, Dilip claimed, the road was so obscured by all the buildings that "you can barely even see it!"[4]

To live in Ghaziapuram twenty-five years ago meant accepting that nothing was given. In the empty landscape that residents described, water, electricity, homes, and general amenities had to be sought out and fought for. Life was different: it was much more difficult. Then, residents requested water—"like beggars!" Asha said—at one of the few export factories. Despite her humiliation at being forced to ask, the companies gave the water without hesitation. Factory managers knew the need of the workers living nearby and were unburdened by providing for the few there. Neetu and her sister had to walk to the far northern edge of the industrial area for water, a trek of several kilometers from where they had settled in Suraj Nagar. The harried traffic in water from afar was marked by a slow parade of people pushing bikes weighed down with buckets of water.[5] Neetu and her sister found ways to make their work into their own adventure, stopping midjourney in each farmer's field to sample their sugar cane. Surrounded by farmland, with no electricity, having to haul all of their water from far away, she said, "It was really difficult (*bahut parishānī hotī thī*)." Neetu's paired images of exhausting hauling and mischievous snacking lent a playful spirit to the work. Though there was so much more labor in collecting water at that time, Mrinalini reminisced about its abundance. With hardly anyone around, no matter what they wanted, they could get! In this empty agricultural landscape, they had managed to find resources to make their life there possible.

Though today migrants can rent a home when they arrive, women were careful to stress, back then there were no such amenities. "All the plots were empty," Hema declared. "These working people took their own bricks and stones to build the *jhuggīs* they lived in." Dilip explained that often men came first, lived in rented quarters, and only later called their families to join them. "People put their money together to construct homes," he added. But as much as there was a pattern in migration, people used flexible strategies and creatively made investments. Dilip's investment in several different *jhuggīs* demonstrated the role he played in substantial development through the entire region. He bought a *jhuggī* in Roop Nagar for three hundred rupees, then sold it and lived in the factory where he worked for a while. Next, he bought a *jhuggī* in a nearby region for 150 rupees and improved it before selling it later for nine thousand rupees. Finally, he built his own *jhuggī* in Hari Camp. "In the beginning it was so small you could not stand up, but slowly we added more to it. It was just *kacchā* (made of dirt and other impermanent materials), but slowly we turned it into a *pakkā* (concrete and brick) *jhuggī*." According to Dilip and other single male "flippers" of *jhuggī* real estate (see also Anand and Rademacher 2011: 1764), they were not exploiting business opportunities, but instead simply building southeast Delhi from the ground up.

For Mrinalini, beginning with a *kacchā jhuggī* allowed her to escape fights with her husband's family. Upon moving to Delhi, she and her husband had lived together with his brother's family in nearby Shikhar Colony. But abuse from her brother-in-law and her sister-in-law's jealousy that she had given birth to a son pushed Mrinalini over the edge. While Dilip had seen investment in *jhuggīs* as a way to make financial gains, the real estate maneuvers of Mrinalini and other women were oriented toward their personal safety and a better environment for their children (Baruah 2007: 2101). For both men and women, seeing the potential of small huts and converting them into modern buildings transformed this area from a jungle to a city with "tentative hope" (Baviskar 2003: 95). With cadenced words, Asha sounded the intertwined moves of migration, growth, and mobility: "They kept coming, they kept developing; they came, they developed. They built *jhuggīs*, they came, they came, they built."[6] Through building, residents instilled their determined sentiment into the material form of their homes and broader encampments.

As Dilip reflected on Ghaziapuram's gradual development, he considered the history of each individual *jhuggī*, one by one—their occupants and which were bought, improved, sold, or split. By explaining the process through which the *jhuggīs* had become the present settlement, Dilip replaced the language of dilapidation with that of intentional, meaningful building. Residents described a historical transformation as much as a creative investment in their homes. From nothing, Neetu explained, they made *jhuggīs* into homes. When she bought her *jhuggī* a little after the year 2000, "It was just a *jhuggī* standing there! The area for washing, the kitchen, bathroom—we made that all. We put in the electric meter, everything." Even though Neetu came to Ghaziapuram much later, she used the same language of pioneering existence that she had for her earlier tenure in the nearby urban village of Suraj Nagar. Some home investments were made to increase their legitimacy in the eyes of the state, anticipating challenges that might come ahead. Durga paid to have an electricity meter installed in her house. Though expensive, she explained to a client of her reproductive health services, it was worth it. Together with her identification documents, this physical improvement would make it harder for the government to move her. To provide their own amenities, residents pooled their money. "Right in front of the factory, near the big peepul tree," Dilip explained, "we put in a water hand pump. Everyone used to use that pump. The water was so good." Over time, such efforts from individual initiative produced extreme variation between settlements in terms of their water access and quality of housing (Anand 2011; Asthana 1995). As they charted the gradual development of the landscape, residents emphasized how their gradual, patient efforts produced urban landscapes from simple dirt huts.

The earliest residents' narratives of their founding had emphasized how the place was "just rocks" and "only jungle," with "nothing around." But their view had its own exclusions, exclusions that placed them rather than others at the helm of urban transformations. In her research on immigrants to California's Central Valley, Leonard (1997: 127) found that their elegiac descriptions of the land depicted themselves "as kings and landowners . . . with kingdoms and capital cities of their own." Yet the silences in their narratives were revealing. She noted how "the whites who in reality blocked them have magically disappeared from the scene." Both their narratives of settlement and their redactions have the effect of placing them "in charge of the physical landscape" (Leonard 1997: 127). Likewise, the emptiness that Asha and her neighbors found in the southeastern Delhi landscape excluded the only other nearby people at the time. These excluded villagers made their appearance in residents' narratives only as hooligans. Across all Ghaziapuram, "People were afraid to go outside at night to go to the bathroom!" Neetu exclaimed. There was violence through the whole area—killing, fights, and harassment—as the new migrants clashed with the villagers who had been living there when they arrived.

Much of this violence, Dilip and others alleged, was "in Gujjar hands," an agricultural caste who lived in the urban villages of Suraj Nagar and Chandpuri long before the large migration waves from rural areas for urban work. "Gujjar people would not let anyone live; they were violent. You would not let your sister or daughters be seen. They looked at them really badly," Asha reported. "The fighting was daily!" While the complaint of Gujjar control of politics and real estate in the area continued in the present, residents argued that their early settlement was defined against the unruly atmosphere that Gujjars had established. As much as Gujjars played a role in the transformation of contemporary Delhi (Chandola 2010: 102–3), residents' rhetorical distancing of themselves from Gujjars emphasized how their migration made them more progressive. They argued that Gujjars' supposed child marriage and disregard for education (see Dabral and Malik 2004) were pointedly different from the personal transformation they envisioned for themselves in Delhi. Mohan, Asha, and Hema explained that, to protect themselves from the area villagers, they formed a collective (*sanga-than*). As families in the disparate *jhuggīs* joined together, they gained strength (*himmat*). "When we were all together, it was different. If one of them came here, then we could throw them out," explained Mohan. Their small groups of *jhuggīs* were held in stark contrast to the destructive violence that was said to characterize the neighboring areas. They, as migrants, were here to work, they said, whereas the villagers living here were satisfied to entertain themselves with primitive violence and crime.[7]

Residents hailed from all castes and from all over India. Most people were from the northern states of Uttar Pradesh and Rajasthan; a few were from Punjab. Others came from the eastern states of Bihar and West Bengal, some from Nepal. There were even a few people, residents told me, who had come from Maharashtra and South India. Even as the identity politics of affirmative action reasserted caste lines, "neither the boundaries of communities are always fully clear nor are all communities structured along the same lines" (Fuchs 2005: 109). Here there were all castes, from Chamar (an untouchable caste) to Thakur (a higher Kshaitrya caste) and pandit (Brahmin). Emphasizing equality as they discussed their demographics, Hema said, "We are not alone. We belong to each other. No one counts others' castes. There are all types of castes, all lands (*desh*)." Here, she continued, "Everyone marries everyone; no one asks who is a lower caste." Rather, people were connected by what they shared in this place: "Everyone is poor. Everyone is the *jhuggī* caste."

Emphasizing the poverty they shared over their ethnic or caste differences, she argued that residents were united by their sincere motivation to come to Delhi from far distant locations (see also Chatterjee 2004: 57; Datta 2011: 755). As different as people found their neighbors in the present (see chapter 2), as they looked back, they emphasized the shared migrant experience. Neetu said, "My sister's *jhuggī* in Suraj Nagar felt just like the city. There, people were educated; good people lived there. . . . Yes, they were good people. They talked nicely, they had good culture. You lived in a way that you felt you could share happiness and sadness." From all different places, they had come to this part of Delhi to begin new lives. These new lives were defined by the uncertainty of needing literally to make their own place in the city. If they did not actually build the walls of their homes, they formed the shape of their kitchens; if they did not personally haul water from afar, they helped bring it in through shared community resources. "Slowly, people built, built, built, and the atmosphere changed some," Asha explained. No longer did people have to fight so hard just to make the place that allowed them to make a living here.

To Akshay, there was something distinct about the people surrounding him in Delhi. "The only people who live in Delhi are money earners (*paise-kamāne-wāle log*). If you don't work here, then how will you eat?" While perhaps people in the village could count on other family resources or their own agricultural land for security, in Delhi whatever you attained was what got you through your own hard work—from wages, to water, to safety. At first, there were only a few factories in the industrial area. But gradually, the factories began calling people to work, and villagers answered the call by migrating in slow, steady droves. Others were pushed from the village rather than pulled by work. Mrinalini recalled her neighbor Durga's experience. Now, she was one of the wealthiest and most respected women in Ghaziapuram because of her midwifery business. But her husband had kicked her out of their rural home, Mrinalini explained, describing the scars he left on Durga's arms. From the train station,

Mrinalini said with admiration, Durga had walked all the way to one of Delhi's industrial satellite towns, "in the only suit she had, to stay with her parents." For many women, returning to live with their parents after leaving an abusive husband would be a sign of shame. But Mrinalini's account of the story foregrounded Durga's stoic will to begin a new life. For awhile, Durga had checked thread in a factory there, but gradually she learned midwifery from her mother.

Still, life was hard. Asha said, "Tell me, with that much income—two thousand rupees—that you got from the company, what can you feed your children, how can you foot the bill, what can you do?" It felt as if they just could not keep up. "A thousand here, a thousand there; two thousand here, two thousand there—with such high prices, we cannot do anything for the children nor can they study nor can we write. . . . What can a poor man do? He can't do anything." Spare time was often spent ruminating on the gap between earnings and the uses to which they must be put. Would enough money in savings magically appear if they shifted their diet, changed their room, ignored their health, or sent a relative home to the village? Jobs often did not materialize despite employer promises; the neighborhood money cooperatives to which men belonged could eat up savings. As residents switched jobs, salaries varied dramatically from month to month, and still there was pressure from rural family to send money home. Particularly in the beginning, large sacrifices had been required. Akshay said, "Sometimes I went to sleep hungry; in winter, sometimes I slept in bad, dirty clothes only." In order to make enough money to support their families, many of his neighbors "ate dinner and then went to the factory at nine and worked until two in the morning." Mohan's neighbor said the pace was "quickly (*jaldī*) get up, quickly eat, quickly go to duty." On his one day off, the roads were so swarmed with other workers that if he were to venture out he was bound to waste away the precious time in bumper-to-bumper traffic. Here in the city, he said, there was no time for anything. As they recounted the difficulty of their work, families charted their persistence in effort, even as they faced uncertainties and setbacks.

By emphasizing the emptiness of the landscape, residents charted their own determination to live here. In building their own homes and hauling their own water, they endured considerable hardship because of their desire to start over here in Delhi. Residents' continued efforts to make a life here in Delhi on their own initiative shows that, even as their awareness of the challenges of Delhi life grew, they held fast to their goals. Now, as they charted the distance between the present Delhi before them and that of their memories, they measured the results of their creative building and believing. Residents' histories paralleled Baviskar's history of Delhi's urban planning, which argues that Delhi's workers were an essential part of making Delhi what it was today (2003: 91). But unlike a story told from the perspective of urban planning, they made their *jhuggīs* into building blocks rather than the shantytowns urban planners saw. In the present, politicians often forgot their promises to protect *jhuggī* residents. Yet in telling these stories residents asserted they had never waited for anyone's promises to be fulfilled. They were going to make it on their own.

"LET THEM BE": CITIZENSHIP AS PASSIVE POLITICAL RECOGNITION

In the minutes after the bulldozers finished flattening the slum, a crowd of residents surged around the two media crews that were there. They held their official documents directly in front of the camera: their government IDs (*pahachān pātr*) and ration cards entitling them to government-subsidized food. Initially it seemed that they brandished these documents to counter the exclusion from citizenship that their flattened *jhuggīs* signified. These documents showed that as much as the government did not recognize them now, it had recognized them before, making them real citizens like all others whose tenure in Delhi was secure. But even if it had been politicians who had given them government cards including them, did that mean that citizenship was granted through the state? Or perhaps as residents held up their cards, were they documenting their belonging in a different way?

Careful attention to residents' narratives about the beginnings of their neighborhood illustrated the fine distinction between citizenship as passive political recognition and citizenship as rights given by a political patron or the state. The gradual building of *jhuggīs* took place with residents' awareness that, at least in the industrial area surrounding

Ghaziapuram, they were living on government and private land without purchasing it. Though they were essentially squatting, their gradual investments in home building indicated that they hardly saw their efforts as temporary. In some areas, like in Shikhar Colony, the land was an extension of the Delhi Development Authority flats.[8] "If the government wanted to, they could take it back," explained Akshay. "They could tear it down if they wanted to." However, he pointed to the government's intentions. As people settled on wide open land in order to work in the factories, Akshay said the government's attitude was, "They're poor. Let them be. The land is clear. People will settle there (*rahan-sahan ho jayegā*). The companies also thought that if the poor people lived here, 'Our company work won't stop. We'll get our work done.'" At that time, it was clear that the city needed the people who put in *jhuggīs*. Even the courts supported this in the 1990s, ruling that eviction of slum-dwellers would not only eliminate their housing but also their livelihood—that "the right to life and the right to work [were] interdependent" (Ramanathan 2005). Without them, the city's burgeoning business would grind to a halt.

To the government, the residents' settlement of open land was a boon to the city's development. In the 1980s and early 1990s, private ownership was less important than respecting the right of *jhuggī* residents, like anyone else, to live. Court rulings at the time echoed Akshay's claims. Outlining several distinct cases, Bhan elaborates:

> In Olga Tellis vs. Bombay Municipal Corporation (1985), the Supreme Court ruled that " . . . the right to livelihood is an important facet of the right to life." In effect, the court argued that " . . . the eviction of the (pavement dwellers) will lead to deprivation of their livelihood and consequently to the deprivation of life." It argued that the urban poor do not " . . . claim the right to dwell on pavements or in slums for the purpose of pursuing any activity which is illegal, immoral or contrary to public interest. Many of them pursue occupations which are humble but honourable." (2009: 134)

Though Akshay acknowledged the lack of legal authority for their settlement, he did not define their settlement through its illegality. Chatterjee (2004) and Holston (2009) both argue that collective advocacy of slum-dwellers, in the examples they use from Kolkata and from Brazil respectively, "spring from a collective violation of property laws and civic regulations"

(Chatterjee 2004: 59). Rather, Akshay's claims are closer to those of Ashu Das, a man Chatterjee quotes in his writing, who explained, "we have collectively occupied this land for so many years. This is the basis for our claim to our own homes" (Chatterjee 2004: 57). Occupying the land was the means through which they established a relationship to the city, which benefited from their labor there. Some descriptions of their life emphasized the opposite—that residents' careful living and saving demonstrated that they were law-abiding. As Asha put it, "We are living in *jhuggīs*, living according to the law, living carefully—saving rental [income] too." Though there was awareness that they lived on government-owned land, neither Akshay, Asha, or Ashu Das privileged ownership or government mediation as they described their settlements.

Asha told of how in those early days a wealthy woman (*madam*) had driven up to her plot, where a number of people had already built *jhuggīs*. The madam began negotiating with the Rajasthani people who were sitting there, and they offered to clear it for her for 2,500 rupees. But suddenly, in a moment of clarity, the madam's intentions changed. "She turned to her father, who was with her and said, 'Let's get some more land; poor people are living here; just let them be.' She said that and then she got in her car and left." Asha depicted poor people who were so determined, even desperate, simply to make a living in the city that they were willing to clear the land upon which they lived. In this story, they neither expected the woman to give them the land nor did they ask for it. Her recognition of their efforts allowed them to continue living there. But in both cases, the desire to work and the efforts for building began with the migrants, who did what was necessary to get their work done. They never lobbied for recognition, but instead their transformative work stood on its own.

As residents told stories of politicians' gradual investments in their neighborhood, they emphasized how the politicians recognized the sacrifices they were making. Mohan explained that their district-level representative had told V. P. Singh, the prime minister at the time, "'Go there and see; look at how the people in the *jhuggīs* are living.' Then V. P. Singh came. After coming here he saw the conditions (*sthiti*). After that, he gave ration cards, tokens,[9] and identification cards (*pahachān pātr*) and told people, 'As you are living, stay.' After that, nothing was demolished. After that, he made sure that there was electricity and water. Before that, no one asked." The residents' gradual building and collective provision of hand pumps had demonstrated they were prepared to provide for their own needs, even with no one asking after them. V. P. Singh confirmed that their contribution was valuable by finding ways to support them.

Politicians added to residents' initial investments in neighborhood infrastructure, knowing that infrastructure served as a visual reminder of their service—and thus encouraged loyalty (Anand and Rademacher 2011: 1752, 1757; McFarlane 2008: 101). In the 2000s, the government began sending one water tanker to Ghaziapuram. At the same time, Neetu said, two different politicians began sending their own tankers. Politicians had bored wells to meet the increasing water needs. These pipes laid through the ground pumped up water that could be used for nonconsumptive household needs.[10] Even when tragedy struck, politicians supported local residents in rebuilding their communities. Hema explained that when there was a fire in one of the local camps of people who collected and sorted trash (*kabārī-wāle*), "the politicians came and gave them some money, some bricks and said, 'Go and build.' Slowly we all made them *pakkā* (homes of brick and lasting materials)." As *jhuggī* residents incrementally built the homes that enabled them to pursue their livelihoods, sincere politicians encouraged them to settle more permanently. As politicians helped them to turn dirt homes to brick *pakkā* ones, brought water directly to their colony, and gave residents official documentation that marked their place in the city, they only furthered the process that residents had set in motion.

In the same way that residents had emphasized good politicians' investment in their settlements, they pointed out the value of sympathetic bosses who invested in their work. Since Mohan had to quit his schooling in order to get work to support his family, years later, Mohan's company sponsored his continued education. Other forms of support were more intimate, caregiving practices. Geeta told me proudly that her youngest son now had a really good job. "His boss (*mālik*) is a very good man," she said. "He says, 'Eat and drink well' (*ārām se khāo, ārām se piyo*), and he takes good care of them." Pointing the length from her palm almost to her elbow, she explained how much milk he had his workers drink. He even had life insurance papers for the whole family that she had hidden away to prevent jealousy from the neighbors. With those, "if anything happens to any of us, then we will get money back." She was not worried that he was spending many nights at the work site instead of doing the time-consuming commute. "I just tell him, 'Relax (ārām karo). Do your work there and then when you want to come home, come home.'" The praise received from good bosses indicated that they recognized the sacrifices their workers had made—Geeta's son made sacrifices of time, and Mohan had sacrificed his education—and valued their individual workers enough to care for them long-term in idealized relationships (Bear 2013). In contrast, women did not always feel the same appreciation. Sunita pointed out the prolonged time and energy that she, Geeta, and other women from the area put into hearing marital disputes for the mahilā maṇḍal (women's council) and other activities at the area NGO. "Staff there make five thousand rupees a month, but the women of the mahilā maṇḍal, who labor on their own, don't earn anything at all," declared Sunita indignantly. Geeta chimed in sarcastically, "Well, they do give us snacks, chai, and laḍḍū (a sweet)." Yet residents balanced their expectations of what they were given by employers or politicians with the assertion of the sincerity they invested in their own work.

Residents' transformation of a jungle into city was evidence that their labor and position were central to the development of the city. Though analysts have argued that the resources provided by the state and employers serve to secure the state's legitimacy (Chatterjee 2004: 47; Gupta and Sharma 2006) or build patron-client relationships (Gupta 1995: 390, 392; Marriott 1976; Wiser and Wiser 1971), residents did not see themselves as passive beneficiaries. Genuine politicians and bosses who recognized the sincerity of their labor also recognized the need to allow them to pursue their basic survival. These claims affirm "the moral rhetoric of a community striving to build a decent social life under extremely harsh conditions and, at the same time, [affirm] the duties of good citizenship" (Chatterjee 2004: 60), but they do not argue for "the government's obligation to look after poor and underprivileged population groups" (Chatterjee 2004: 60). It was good and right when politicians or wealthy people supported their basic act of living in the city. But residents' narrative of their building and pursuing their work—even without any politicians asking after them—demonstrates that their desire to get ahead was not dependent on the support of patrons or the state. The length of their tenure mattered, but it was situated within larger narratives about building and work that highlighted action over this historical time period. As they brandished their government documents, residents presented evidence of their long history in Delhi and cast doubt on whether in the present their citizenship could be so easily revoked.

GLOBAL DELHI AND THE COSMOPOLITAN LIFE

"How much does this cost *vahān* (there)?" Darshana asked me, referring to the shirt on which she was attaching sequins. Nearly everyone in Ghaziapuram had either worked in the factories of this industrial zone or had their hands in some informal labor sent beyond factory walls to arrive on their doorstep. With fabric tied across their faces, women gathered under tarps in the sun to sort remnant scrap material from clothing to be sold for reprocessing. Stacks of boxes filled with empty medicine tubes were distributed to families who stayed around during the day; women, unemployed men, and kids home from school circled around to gossip and screw tops on the tubes. Upon seeing me, Darshana and others connected the burning of their finger pads worn from tops and needle pin pricks that earned fractions of a cent to *there*, the Western countries where the bottles would be squeezed and buttons closed. Whether to condemn the inequality of global production or to comment on their own cosmopolitanism, people pointed out to me the international reach of the companies they worked for.

Men in particular used their uniforms, office buildings, and products to confirm their connection to a broader world. When I accompanied Mohan's son to meet Mohan where he worked as a security guard, the son pointed to the surrounding factories, many which had commanding glass fronts. "These are the biggest companies in the world and big exporters," he said while he rotated around. "And this company," he said, pointing toward Mohan's company, "is one of the biggest and best companies. They make lots of money!" At home in their *jhuggī*, Mohan's daughters showed me the brochures and promotional material of the company. As a security guard, their father was a part of something much larger than himself. His desire to work had connected him to international prestige. Working for international companies in Ghaziapuram and building an increasingly global city made residents instigators of India's global transformation.

I often came to people's homes on Sundays, everyone's day off of work, in hopes of prime availability for interviews. But more often on Sundays, wandering (*ghūmna*) seemed to preoccupy the families I knew from the *jhuggīs* (Datta 2011). There was a big world to explore; no one wanted to always talk about serious things. "Let's wander," Neetu would say as her eyes bulged with excitement. We could go to Vrindavan, Krishna's home in Mathura, or to the Sai Baba Temple in Noida. Mrinalini's daughters gathered in a flock with their friends as we joined the Sunday swarm at the Kalkaji *mandir* (Hindu temple). Geeta was more discreet as she left for *ghūmna* with me, pulling out her suitcase of nice clothes and draping herself in clothes I had never before seen. She always made me look bad in comparison. She and other women tucked away the small items that they bought at roadside stands—lipstick, bangles, special clothes—as objects of consumer identity that they could strategically deploy (see also Lessinger 2002; Lynch 1999; Srivastava 2010). As we enjoyed the pleasures of the city, it became clear to me that though my freedom to move was greater than most women's, Delhi was what they had built as much as what they enjoyed (compare Farquhar and Zhang 2005). Some of the massive construction projects to build recreational spaces and large infrastructure in contemporary Delhi had felt exclusionary (Dupont 2011; Ghertner 2010), but in other ways, it was a sign of a modern city whose global nature they had initiated.

Geeta traced the similarities in her character that allowed her to be independent when she lived in her husband's extended family rural home (*sasurāl*) and here in Delhi. Then, she had decided on her own to be sterilized after she gave birth to her two sons. Her sisters-in-law (*devrānīs*) had asked her if she was scared. "What is there to be scared of?" she said, as if answering the most obvious question. But after she went, she chuckled, every single person in her family followed. Here, in Delhi, she told me she adopted the same attitude. Some women never left their homes—they were afraid of what would happen or what people would think. In truth, many women's excited imagination of movement was more common than their actual practice of it. Women knew that being in public both exposed their reputation to public scrutiny (Chandola 2012a) and exposed them to danger in public places (Ali 2010). Their practical need to be home when their children arrived from school or when the unpredictable water supply jolted awake often trumped their ability to leave. Husbands, brothers, and male children often got to do more than their fair share of roaming. Nonetheless, women's active imagination and occasional practice of movement constituted women's sense of themselves as cosmopolitan, giving them freedom and imagination that they often rarely had in rural places with heavier scrutiny of family (Chandola 2010: 195). Even impersonation helped connect them to the new cultural and material impacts of liberalization (Appadurai 2000: 642–43; Mankekar 2010).

Always tied to their rural homes and changing in new ways in their urban worlds, residents expressed their excitement to be able to navigate both worlds, defining them both as essential parts of India. "You must have seen it—white radishes, spinach— . . . in the morning they are sold and then you eat them right afterwards," Sunita told me passionately in the bustling streets of the *jhuggīs*, with neighbors at arm's length. There, in the village, "water flows from the well, you wash the vegetables in this water, grow them in this water, there is no *gandagī* (dirtiness), it's pure. Eating such food brings taste to your mouth."[11] Like Sunita, others would dreamily talk of the village. They placed a hand far in front of them and slowly panned across as if pulling a curtain to reveal endless fields filled with wheat, mustard, sugarcane, and vegetables in place of the *jhuggīs*, factories, and urban landscape that surrounded them. Describing the rich rural landscapes and fields, they argued that I needed to see and feel the other places to which they could travel. As residents reflected on their physical mobility, their connection to both places diluted firm distinctions between village and city (Holmström 1999), but also emphasized their inclusion within the whole of society. They could navigate Delhi as well as their distant rural homes. Knowing the differences between the two helped them to demonstrate their "urban self" (Datta 2011: 754). This self was changed since migrating but aware of India's rural world in a way that showed their knowledge of contemporary India to be superior to that of urban middle-class people. "The nostalgic landscape is not the village or the hometown," writes Chandola about residents in another low-income community close to Ghaziapuram. Rather, it is the "imagined sensorality—in the way of uninhibited mobility and interactions . . . promised by the 'city way of life'" (Chandola 2010: 195).

As people elaborated on their industrial work and physical mobility, they shaped a cosmopolitan selfhood. They answered my questions about their otherness by pointing to our mutual proximity. They knew about my world as surely as I knew about theirs (Snell-Rood 2013b). They could navigate multiple worlds, urban and rural, foreign and Indian, in the *jhuggīs* and in global Delhi. While it is easy to emphasize the tragic unattainability of these dreams of mobility (Srivastava 2010), to do so is to neglect the true profundity of slum residents' personal transformations, the inclusions that they powerfully shaped in spite of ever-present exclusions. But measuring change through income alone fails to recognize how, through their moral citizenship, residents reshaped their social dignity (Kapur et al. 2010).

RIGHT AND WRONG WAYS TO GET AHEAD: WOMEN MEDIATING MALE ASPIRATIONS

"There is tension," Mrinalini explained, exhausted. Earlier (in chapter 1), I described "tension" as embodied burden that women bear as they care for their families. Mrinalini's account of tension captured how this weight intersected with her family's pursuit of mobility. For her, like many other women, "getting ahead" was always a task of the family. It was a sum of individual efforts that often were differential. She clarified: "My husband drinks alcohol; because of the alcohol, tension stays in my mind every day. The tension never leaves my mind. Why does my husband drink when there are six children?" She connected her husband's habits to the needs of the whole family. She amassed the tasks that their household must accomplish to both sustain their regular needs and their long-term plans. But, instead of him looking ahead, "He does not even know the responsibilities in the house, what needs to be done, what doesn't." And she felt his habits made him absent, shifting burdens unfairly onto their children, those who they had hoped would have a different life: "There is my oldest son: all the weight is on him. I do not do any work either, I sit at home. From one boy's income the whole house is run." All of this neglect caused her to ruminate on this stress, which then flowed throughout her body: "Now because of this I take tension. My husband has no tension at all; he does not even care. The tension is of the mother. Because of the tension in my head, I will get dizzy and fall. Because of tension, my heart is upset, that maybe one day I'll have a heart attack. I feel like that."[12] For women living in poverty, like Mrinalini, illness was not just a product of deprivation, but also of the fears and brooding over how to provide for their families (Ramasubban and Singh 2001: 22–25).

In their daily interactions, women steadily reminded me that the visions for transformation that their family members and neighbors glibly expounded were not as easily achieved in practice. In Delhi, residents suggested, anyone could transform him- or herself. But for people who were poor, they warned, there was less room for missteps. Geeta complained to me that her son was dazzled by mobility but neglected the disciplined steps that it required. She had made substantial investments in order to hold firm to the goals that motivated her migration to Delhi, one of which was her sixteen-year-old son Dev's education. With his exams a month away, in the small room that Geeta's family had moved to right after demolition, he playfully invited me to come with him to Mumbai. He wanted to see movie stars, he smiled. Geeta exploded. "You give your papers in April—why not just go after that? He's stupid, thinks he can do anything. Look now, he's angry," she said, her words dissolving into seething mutters to herself. She huffed at the prospect of what he was saying: "He wants to go to Mumbai so he can meet Akshay Kumar" (a famous Bollywood actor). She repeated his desire with disgust to imply the ridiculous thrill that he suggested at the expense of his education. But she redrew the frame, restating that significance of getting ahead, as if to remind him that moving to Delhi was not simply about fun imagining. She explained to me all of the costs that were related to his education: almost six thousand rupees a year in all between his tuitions, his private schooling, exam fees, and books. "Look what happens if you aren't literate (*paṛhī-likhī*)," she said as a terse warning. "You cannot do anything." When I tried to revalue the people to whom she was referring—namely, nearly everyone in the *jhuggīs*—she tersely shut me down. She turned to me and explained that she had not been able to continue her own education, and now see what happened. With her silence, she summoned the many conversations in which I had noted her amazing skills with children and that she would be an incredible teacher—only if she had education, we both knew.

Geeta had built her plan for her family to get ahead with this approach of slow progression in mind. She knew that others discounted such tactics. Sunita had grilled Dev's younger brother on the job he had just started. What exactly was he doing and what was he making? she asked him with a slanted eye. Geeta had emphasized that while his salary was small for the construction work he was doing with her son-in-law, he was learning skills that would enable him to make three- to five-fold after his apprenticeship. "It is a good job," she underlined coolly, defining work's value not through immediate gain but through long-term security. Now, as she sat with Dev, she upheld the same doctrine of patience. As if her point were not yet proven, Geeta further mentioned to her son that Sunita's son Sagar had almost completed his studies but stopped short. Her point: he would never be the big shot he pretended to be. But the difference was that he could always get a job through Sunita's powerful connections. "If you study, then you can get a good job and do whatever you want. If not, what will you do? Tell me," she said to him. And then toward me, "His mind is strong. But his brother's is not and that's why he works instead." Though tears had slowly gathered in her son's eyes as she harped on, Geeta did not relent in her lecture. For her, the meaning of their work now was that her children would get ahead in life (āge baṛhānā). Though they had built something they were proud of in the city, Geeta argued that without her sons pushing what they had built even further, it was a waste. While her son Dev already worked two jobs—delivering newspapers and doing security guard work at a home in a wealthy neighborhood—it was insufficient for them to have sacrificed so much for him merely to make ends meet, as they did now. For residents of the *jhuggīs*, the goal was not to build a life and community within the *jhuggīs*. The goal was to use their place in the city to change their lives as others before them had changed rugged jungle to possibility.

It was one thing to get ahead as Akshay had described, deciding for himself and venturing alone to the city. But what of families who had multiple visions of what they could become and different degrees of devotion to those visions? Geeta had emphasized how important it was to stay focused on the shared goal, but Shaista articulated how exhausting it was to be the lone engine of discipline steering their families. Shaista's family was different from many other families in the *jhuggīs* because rather than seeking upward mobility, Shaista sought to return to the lower-middle-class status of the rest of her family. She and her family had come to Delhi after an explosive fight between her husband and father-in-law. Shaista was mad that they were in the *jhuggīs*, but she seemed more upset about the restrictions that her husband placed on her work, impacting not just her but their sons. Her husband told her not to work as a teacher at an area NGO, so she found work in a factory instead. With those diminished wages, she had to make her two sons work in order to have the money to put the other three in school. When she later attained a better job at the factory, she could send them back for more schooling, even if they had missed out on some.

Now, when I knew them, with Shaista and her two oldest sons' wages, they sent the three younger sons to private school and supplementary lessons—something that only a few families from the *jhuggīs* could afford. During my many visits, when Shaista was cooking dinner, she sorted out their family matters in anxious worrying that only occasionally surfaced in speech, particularly her frustration with Aamir's repeated bad choices. In the present, her husband was still often away for days or weeks at a time, leaving her with much of the responsibility for the daily getting ahead. Like many other women living in slums, she bore the responsibility for providing for their family but received less of the credit than he would have (Ali 2010; Das 1994; Roy 2003). Her son Adil said that sometimes in the middle of the night when his father came down to their room from where he slept on the roof, his mother would begin fighting with him, angry that he never made enough money to support their family. Perhaps her anger was because Aamir's actions had destroyed her sons' educated status; they were locked out of her family's respectable background (see also Bear 2007: 176). Getting ahead should have been easier. But in addition to that, Shaista felt that if her husband had fulfilled his own work responsibilities and supported her, her family would not be struggling in the *jhuggīs*. Even as she wondered how things could have been different, her worrying was deeply practical, focusing on each son and how he would reach the goals she envisioned for him.

Some women pointed out how their husbands' grand visions of their mobility far overwhelmed the poverty they continued to live in now. Saraswati's husband was between jobs, having argued that his employers did not properly remunerate him for the skills that he had. Although her husband gave me interviews about the value of work, as Saraswati and I talked later, she said that she no longer believed his earnest talk. "Every day he says he is going to go out to look for work, but the thing is that he has work, why does he need to look for it?" she asked. In the meantime, she kept working and he kept spending. She pointed to the brand-new DVD player on top of the TV and said, "Look what he just got." She looked annoyed. She just found out about her sister's wedding; it would require at least ten thousand rupees for gifts, and here he was buying stuff they did not need. "Fine, I'll cook, I'll take care of the children—but if he is going to stay home all day?" she trailed off.

Saraswati guessed that he was no longer committed to what he was doing in Delhi, satisfied to go back and forth from the village making a little money here and there while telling his family that he made plenty of money. He seemed to come up with new schemes all of the time. One was moving to Agra, where he claimed the pay was better than in Delhi, where, he said, "You can't get paid what you are supposed to." Another was starting a computer course that would enable him to demand higher salary. But this was overly ambitious, she reasoned. "He's hardly literate; he has barely been to school!" she explained with exasperation. "What he knows, I taught him."

But Akshay represented himself differently—his plans were not schemes, but attempts to get what he deserved. True, when he arrived in Delhi so many years ago, he admitted, he was naïve. It was a fight with his father that brought him to Delhi at the age of fourteen, he told me with a smile as he considered his innocence in making the 250-kilometer journey from his village. He said he had decided at that time that "I was going to make it with my own hard work." On the way, he had met a young woman on the street, sad and sitting alone. With his "villager's mind," as he put it, he had asked her, "Why are you sitting like that? I came in this way and I want to know how Delhi is. What are the people here like—how bad or how good are they?" She took him to her family house, fed him in the morning and suggested work he could do in Delhi. From where he sat now, Akshay looked back at his intentions from that time differently, and they made him laugh. His own ambition and naïveté embarrassed him from the distance of his years of Delhi living. Since then, he had become a completely different kind of worker. He described the excitement of learning new skills, from manufacturing watches, to learning stitching, checking,[13] and computer-based embroidery. The more skills he learned, the greater the salary he could expect.

Yet he embedded this description in his narrative of the past. These days in visits, he talked more about his frustration with the fact that he could not find a position that would allow him to use the more advanced stitching skills; the factories only seemed to want the lowest skills so they could pay the least. He kept talking about the village: maybe he could return; maybe they would return. It seemed that his uncertainty about the watered-down work around him pushed him to look elsewhere. To Saraswati, Akshay's big dreams were fine if they were backed with persistence. Saraswati's hope in her husband's drive was depleted. By now, he was so used to thinking of himself as already ahead that he believed it. But as much as Saraswati was also excited to show his family their new riches, she felt tethered to how far they were from wealth right now. The struggle of getting ahead was still their present occupation—so how could she convince him of the continued need to push for it? As a result, some women simply began to hide their resources from their husbands, putting money and their jewelry in cracks and corners of their *jhuggīs* to make their own security. They would try to curb family members' schemes to push ahead faster by moving on and out in circumstances that they imagined would always be easier. They would rein in their families, whether they were aware of it or not.

Now, as they used their work to claim their citizenship in Delhi, residents only continued terse debates that punctuated their daily lives. In their fraught commentary on how they, their families, and their neighbors got ahead, residents—and women particularly—grounded the grand vision of migration in the mundane. These conflicts complicated the romanticized histories of their urban transformation. As much as their work might connect them to the world, women emphasized how much work remained. There were tests to study for, money to be saved, and children whose futures still seemed open. Women's critiques of their family members' efforts indicated that their family members were sometimes content to use getting ahead as a moral discourse that was empty of action. They reminded themselves that, as quickly as aspirations for mobility could blossom in Delhi, they could rot into dangerous desires that made them neglect their ethics and seethe with unhappiness. To combat this, they paired their attention to intentional action with an awareness of its limits. From each angle, women reordered their sense of themselves. Their poverty was a temporary sign of their commitment to get ahead; their poverty was a sign of their hoped-for mobility; their poverty, as fate, was a sign of the God-given wealth they were obliged to recognize. Yet, in all of these stances, women placed moral accountability squarely within their homes.

FICKLE POLITICIANS AND RETHINKING POLITICS

As residents questioned the selves they sought to transform, so too did urban planners and middle-class Delhi-ites question the evolving character of Delhi. Beyond the cosmopolitan excitement through which residents roamed, there was another side to the global vision of Delhi that residents felt less a part of. Politicians like V. P. Singh had hoped to improve the security of housing for people living in poverty, but his short tenure limited the reach of the efforts he had initiated (Ramanathan 2006: 3194). As Delhi developed for the 2010 Commonwealth Games—sinking billions of rupees into infrastructure projects like the Metro and large sports arenas—it also was clearing thousands of slums all over the city.[14] While the city had hoped that the games might attract foreign investment, middle-class people hoped to use this vast urban development to enact their own changes. This demolition and many others before it were ordered by judicial rulings from public interest litigation (PIL), rather than being ordered by urban planning bodies (Bhan 2009; Ramanathan 2006). Through their residents' welfare associations, middle-class people sponsored PIL suits because they were tired of having so many poor people in Delhi. Residents felt they were being pushed offstage, an embarrassment to a city that wanted to be modern. If, previously, "letting them live" had been the engine driving the city's very modernity, then it seemed hard to believe that now that demolition of their homes was the next step.

Residents admitted that the contemporary political landscape had shifted. "Look, at the time when people came, at that point there were not

any companies," Asha said, to review the history. "People [from the com-
panies] came to homes to invite them [to work]: 'come to our place to get
work done.'" Migration, in this narrative, was by aspiration as much as
invitation. But the invitation was rescinded, she explained: "These days,
we're here and [the companies] are sealed, so nothing is given in the company. The number of people has grown, but the work has not grown much.
And today there is a lot of unemployment."[15] From feeling like proud citizens, they now felt stereotyped as the burdensome poor. As the demolition
date approached, people turned from their piecework to point to the five-
star hotel being built down the road. Geeta and her neighbor observed
grimly, "They want to clean Delhi so that the foreigners staying in the
hotel don't have to see our poverty." Although they had played their role in
transforming this place from a jungle, as people sat in front of their homes
on their cots, they asked me, "What is going to become of us when they
make this city Paris—it will just be for you foreigners and for rich people."
Indeed, government funding had been reallocated from public goods
like health, education, food subsidies, and housing toward large roads,
the metro with its prohibitive fares, and sports complexes for the
Commonwealth Games (Baviskar 2003; Ghertner 2010).

Where residents had continually emphasized their honest desire to work
and legitimate claims to the city, now the court, in *Dhar vs. Government of
Delhi* (2002), "differentiated between the justice deserved by slum dwellers
who are 'unscrupulous citizens' and the 'honest citizens who have to pay for
land or a flat'" (Bhan 2009: 135). Thus the pairing of demolition and resettlement, formerly taken for granted, now had an entirely different meaning. In the case of *Almitra Patel vs. the Union of India* in 2000, compensation to residents of slums in the event of demolition was labeled as a form
of "rewarding an encroacher on public land with an alternative free site,"
akin to "giving a reward to a pickpocket for stealing" (Bhan 2009: 135).
Rather than the government needing their labor to build this city, a juice
maker said, "They think that the trucks and factories bring too much pollution to the city, so that means that the factories will keep getting shipped
out of the city."[16] Times had changed, Akshay said, and "now the government realizes that it doesn't have much land left; . . . now it thinks this
should be cleared" (see also Baviskar 2003: 92).[17] From being engines of
Delhi's growth, the courts now defined their way of life as illegal and their

continued existence in Delhi as a source of nuisance that harassed middle-class residents (Ghertner 2010; Ramanathan 2006: 3195–96). Now the fact that there was a time when they had been called to Delhi was forgotten. Instead, court justices denied this process ever happened as they claimed, "no one forced you to come to Delhi . . . if encroachments are allowed, there will be anarchy" (quoted in Ramanathan 2006: 3197). When Akshay's comments stood alone, it seemed that good patrons had become bad patrons, forgetting their end of the exchange.

But *jhuggī* residents' continued engagement with politicians in the weeks leading up to demolition disputed this scheme of historical decline. It was not as if politicians of yore who supported them had simply faded into money-grubbing politicians of the present at their doorsteps. Even though residents were aware of the larger sea of changes in middle-class and urban policy, they still distinguished the activities of individual politicians from this trend. Indeed, bureaucracies *were* complex organisms whose parts were often not coordinated. The result was that "major policy shifts at the federal level were not necessarily transformative for lower levels of the bureaucracy" (Gupta and Sharma 2006: 278). But the complexity of the state bureaucracy alone did not account for such inconsistency. The way that politics intersected with their ambition to get ahead was more complex. Regardless of whatever overall shifts may be taking place in the city, Vijay explained that ultimately it was not what was written in the law that mattered, it was what the politicians decided to do. Vijay speculated, "If in the past, Indira had helped us, then Rajiv Gandhi, then V. P. Singh, then why could not Sonia Gandhi do something now?[18] She is the one who should give us land." Residents continually reminded me that politicians had saved their settlement two times before when notices were posted. It was common enough that *jhuggī* clusters that managed to stay around for longer were more likely to be regularized by the government (Baviskar 2003: 96). Residents affirmed the strategy of lobbying multiple politicians. It worked because in South Asia, the state does "not reflect a single underlying rationality or form of rule but a highly differentiated institution operating according to multiple rationalities" (Anjaria 2011: 64). Vijay implied that the multiple rationalities of the government did not play out randomly. The sentiments and ambitions of politicians were key. If politicians wanted to preserve their settlement now, they would.

There were times that residents mentioned good politicians and middle-class people, those who had supported their efforts here. But outside of a few local people whose leadership made them perhaps more sympathetic, most people did not believe that the government had a profound interest in helping them (contrast Gupta 1995: 391). They emphasized that the hope for political assistance was rooted more in politicians' personal interests. They were at least safe until the next election—politicians needed their large voting blocs. It was assumed that their continued presence there, like the bribes that street hawkers paid, were "an exchange, an arrangement, and a negotiation" that had "a certain public, and almost structured, quality" (Anjaria 2011: 62). This was not outside government practice but an essential building block of it. From the "field of negotiation" that constitutes political corruption come "at least momentary claims to urban space" (Anjaria 2011: 63). Perhaps they were now deemed illegal by the courts, but illegality was everywhere: "The mapping of functionally specific land-use zones is obliterated by a spectrum of unauthorised practices: workers without shelter (and unable to afford commuting costs) who crowd around their places of work; a land mafia that brokers deals between municipal authorities and those with the capital to acquire and use land illegally; and political leaders who encourage encroachments with an eye towards cultivating vote banks among insecure squatter settlers" (Baviskar 2003: 93). Being in a grey area provided some hope for flexibility. Yet the prominent place of slums in the public eye often counteracted the flexibility of this position between legality and illegality, with the result that "state (and private) interventions are often just as likely to take the form of violence" (McFarlane 2008: 92).

The haziness of the legal categories of entitlement cast doubt on every aspect of demolition: whose home would be demolished, who could receive compensation, and who was in charge of the whole process. The lack of certainty was so widespread that even in the months after demolition, residents continued to speculate about its causes and aftermath. In a meeting at the now-flattened *jhuggīs*, Mrinalini felt buoyed that they really would be able to get something—that is, those who, like her, had a ration card from before 1990. The original notices that had been posted a few weeks before demolition had said that the *jhuggīs* violated "right of way" by obstructing the industrial zone's plan for a road. But, Mrinalini reasoned, "if the government really felt right of way, then why did they provide ration cards, V. P. Singh cards, and electricity?" These tangible signs of citizenship were evidence that the government had never really planned on exercising right of way. As further evidence, she pointed to the inconsistencies in the actual practice of demolition. To make the road that the PIL suit had argued in favor of, technically only a narrow strip of *jhuggīs* needed to be cleared away from the overall settlement. But there were homes behind this perimeter that were demolished nonetheless. On the day of demolition, these families had pointed this out to the demolition workers. But no one heard what they had to say. The police, Mrinalini said, had just decided that they were going to "clean" the whole thing. All of this made her wonder whether someone else might step in now to correct what was an obvious series of mistakes. She searched the logic of demolition for inconsistencies that might show competing interests amongst the powerful—particularly those that might swing in their favor.

Sunita and others knew that, in the present, their negotiations and promised votes to politicians were not outside of political practice, but intrinsic to it. Only what politician to depend on, or whether they could be depended on at all, was left up to question. Even Sunita, who had claimed the importance of choosing the right party, argued "politicians only decide what they do based on who gives them money." At one point, she had reached into the side pocket of my bag and pulled out the card of the Bharatiya Janata Party (BJP) politician who had won. Having received it during the elections in November, it now was a scrap of paper that I had forgotten to clean out. She whispered, "You know, this demolition is because the BJP won. They gave money to the right people and now this is happening." Politicians' capacity to save their neighborhood was likely tied to their dreams to amass political power—but it was accepted as such. The key was to find a politician who might help them now.

As the days drew closer to the demolition date listed on the notice, there was excitement whenever news arose of a different politician's impending visit. I could not keep track of them at all—former and present politicians of their district, Bahujan Samaj Party (BSP), BJP, and Congress. To host them, local leadership set up large stages from rough benches and rugs and sent young men to string up powerful lights in the larger trees. At night, with lights shining bright on them, politicians proclaimed that this city would never forget the *jhuggī-vallahs* (people living in the *jhuggīs*) and always need them. Residents responded with approving chants of "*Zindābād, zindābād!*" (Live long!). But the next day, the same uncertainty resurfaced. Aamir, who had been smiling in his nice clothes the evening before, now said bitingly, "The politicians just come here to say how great they are and how they are with the poor and to get us to [he made the sign of stamping a thumbprint that illiterate people use to vote], but they won't actually do anything for us." When I expressed my frustration to Geeta, she told me that although others last night were loudly chanting in rhythm, "*Zindābād, zindābād,*" she shouted in tandem, "*Marnābād!*" (Die!). We both laughed at her clever reordering. Everyone wanted the politicians to save them, but their faith varied in politicians' promises to follow through. The local powerful people, many of whom partnered with politicians in their role as *pradhāns*, spoke confidently of the politicians. Others wanted to believe, but knew better.

While they all comprised the *jhuggī-vāllāhs* that the politicians professed to save, residents were hesitant to look toward each other for a solution to impending demolition. If even their households were not unified in getting ahead, there was little hope left for neighbors whom they automatically viewed with even greater suspicion (see chapter 2). When I suggested to Durga that there was potential in collective organizing (i.e., Appadurai 2002; Chatterjee 2004; Holston 2009), she abruptly rebuffed the suggestion. Her neighbors were *aise log:* that *kind* of people. She said they were too uneducated and unmotivated to have the will to stop demolition. Even if people wanted to stop demolitions, coalitions rarely stayed together because of the need to guard one's own security (Baviskar 2003: 96; Harriss 2010: 104)—let alone accommodating the needs of others. In Durga's view, their eyes were set squarely on their daily work of survival. Some migrants sought betterment here, but others were simply here to feed themselves. As Durga put it, "People here . . . don't care. They just sit around, do their work, and then that's it." Neetu had praised the "Lucknow" culture of the neighborhood in the industrial area where she had lived in as a child with her sister—referring to the habits of respect associated with the Uttar Pradesh town. But when it came to Ghaziapuram, her praise ended: Neetu said, "In our *jhuggīs* it wasn't nice." After demolition, she claimed that she had been ready to leave.

I asked Geeta to join me in gathering names to contest the demolition, as my friend Pushpa had suggested. As we went from door to door and explained the process, many women became confused. Frequently addressed by nicknames or kinship terms, many could not tell us their legal names that we were requesting. Their shy, submissive confusion with which they handed over their government documents was too much for Geeta, whose moderate literacy made her stand out from most women. She stood back in exasperation and yelled, "This is why our country is so backward (*pīcche*)!" People like Geeta and Durga saw themselves as victims of bad circumstances, but their illiterate neighbors for their embarrassing failures to get ahead.

More talk veered toward suspicion that local *pradhāns* might be usurping this tragic moment for their own benefit. After demolition, people whispered that the eighty thousand rupees that three local *pradhāns* had collected from them to challenge demolition in court had simply been pocketed. This hypothesis had analogues in what residents told me they had already seen in the local NGO. One resident, they said, had used the local NGO as another avenue to build her power. Numerous people told me that she had demanded payment from the NGO even when none of the other local women from the slum got compensation for their work in the women's collective (*mahilā pañchāyat*). Others argued that she used her position there so that she had a title to throw around, introducing herself to outsiders, politicians, and journalists as working for the NGO when in reality, they argued, she was merely involved in the way that everyone else was. For this very reason, feeling sidelined by this resident or refusing to accept the authority that she claimed there, many women refused to join the NGO.

In the few months that followed demolition, residents asked after the *pradhāns'* efforts in court to lobby for resettlement. Eventually their hopeful questions faded and instead of asking they stated, "We won't get anything." Months after demolition Akshay said that demolition went forward because people in government jobs had no reason to stop it—it was only for personal benefit that leaders would act. "This is Indian politics. Lovingly get your work done (*pyār se kām nikālo*); then when it's accomplished, hit the people who did your work. At election time, they tell us to join, then choose, and then after the election, no one asks." The politicians had got their work done and now they were gone. Asha pointed to the

violence with which they struck: "They come and tear it down with force—
mightily, with sticks they win. It doesn't make a difference to them [that
they break people's homes]. They just break them." Afterwards, those who
had ordered it hid behind the force they hired to do their work. They "hid
in the police station," Asha explained, "feeding" the policemen with power
while remaining unnamed.[19] Others repeated rumors that the companies
had engineered the demolition. Neetu explained that the daughter-in-law
of a deceased factory owner had convinced her husband they should clean
up around the factory. This generation of factory owners was different.
Nothing was too dirty for powerful people who wanted more power.

After all, dirty political work had its precedents. In a resettlement colony north of Delhi, a friend of mine who did community work was not
surprised that a fire had broken out in the poorest part of the settlement
in the weeks leading up to the spring election. "This happens a lot at election time," she said. "You just wait and see, there will certainly be a lot
more fires in the *jhuggīs* before the election comes. Politicians set them
and then take advantage of how vulnerable people are—they have nowhere
else to turn, and who ends up offering them stuff?" In some places, activists made sense of such webs of power as land mafias "to describe the
powerful nexus between landowning elite, local government functionar-
ies, and organized corruption and crime. Upper-caste landowners get
common lands titled in their own names with the help of local officials.
These men routinely threaten low-caste women who challenge them, and
hire goons to beat or rape them or tear down their houses. The police and
local administrators are in cahoots with the landowners and do not prevent land encroachment and violence, or assist low-caste women in bringing cases against upper-caste men" (Sharma 2010: 81). Such powerful
networks made it clear that people could stand to lose much more than
their homes. As much as the idea of relying on support from politicians or
middle-class people had appeal, *jhuggī* residents knew better. Those who
stood to benefit from political alliance, like *pradhāns*, sought their favor.
Those who did not attended rallies, gave votes, and put in their money
when necessary. To the extent that residents could use politics to get their
own work done, they would. Yet this was done carefully. In an era where
every house could have its own *pradhān*, any interaction with neighbors
could be an unwitting connection to larger political forces.

In order to get water at the tanker every day in her new neighborhood after demolition, Saraswati had to have a connection to a local landlord; they were the ones who controlled the water hoses from the tanker and determined whose water buckets would be filled (see also Anand 2011). When she first moved there, she would only manage to collect half a bucket for all of their needs. But with time, as she ingratiated herself to an area landlord, her water needs were attended to. But this connection had its limits, particularly in the summer when water ran drastically low. A woman from the neighborhood came by Akshay and Saraswati's door and asked them to put in twenty rupees for water so that the tanker would come. Akshay insisted, "We did not put any money in at Holi[20] [when another tanker was ordered], and we won't now." The neighbor returned a little bit later and asked again. This time, Akshay reluctantly gave ten rupees and told her to get the remainder from the lodger whom they fed. Once she left, Akshay hesitantly speculated that the money would not go for the tanker but instead directly to politicians. Sometimes, if the water did not come, these local leaders called politicians to provide them with more water from the Delhi Jal (Water) Board (DJB). At election time especially, political parties sent tankers for their supporters. Because it was common knowledge who supported which political party, loyal supporters ensured that they were the only ones allowed access. In other cases, politicians stopped regular water tankers from arriving.[21] These acts in the present indicated that past political collaboration had been appreciated, but not expected—at least not expected to be motivated by politicians' altruism. People might be quite politically active, in fact more politically active than the middle class (Harriss 2005). But perhaps it makes more sense to think of their political action as hedged wagering, rather than faith in politicians' promises.

There were times when residents could avoid having to rely on inadequate government services, if they could. Some Ghaziapuram residents reported going to the hospital daily to receive treatments that they felt did not really even make a difference in their health conditions, whether extreme constipation or persistent fever. Saraswati bemoaned the fact that when she went to the government hospital to get care to help with her son's chronic ear infection, she had to pay to get a ticket to even wait in line. That was only the beginning of the fees, which continued with a doctor's charge, a long list of medicines they had to buy for his ear, and then orders to return to have the ear cleaned in another two weeks for another high fee. And, as if to top it off, she said, "It's a bad hospital!" She preferred a private hospital that was close by. There, instead of paying for a ticket to stand in long lines, she explained they had a nice waiting room with air conditioning and TV monitors that broadcast information about ear and nose health. "You can just sit there and learn so much," she said, "It's so much better." Going "private," as people commonly said, meant taking control of how you were treated, even if that meant you had to pay for it.

In this setting of powerful political and economic possibility, residents were hesitant to depend on others. Recently, anthropologists have attempted to reframe the corruption that is widely believed to be endemic to Indian politics. "Illicit, 'unofficial' transactions with the state," writes Anjaria, "constitute the terrain on which new forms of politics are worked out" (2011: 68). There is a common optimistic strand that surfaces as Anjaria (2011) describes street vendors' routine bribing of municipal officials as political possibility, as Witsoe (2011) elaborates the popular support of corrupt politicians (like Bihar's chief minister, Lalu Yadav) "as a means to caste empowerment" (Witsoe 2011: 77), and Chatterjee asserts that slum residents associations' extralegal negotiations demonstrate that "freedom and equality" must not be "imprison[ed] within the sanitized fortress of civil society" (2004: 74). These authors argue that citizenship and politics that include corruption and the ownership of illegality deserve consideration as the new democratic forms of politics.

But what of the local ethical models that evaluate different forms of social participation? Only by paying genuine attention to the "squalor, ugliness and violence of popular life" that are also part of political society (Chatterjee 2004: 74)[22] can we understand that not all forms of political engagement are equal. Because of the danger that working with *pradhāns* poses, some residents of this slum considered themselves to have greater autonomy but fewer state entitlements, as long as it meant that they were not allied with poisonous others. Thus, alongside "devising new ways in which they can choose how they should be governed" (Chatterjee 2004: 77), slum residents are also choosing *not* to be governed by anyone other than themselves. Residents were attached to what they had built in this city, but they were more attached to what they had come here for in the first place. As Asha, a former *pradhān,* said to me forcefully, "You cannot buy my vote. I don't need *pūrīs*[23]; I don't need sweets; I don't need anything; I just want security *(surakshā).*" She made her independence starkly clear: "I don't drink anyone's water or eat anyone's food. Whatever I am capable of doing for the people is the service I render to them, nothing else. This is our place; this is our history."[24]

Until February 4, the day before demolition, some residents continued to lobby politicians. That afternoon, a final group of residents left for a meeting with politicians at their offices. When they came back to the neighborhood around 4:00 p.m., the streets were flooded with residents packing and dismantling. Most people had held out hope gingerly, knowing that if something had come through, it would be because politicians found it in their own interest. Before, it had been in their interest to support *jhuggī* residents because the city needed to be built. Residents recognized that politicians were now eager to take advantage of the changing attitude toward them, from valued workers to the "poor people problem." Now, it was anyone's guess whether it was in politicians' interest to support the large vote banks in slums like this one or to answer the middle-class Delhi residents and factory owners who felt the city was now their own. While a few powerful locals held out hope for the politicians' intervention, most felt that these political battles were out of their hands. They engaged in politics when it might be useful, but never depended on it as a stable resource. What was in their hands now was what always had been, before there was a city here or even homes: their vision of transformation.

ON GETTING AHEAD WHILE ACCEPTING ONE'S *ROṬĪ*

I had initially been perplexed at Durga's resigned sigh in the face of the demolition notices, one of which was posted between her storefront and front door. I had argued that this was the moment for political action. But Durga sighed sadly, "It's our *kismat* (fate). If God wants us to eat *roṭīs,* then we will eat *roṭīs;* if God doesn't want us to eat *roṭīs,* then we won't eat *roṭīs.*" Some suggested that she took this stance because she had the money to afford a new home. But Durga's waffling back and forth between considering political action or surrendering to the circumstances asserted to me that she said this to urge herself to accept these circumstances, rather than remain distraught.

Women in particular emphasized how what they achieved was tenuous. This fragility was due to their own dedication to their ambitions, but it was also due to humility and accepting the limits of their agency. Residents had emphasized practical planning: Geeta's careful saving for her son's education, Akshay and Saraswati's careful scheme of nonalignment with local politicians, women's careful hiding of money. All of these strategies allowed them to stay closer to their plan to get ahead. They were the basis for a form of moral citizenship that asked for no precedents from earlier generations or support from politicians and factory owners. For women, these strategies helped root themselves in something larger as they dealt with the straying paths of husbands bent on unrealistic schemes for mobility, abuse that knocked down their plans, and migration journeys guided by others' whims that led them back and forth. But as much as they carefully, painstakingly sought to take control of their visions for themselves, they also acknowledged that it was presumptuous to put one's fate entirely in one's own hands. There was the worldly work that they reflected on now, but there was also a parallel belonging in which one's self was subsumed within a larger cosmic force, dissolving one's individual feelings and one's ability to control. Surrendering to this reality was usually the work of Hindu renouncers. But as Durga reflected calmly on her hands, she too advocated for surrender, "living for the moment without worry rather than planning for the future" (Khandelwal 2004: 87). From the time she first fled her husband's abuse to arrive in Delhi until now, she said, "It is written here," with a finger moving across her forehead, "I will have to earn money myself." But as lonely as Durga or Saraswati might have felt as they pushed their families ahead, both of them grounded themselves in prayer that placed God as a more powerful agent than themselves.

Saraswati tucked away money because it was practical, but she and other women also mused on the way that their aspirations could morph into dangerous desire. As Padma said, "If we become envious after seeing others, then we should not do that. [We should not think that] I could wear this, eat that."[25] To think bad thoughts about others, to be jealous of what they had, other women agreed, would bring danger back to their own bodies, a type of danger that could not be removed with any type of medicine. Yet sometimes it was difficult to accept what they had. After looking at what others possessed, Padma admitted, "We see them and are envious. But we don't get anything. Just our body will burn, be envious."

In this orientation, women drew attention to the way that their emotions caused their bodies to burn. In her "we," Padma spoke as herself, who was tempted to look enviously at the surrounding wealth in Delhi. She urged that acceptance allowed her to reorient her emotional reaction to her environment. She suggested that, "we should live by having faith in our own lentils and bread (*dāl-rotī*). We get okay clothes; we get food. . . . What God gave us we should be proud of and sit still. We should not look at others' *rotī*. Eat from your own salt; that is good." This more tempered perspective aspired to avoid comparison and proclaimed pride with where they were, rather than where they hoped mobility would take them. Sunita's neighbors recalled the screaming fight that spilled outside their *jhuggī*'s walls when her son Sagar came home to tell her that he didn't want to live in the *jhuggīs* anymore. They recounted, "He thinks that they are too good for the *jhuggīs;* that their kind of people don't live here." No one *wanted* to live in the *jhuggīs.* Sagar's neighbors wryly commented that, by removing the *jhuggīs* from his path of mobility, Sagar only brought himself misery.

In this orientation, women did not ask for a change in circumstances but drew attention to the way that their own actions were the cause of their bodies' burning. "The very body itself comes from God," said Durga, "who gives the age, and who gives the life depending on one's *bhakti* [devotion]. But regardless of what is given, it must be endured. This is the biggest wealth that God gives, regardless of how it comes." Like Padma and Neetu who had emphasized the importance of accepting their fate of clothes and food, Durga applied the same acceptance to bodies, even as she connected the gift of the body to one's actions in a past life. Surrounded by people all exploring how they might transform themselves, the temptation was constant. In this atmosphere, women made starker requests. "All I want," Asha explained, "is one place to live. There is no need for two places to go to." She further emphasized her ascetic self as she continued, "I don't need alcohol or meat or money or *pūrīs.* I don't need anything! All day long I wash dirty plates for the sake of my belly as well as to give lovingly to my children."[26] To have faith in simple food and daily work was to free one's body of the pain of wanting more. In this contemporary age, reflected one renouncer (*sanyāsanī*), no one was free from the burden of desires: "To the degree that desire (*vāsnā*) and happiness (*sukh*) have increased, to that degree disquiet (*ashānti*) has also increased. Today there is no one in the mountains who doesn't have money; whether less or more, everyone has it. But there is no peace (*shānti*). Those who lived in dirtiness, let's say, or in poverty, had a peace that does not exist today" (Khandelwal 2004: 128). Although they lived in poverty, women still argued that they were haunted by desire.

Although turning inward to check dangerous desire was congruent with women's practical strategies to keep themselves focused on getting ahead right, turning inward to check dangerous desire clashed with women's imaginations of their transformations. Perhaps they could purify their intentions in getting ahead; but was it possible to detach themselves from the fruits of their actions? Neetu wavered back and forth between what she imagined she might become and how she lived in the present. But, in mentioning her fate, Neetu dampened her aspirations for mobility. "I understand that in my fate (*nasīb*) there is not gold, in my fate there are not such [nice] clothes, in my fate there is no car, no touring (*ghūmna*), that I cannot live in a palace."[27] Now living in a lower-class neighborhood where her neighbor had asked her recently why she did not wear nicer clothes or jewelry, such acceptance was hard won. Particularly from here, outside the *jhuggīs*, Neetu could see what other people's fate had endowed to them. She continued. "So in this way, I have understood my *nasīb*, that God did not give such a *nasīb* to me, so why should I look at others and be jealous?" In grounding herself in fate, Neetu turned from impossible dreams to the boons already before her. "But God has given me so much so that I can eat my *roṭī*, sleep in my house, so that my children can eat, so that we can work."[28] By accepting her fate, Neetu reworked her circumstances. Rather than a fate *without* gold, clothes, or car, she said God had given her "so much." In Neetu and Asha's turns inward, they articulated the struggle of balancing their ambition with detachment. They urged themselves that their continued distance from the nice clothes and cars of their fellow Delhi citizens was not evidence of their failure to be mobile, but evidence of the divine origins of inequality—God made it that way. Action had its limits. As residents had emphasized the simplicity of their lives as they began in the city, so Neetu and Asha urged them to stay grounded in it.

But this was not easy. Women asked many questions before and during the acceptance of their circumstances. Although Geeta accepted that God had given different circumstances to Delhi's residents, there were limits. As she told me, "*Ūpar-vāllāh* (the one above) has made us so we're all different. That's fine, you're rich, I am not, and that's okay. But the thing is, it should not be so different that people are dying of hunger. That's wrong. It's fine if we aren't the same (*barābar*), you have one thing and I have another, but it doesn't mean that it has to be like this. But what can we do, it's not in our hands." Geeta was frustrated with acceptance. It did not change the fact that some things were simply wrong in her eyes.

As she hid away money, provisioned a new home, and struggled to keep her family in line, she lost patience with God: "You know, if he came down here, I would really be mad at him; I would hit him. He's sitting up there comfortably and I am down here homeless (*beghar*)." After demolition, when she had tried to make so much with what she had and insisted multiple times that it was just fine, there were moments when she lost patience. She and others had pushed so hard to create peace with their limitations that sometimes their faith ran out. Some inequality was fine, but what was the purpose in this much inequality? For Dilip and Padma, their faith in God had run out: they refused to talk about God with me.

Sometimes it was easiest for people to focus not on what they had accomplished or aspired to in the future, but on their own morals right here in the present. Before demolition, as people had pondered their own future, they also worried about the puppies that waddled around the remnants of an abandoned *jhuggī* next to Padma's house. Now, two days after it was all destroyed, as people sat on the cots they had laid out on the bricks that used to be their homes, four women became preoccupied with feeding the one puppy that had survived. They forced the puppy's mother to lie down to give it milk. When she refused, they bought milk and fed the puppy. First, they tried to put the puppy's mouth into the small plastic cup, and when that did not work, Geeta fashioned a spoon out of an orange peel on the ground, and her son held the snout of the puppy while she spooned milk in. I said to Geeta, "Look, everyone's homes have been torn down and here everyone is worried about one puppy." "We still have clean hearts," Geeta said with defiance. "But the rich people (*paise-vāllāh log*)," she said as she nodded toward the factories, "have money for their hearts, rather than hearts themselves."

Padma contrasted her anger with wealthy people she saw as greedy with a karmic vision of generosity on behalf of the poor. She played with how she knew that rich people saw them: "You know, the ones who live in mansions—they have one child and then they stop. Poor people can have ten children—even ten is fine. 'They don't have anything, just a *kacchā jhuggī*, that's all. Some don't even have a *kacchā jhuggī*, but they have a shirt. Some don't even have a shirt.' That's what rich people say." Then, toward the rich people she was discussing, she answered their criticism, "They don't have anything, but no one is begging for anything from you! Whether someone covers himself in one rupee or two rupees. How he feeds himself, how he does not—what difference does that make to you?" Still, she faulted them for not even thinking about giving anything. "You could give them at least a rupee, you could at least give that much to the poor!" Then she connected this feeling of greed to what had just happened to them. "It was the rich who just did it, who had our *jhuggīs* torn down. Those assholes just had our camp cleaned up. Did the rich people think about where the poor people will go? No, they were just proud of their wealth. One day when they die, they will put their hands on their cunts as they go, but they will go having left everything here."[29] Her words mocked the fact that rich people did not understand the difference between this world and the other—they would clutch their earthly possessions for as long as they possibly could, having mistaken them for the moral worth they could have built in this lifetime.

These families had come to Delhi with big dreams about self-transformation. As much as politics and a powerful sense of belonging informed their ambivalence as demolition approached, in many ways demolition showed the limits of their everyday striving. Residents grounded their practical work in the awareness that much of their future and present was beyond their control. Unequal circumstances and success were simply part of divine agency, even if divine agency was unfair. Rather than arguing for fatalism, such a perspective argued that the current fortunes of politicians and the wealthy did not originate from their talents, but from temporary luck and bad actions. Standards of living would rise and fall for those living in poverty (Cavalcanti 2007: 28). Now the water infrastructure that they had fought for and gradually built slowly deteriorated, and the government water tankers stopped coming. The few people who had moved to *jhuggīs* in a small strip of Ghaziapuram that had escaped the bulldozers saw their water slow to a slow drip. Now they, like the first migrants here, had to trek to far places to collect water that they had to pay for. As they had slept in dirty clothes and hauled water long distances before, now they would search for homes and begin another period of hardship that they hoped would lead to something different. Even as demolition struck at the core of what migrants had built for themselves in the city, they emphasized that their most precious resources endured: clean hearts.

ALWAYS BUILDING

The disenfranchisement of people living in slums stands out poignantly—often uncounted in censuses, unattached to the urban sewer and sanitation system, poorly connected to health care services, and pushed out of the very city itself. Yet the ways that Ghaziapuram residents described their disconnection to the city and society as a whole were more complicated. As migrants to Delhi, most residents argued that they had built the international reputation of Delhi as a global city and erected the community that urban planners and the middle class now used to justify their removal. During their gradual building of their *jhuggī* neighborhood, politicians and the middle class had tacitly supported them, undergirding residents' own sense that they intrinsically belonged in Delhi. Residents took pride in the fact that having come to Delhi to make a new future for themselves, they could now navigate the contemporary Indian landscape, urban and rural, and its global economic ties, in ways that few others could. Their *jhuggīs* were a sign of their poverty, yet they also signified the struggle symbolizing their dedication to their aspirations for mobility. Others had benefited from and sometimes even supported their efforts. Yet residents had counted on themselves to engineer their own resources rather than counting on the beneficence of others. Where researchers and activists demand that the state must recognize the urban poor through providing the "stuff" of citizenship, here residents stressed that they did it themselves.

In contrast to the histories of most male workers, women's descriptions of getting ahead recounted a continued struggle in the present, both material and moral. Women's worried narratives show the complicated relational dynamics involved in pulling out of poverty. Not only do men and women have differential access to resources, goals and strategies for mobility are also quite gendered. Their cautious warnings and sometimes abrasive complaints indicated that, even as they face continued gender inequity, women exert authority within the household. In all of these ways, women elaborated a theory of action that must be morally accountable, but also limited. Here, women challenged the idealized *jhuggī jāti* (*jhuggī* caste) in historical narratives of their community, arguing that the ways in which migrants made their new lives were diverse, and the obstacles constant. Although claims that they had built this city emphasized societal belonging, women's emphasis on their continued efforts revealed the deep cleavages in vision that were rooted even in their families. I suggest that some of residents' ambivalence in the face of demolition was because of how deeply women were embedded in these more intimate questions of citizenship. For them, the question of whether they would keep their homes was important. But they were also preoccupied with the larger questions of the ethics of their own efforts to get ahead.

Residents knew that, in the present, middle-class people and politicians did not recognize their true belonging to the city and perceived them as a nuisance that threatened their future in Delhi. But residents were also realistic about the uneven landscape of governance and knew that as much as the tide of history was shifting against them, politicians had historically needed them and occasionally supported them. Most residents withheld faith in politicians but still hoped for their intervention. Yet when demolition proceeded, no one was surprised. There was no preexisting exchange that had failed; politics worked like this. Ultimately residents argued that their spirits remained, even if their homes did not. By looking toward fate, they emphasized the impermanence and randomness of all that transpired. They were poorer now, but they could be sustained again by their efforts to get ahead. The factory owners, politicians, and middle classes who benefited from demolition had what they wanted, but this was neither permanent nor was it earned. In injustice, there was a theory of justice.

Here, by describing getting ahead as an emic concept of moral citizenship, I seek to highlight the strongly held political morality that was deeply embedded in what appeared to me initially, and naïvely, as fatalistic political apathy. By getting ahead, residents offered a nuanced approach to agency—or action—that invested in their personal transformations, while cautiously distancing themselves from desire and emphasizing that, ultimately, all action was temporary and limited. In this type of citizenship, residents argued that their belonging to city, society, and the world was mediated through their own ambition to work and build and therefore could not be taken away even as their most intimate physical markers of their citizenship, their homes, were. Sometimes the political fight was not the most important one to fight. Preserving their efforts to get ahead rightfully could be far more precious—and even harder to fight for. Residents interacted with the powerful cautiously—from the middle class to their factory bosses to politicians' local allies, *pradhāns*. Residents knew that these powerful people could be conduits to further bolster their self-made foundations of citizenship, but the powerful could also use residents for their own benefit. Even as the moral citizenship of getting ahead appears to endorse the self-reliance of contemporary neoliberalism, narratives of the past and present show that the social landscape of people living in poverty has always required strategic caution and extraordinary drive. Yet this caution and drive often did not have large effects on health, much less on broader social conditions that shape health. But researchers and activists who advocate for dramatic social action may not have fair expectations for the caution that poor people must sustain (i.e., Chaplin 1999: 157).

The answer of "what could be done," as was asked longingly as demolition approached, ultimately was answered by residents of Ghaziapuram—even if it was moneyed hearts of the powerful who should have answered. Their moral citizenship, rather than the tattered provisions of formal citizenship, was the answer. Through moral citizenship, women could claim equality with the very people that excluded them from the city: equal not in circumstances or in moral fiber, but equal in deserving to be counted as part of society. In so doing, they could proclaim the poverty they endured, but also be more than their poverty. I agree with other scholars who have been hesitant to endorse morality of this type as a form of agency because it can distract attention from the larger social determinants of health that require social reform. Yet in seeing "getting ahead" as a relational strategy that promotes inner well-being, we can concentrate on what it makes possible in everyday life. Deciding who to count on and how much, when to push and when to accept: these decisions must be made regardless of whether the state more equitably enables social provisions for health.

Despite the hundreds of police that had been gathered on the day of demolition to clear off the site for the bulldozers, most residents still found their way back in. They had taken their homes apart the night before, but many of them still wanted to see the final step. Residents murmured the names of each house as the arm of the bulldozer pushed it down, as if taking attendance for each building they had gradually built over the years. People whispered about who put money in whose pockets and scrutinized the movements of *pradhāns* interacting with their neighbors, policemen, and the media. Then, gradually residents made their way to their new homes, rooms in surrounding slums on streets they did not recognize. Padma sent her son to school. Neetu stacked her metal plates. People went to their factory jobs. There was work to be done.

4 To Know the Field

SHAPING THE SLUM ENVIRONMENT
AND CULTIVATING THE SELF

Geeta tired of Sunita's complaints about the slum environment they shared. Like her neighbor Sunita, Geeta longed for the open rural environment of her youth, but she looked to where she sat now: a small *jhuggī* to which she had just moved clustered among many others. Their slum had just been demolished a few weeks ago, and now Geeta stayed in an unauthorized hut built nearby in the industrial area. With a cartoonish nasal voice, Geeta impersonated Sunita's critical comments on her new room. "'I need a latrine, I need more space, I could not have a room like this,'" she parroted Sunita's disapproval. "So what?" she began her imagined response. "I have no problem in going to the [government] latrine.[1] And so I take my bath in the open and must cover with my clothes—no problem," she said with a reproving hmph. "There is no trouble (*parishānī*)," she said to rebuke Sunita's complaints. Geeta felt that Sunita used her renewed critique of the slum landscape to elevate herself above the slum and to complain about the obvious insufficiencies of an environment that they all faced. For both of these women, environment had as much to do with where and how they lived as who they were.

For both Geeta and Sunita, their disagreement explored their selves through the environment. Sunita, in Geeta's view, looked at her slum

Figure 5. Chicken Curry. Photo by Mayank Austen Soofi.

environment with dissatisfaction because of the exclusions it represented. She frequently complained of the inadequate toilets, the stagnant air, the cramped conditions of spaces available to poor migrants like herself, and the insecurity brought on by demolition. These physical conditions marked her as a slum-dweller and became embodied in her daily work to survive in this environment. Sunita had migrated to the city to improve her quality of life, yet the environment before her demonstrated her decline. In contrast, Geeta reckoned that focusing on environmental insufficiency was fruitless. "Why cry?" she would say. "Nothing comes from crying." She had little faith that any complaints about this environment would provoke structural reform. And with that, she pointed to her quiet efforts to make this environment suit her own purposes despite what she wished changed. By patching her own home, she saved money for a property elsewhere, and, where possible, she pointed out the positive features of her surroundings she had learned to notice in the years since she arrived here. If she was to embody the environment—and all of its constituent water, housing, and the health that followed from them—then she would try her damnedest to do it on her own terms.

SLUMS AND THE SELF: EXCLUSION AND INCLUSION THROUGH THE ENVIRONMENT

Geeta, Sunita, and other people living in slums, more than any other urban people, are defined by the place they live—as "slum-dwellers" (Roy 2011). Popular parlance conveyed distinctions of class as poor (*gharīb*) and rich (*amīr*), but Padma and others frequently distinguished between groups through the types of homes in which they lived—the *jhuggī-vāllāhs* (those living in *jhuggīs*) and the *kothī-vāllāhs* (those living in mansions). Padma's distinction more closely approximated the law, which defined slums not through their poverty as much as through their physical features. According to Delhi's Slum Area Improvement and Clearance Act of 1956, slums are those places "where buildings are unfit for human habitation by reason of dilapidation, over crowding, faulty arrangement of streets, lack of ventilation, light or sanitation facilities" (Tewari et al. 2004). Since the colonial era, poor people in Delhi have had less access to water and sewerage than the middle class. While the British and affluent received sewage lines, flushable toilets, and city services, the poor, seen as incapable of using advanced sanitation technology, received few public toilets, waste collection by scavengers, and little water (Hosagrahar 2005; Mann 2007; Prashad 2001).

In the present, Delhi's urban planning regime has continued this historical inequality. Most of the sewage of middle-class neighborhoods flows by the settlements of the urban poor (Sharani 2002), while lines are not extended to service those very areas (Chaplin 1999). Aamir bemoaned the fact that the workers charged with cleaning the drains in their neighborhood were worthless. When he complained to them about their negligence, they asked for bribes to do the work. Women living in Delhi slums spend an average of forty minutes to two hours *each day* collecting water from municipal water tanker trucks, groundwater pumps, and neighboring settlements (Tovey 2002). When they are not fighting to make sure they have enough, women have to worry about the quality of the water, which can be contaminated with dead animals or fecal waste (Tovey 2002). Furthermore, in slums located in industrial areas, many people face exposure to chemical contaminants (Shukla, Kumar, and Ory 1991). Though the risk for cholera and the pneumonic plague has significantly declined in recent years in India, gastroenteritis, diarrhea, dysentery, malaria (Chaplin 1999), skin infections (Rashid 2007b), tuberculosis, fevers, and stomach problems persist to the extent that illness is ordinary for people living in urban poverty (Cohen 1998; Das and Das 2006; Karn, Shigeo, and Hideki 2000). If these health problems are so extensive, and the environment plays a large mediating cause, what did it mean for Geeta to affirm her *jhuggī?*

Even before slums were widespread in India, anthropologists of South Asia argued that the symbolic meanings of environmental substances played a central role in asserting social hierarchy. Dumont's (1980) seminal work on caste elaborated how lower-caste people's contact with food, water, and other environmental substances is polluting, a proposition echoed in other analyses of intercaste transactions (Harper 1964; Marriott 1968). Since then, postcolonial scholars have critiqued this argument for privileging upper-caste views (Chatterjee 1993; Khare 1984) and for institutionalizing a colonialist perspective on caste that emphasizes contamination (Charsely 1996).

"Those people are dirty!" a factory owner I met in Old Delhi's Chandni Chowk told me when talking about the people he employed in his Ghaziapuram factory. (Geeta and Sunita chuckled as I relayed the story, including my reflection to him that actually I found the people I knew in the *jhuggīs* of Ghaziapuram to be very friendly and I enjoyed spending time with them.) His feelings had their own heritage. The assumption of "crowds, dirt and disease" that fueled Orientalist constructions of Indians as environmentally unaware has always been deeply classed (Chakrabarty 2002: 65; Hosagrahar 2005). The same language used to indict the lack of a culture of public citizenship over the environment continues to be used to indict the areas where poor people live: chaos, garbage, lack of order, narrow disordered *galīs* (lanes), public urination, and dirtiness. Delhi Development Authority reports described how some *jhuggī* residents heaped trash in their settlements; public health campaigns assumed people did not know how to wash their hands without tap water; middle-class people urged me to pack my own sandwich when I came to the *jhuggīs*, noting that women there might not know how to clean food well. NGOs, remarked Aamir, had all kinds of suggestions for people living in *jhuggīs* to improve their sanitation: "In every city and village, 10 or 20 people come together in these organizations from which they sit and explain, 'Look, keep your water right, bathe and wash from that clean water, keep your children healthy.'" But, he remarked with a twinge of irony, in many households, "There is no clothing, there is no soap, there is no fuel to boil the water to keep away this bacteria."

Middle-class urbanites have transformed notions of caste contamination through the language of health, arguing that their poor domestic servants' supposed dirtiness threatens their homes' sanitation (Dickey 2000; Hancock 1999; Ray and Qayam 2009; Waldrop 2004). Researchers at times have inadvertently reproduced this bias. Some researchers suggested that the environmental conditions in which the poor live indicate a lack of concern for public health (Chakrabarty 2002: 78–79), or perhaps they had an entirely different conceptual system, in which filth and disorder did not pose matter out of place (Kaviraj 1997: 107). In both cases, however, the environmental practices of the poor are characterized as of a different order, one that has deteriorated civic culture (Kaviraj 1997) and put their own health at risk (Chakrabarty 2002).

Yet in spite of this stigmatization, environment also plays a central role in the *inclusion* of slum-dwellers into broader society. For people living in low-income urban neighborhoods in India and elsewhere, decisions about the home environment have important consequences for their ability to save, legal rights, and long-term security (Anand and Rademacher 2011; Cavalcanti 2007; Chandola 2010). India is replete with examples of urban pioneering that have transformed landscapes in Delhi, Mumbai, and Kolkata. Against a background of structural inequality, the individual initiative of slum residents has resulted in variable conditions between slum settlements (Asthana 1995) achieved in part through building strong political relationships to secure improved environmental necessities like water (Anand 2011). Over time, improving housing can transform residents' status from illegal slum-dweller to legal slum resident, with improved urban amenities and the right to compensation in the event of demolition (Anand and Rademacher 2011; Appadurai 2000; Chandola 2010). (See more in chapter 3.)

In contemporary India, many lower castes and Dalits have not left behind traditional caste occupations that involve handling substances labeled polluting, like leather and human waste. In fact, the municipal sweeping jobs reserved for particular Dalit castes are frequently more secure and have better benefits like pensions than work available in the informal sector that does not involve these stigmatized substances. These groups emphasize that leaving behind the demeaning ideas tied to this work is sufficient to feel transformed (Khare 1984; Kutty 2006).

Neither "environment" nor its Hindi translation *vātāvaran* was used in Geeta and Sunita's community, yet the women with whom I did research commonly discussed their physical surroundings through terms that resonate with research on public health and urban planning policy related to slums, environmental symbolism in South Asia, and South Asian medicine and agriculture. In particular, they stressed particular aspects of the physical environment that are emphasized across these conceptualizations—like water, air movement and quality, and food quality, for instance—while stressing housing in particular, a theme vital to public policy research on the slum environment, and weather, a theme particular to South Asian medicine.

As described in anthropological accounts of South Asian medicine and agriculture, women's conceptualization of environment stressed how interactions between water, land, weather, medicine, food, and the body changed the qualities of each constituent environmental part, so that individuals could manipulate the environment to produce physical conditions that would improve health (Alter 1999; Zimmermann 1987a). Women applied South Asian moral-religious principles to the environment by arguing the importance of seeing beyond exterior physical characteristics to judge inner potential (Aklujkar 1992; Egnor 1984; Khare 1984). As I examine the environmental practices of women in Sunita and Geeta's community, I use environment as an analytic term guided by cultural categories to encompass the moral-symbolic effects on their selves that women enacted through manipulating the homes, water, food, weather, and air that surrounded them.

In the conflicting perceptions of Geeta's home as simultaneously inadequate and *not* a problem, I explore how women's claims about the slum environment are also claims about themselves. The tension between Geeta and Sunita about the state of their environment and what it meant for who they were illustrates how, for those living in slums like Ghaziapuram, the self is a source of nervous transformation. For them, living in slum approximated "two oppositional processes, a process of stigmatization and demarcation, pushing the slum and the slum dwellers outside society or its margins, and, at the same time, a movement into society ... into what is considered the mainstream" (Fuchs 2005: 104). For women, this tension takes on deeper significance. The environment is at the core of the daily activities of South Asian women living in slums, especially because of their responsibility for domestic respectability and their caregiving obligations. Women's obligations force the self to become "radically fugitive and forever fragmented— invested more in the stories [of popular culture] than the story one is compelled to live" (Das 1994: 62). What results is a "deeply divided sense of self" (Das 1994: 56), torn between how women see themselves and what they are obligated to be. I examine how, in this setting of tense exclusions and transformative inclusions, self and environment are dialectically created, following work on environmental relationships (Ingold 2000; Milton 2005; West 2005) and extended in conversations on emotional geography (Bondi, Davidson, and Smith 2007; Davidson, Smith, and Bondi 2007; Davidson and Milligan 2004). In contrast to research on the collective claims of self by scholars analyzing citizenship in slums (Anjaria 2011; Appadurai 2002;

Chatterjee 2004), this chapter explores environmental claims to self that occur on a smaller, less public stage but lay the groundwork for changing the dignity of entire households. I demonstrate how environmental creation is an essential site to understand women's self-definition in a context defined equally by its exclusions as by its hopes for inclusion.

Regardless of the sources of their annoyance, in their own respective homes, both Sunita and Geeta tried to survive in a challenging, stigmatized slum environment while making plans to transform their lives in the broader city in which they lived. Within the self, women's environmental efforts created a new space of inclusion for themselves that both reinforced and challenged society's environmental heart.

HOMEGROWN FIELDS: EXPERIENCING THE ENVIRONMENT

On a spring morning a few months after demolition, I stood with Aarti's thirteen-year-old daughter looking over the railing of the third floor of their large apartment building. In the following months and years, headlines proclaimed the collapse of buildings like this that housed underpaid migrant workers working in the area's factories, denouncing the shoddy construction and lack of regulations that engendered this devastation. But now, as we stood there, we looked below at the bustling walkway through Hari Camp, and ahead were the four busy sets of railroad tracks that formed the boundary of the neighborhood. On both sides of that scruffy path leading out from the neighborhood rose green tall grass that blew in the wind. The sky was huge and blue and, for that moment, it felt that everything was quiet. A nice wind blew, cooling our skin. "It's just like the village up here," Aarti's daughter said in a voice scarcely louder than a whisper. From Aarti's daughter's peaceful view, our backs were turned on this fragile building; I had forgotten about the industrial area I traversed to get here. Was this peaceful feeling just as real as the larger environment that surrounded us? Or was it as transitory as the breeze that would soon leave us?

Urban planners, environmental historians, and geographers have illuminated the scale of exclusion faced by those living in slums. This scale encompasses the compounded effects of environmental inequality, comparison between slum settlements, and the policies that generate and perpetuate slums. But such macroviews of the environment conceptualize it from the outside, "as an object of contemplation, detached from the domain of lived experience" (Ingold 2000: 210). This approach seeks meaning in representing the environment as a whole. The cost of such holism is that "the world as it really exists can only be witnessed by leaving it" (Haraway 2007; Ingold 2000: 213). As an alternative, Ingold suggests that environment be understood from the level of perception and practical experience "with components of a world that is inhabited or dwelt-in" (2000: 216). Although from the scale of the global this view is incomplete, Ingold argues that perception of the environment shows a different form of unity by showing how people participate with their surroundings (2000: 212). Participating with surroundings did not always yield the positive view that we had on the stoop, and often approximated the conflicting interpretations held by Geeta and Sunita. Yet this was the environment as it was felt: frustrating, beautiful, and everyday.

Personal histories and identities guided how women felt the environment that surrounded them. *Gandā*—dirty—that is what Durga said about the family whose baby she had just delivered on my first day back to her home after a year away, as if to explain the urgency with which she filled a bucket with water for her bath. In careful synchrony, her neighbor Padma topped off the bucket with a pot of heated water and pulled shut the curtain behind her to enclose us in Durga's focused bathing. "I always do this after a birth. It's dirty work," she said as she stripped down and lathered up, narrating the blood that was on the floor when she arrived and the home conditions that were so dirty that even their poverty did not excuse it. As Durga washed her body of the blood of the babies she delivered, she scrubbed away allusions to caste pollution. Rather than seeing Durga's feelings as merely her way of experiencing her external environment, we should not presume that people and their environments are conceptually separate things (Milton 1997; West 2005). Washing, cooking, cleaning, building—in all of these interactions, humans become composites that include the environment, "creating themselves, others, and environments in a series of dialectics" (West 2005: 640).

Durga's visceral response to blood is only one example of the powerful meanings embedded in physical substances from blood to dirt to *ghī*

(clarified butter) in this region. Following these rich meanings, anthropologists of South Asian medicine and agriculture have long explored a
perceptual, practical, and dialectical relationship between self and the
environment. South Asian medicine illuminates the impact of the environment on the body, and South Asian agriculture links the cultivation of land
to the cultivation of the body (Alter 1999; Gupta 1998; Kurin 1983; Nichter
1980; Nichter 1989; Vasavi 1994; Zimmermann 1980; Zimmermann
1987a; Zimmermann 1987b). At the heart of both is an emphasis on how
the caregiver realizes the potential of the body and the environment. This
tempered philosophy emphasizes that cultivation of the body and land, by
itself, creates the conditions for health to follow.

Pay attention, women implored, as they explained their routines to promote health. Padma warned me that my habit of eating food in whichever
house I visited would make me sick. I ate whatever was given, without
attention to the order of how I ate it or whether the foods went together!
Saraswati looked with disgust at the bottle of water that I had offered her
over the water from the vendor on the street. After the water I offered had
sloshed around in my bag all day and heated to a boiling point—why
would she drink *that* when she could drink water pumped freshly before
her? Taste of water, amount of grease, feeling left in the stomach pointed
to qualities of environmental substances and their potential effects.
Observation is key to both farmers and caregivers to monitor the impacts
of weather, the type of water and food consumed, the quality of air flow
(Kurin 1983: 287), and to measure the qualities of ecological elements and
their changes through interaction with other elements (Zimmerman
1987a). The farmer's careful observing, tending, and balancing of the environment in "an inherently and naturally imperfect world" (Alter 1999:
s45) is an art as much as it is an honor, for the farmer is "custodian of the
earth's potential for 'reproductive prosperity'" (Moreno 1992). The onus of
the self to recognize environmental potential privileges an individualized
perspective that echoes South Asian religious perspectives (Khare 1993).

Yet beyond their significance for individuals, environmental acts have
social consequences. While we were visiting another resident, Saraswati's
three-year-old son told her he needed to use the bathroom. Her neighbor
took him around to the latrine shared by a number of residents in their
building. Later, Saraswati told me, laughing, that her son had refused to

go. "He looked at that dirty latrine," she explained smiling, "and turned to me and said, 'This is *chī chī* (gross); I am not going to go.'" She was proud of his ability to recognize the dirtiness of surroundings, even though it meant that he was not able to relieve himself. Saraswati's pride in her son's refusal to accept this environment demonstrated his refined environmental sensibility. But, more than that, it reflected *hers*, as the mother who taught her son these environmental values.

Saraswati questioned more broadly the domestic environmental skills of the women surrounding her. When I announced that I was beginning a series of interviews on home remedies (which drew on Ayurvedic concepts), she shut down my enthusiasm, explaining flatly to me, "Most women aren't going to know about that." People who were educated knew such remedies, she said, but many people in the *jhuggīs* did not. For Saraswati, home remedies and strict sanitary efforts signaled refined domesticity; lack of remedies and dirty conditions indicated apathy caused by environmental ignorance. In South Asia, as in many places, the domestic sphere has particular political meanings for women. Nationalists emphasized that women's domestic mastery protected intimate cultural values from the dangerous foreign values present in the public (Chakrabarty 2002; Chatterjee 1989). Although at times women's domestic responsibilities are in the name of health, they also serve to guard their class (Dickey 2000). In defining their household for the outside world, women have special responsibilities to depict themselves and their households as respectable (Das 1976; Nair and John 2000).

Domestic environments, whether the home remedies applied or the state of the shared latrine, were a window into which others could see. As Das and Addlakha put it, "the domestic, once displaced from its conventionally assumed reference to the private, becomes a sphere in which a different kind of citizenship may be enacted . . . always on the verge of becoming the political" (2001: 512). Whatever neighbors and the broader public perceive in women's domestic qualities is communicated through rumor and entrenched in widely known reputation. So though homes may be limited in space, women's home environmental actions are always communicative, whether intentionally or not. With me, Saraswati emphasized her dual awareness of Western and Ayurvedic conceptions of health. But when engaging in small talk with her neighbors, she complained about water access and the habits of her neighbor whose dirty dishes stacked high into a neglected tower. In slums especially, what identity claims are communicated varies by contextual reference (Fuchs 2005: 110) and by audience (Chandola 2010: 57–58).

Peering through the window to see women's daily environmental practices, I focus on the meanings women drew out of them, rather than measuring the degree to which women were able to transform their environment. First, I examine how women refined their emotional reactions to the slum environment and thus commented on their ability to find environmental potential. Second, though women faced chronic health challenges, I describe how their efforts to strengthen the body through managing the severe climate disputed the logic that inequality alone determines health. Third, I examine how women's efforts to make a home in the slum created microenvironments that allowed them to ideologically and physically separate themselves from the slum around them.

Each section illuminates a different comparative view of the slum environment through its different aspects: slum appearances and their contrasting inner value, health-harming weather and the strengthened bodies it shaped, and contaminated landscapes and insulated home environments. Through these comparisons, women defined environment to include their perceptual scale: that which they could resee and manipulate, not merely that which could be measured in community-level health outcomes. Rather than effecting total transformation of their self and environment, these acts enabled women to strengthen themselves and experiment with reenvisioning their environment.

TO "KNOW THE FIELD": RECOGNIZING ENVIRONMENTAL POTENTIAL

Durga said that her sons in the village earned nothing, but they insisted on staying there anyway (for more, see chapter 1). She patted the walls of her *jhuggī*. It was easily an eighth the size of her youngest son's village home and had a thin tin roof that rested low on the house. Outside were rows of *jhuggīs*, some with tarps over their roofs, and roads that turned to mud in the monsoon. Though her sons did not cover their noses like some NGO workers who visited, she knew what they thought. "They don't want to live in this type of house. They have pride in their temples back at home. There are none like that here in Delhi." As she looked around her house at this *jhuggī* landscape, she disagreed with her son's perspective: "You should not need a temple, because God is everywhere."

Whether temple or *jhuggī*, place was important, but its appearance should not be mistaken. When thinking about lush environments that they knew from rural homes and from green streets not far from Ghaziapuram, it took bravery to affirm one's place in the *jhuggīs*. For many people, poor as they might have been in the village, their village lives were filled with trees and opened by space. As many women told me, moving to the *jhuggīs* had felt odd at first, not just because of the strange new people, but because of its unattractive environment: weather was irritating, food was low quality, good homes were hard to find, and good living conditions impossible. Her son confused physical appearances with substance, but Durga posited substance in what she could recognize anywhere: God's presence, unmediated by physical conditions.

Like Durga's changing orientation toward the lanes before her, "through their engagement with different environments, people learn to love, hate, fear, or be disgusted by different things, so their bodies react differently when these things are encountered" (West 2005: 36). Here Durga contended that environmental emotions could be relearned and reconfigured. Where grand temples inspired awe and slums provoked Durga's son's disgust, Durga's interpretation pointed to her capacity to relearn her reaction to environment. The physical place, Durga argued, should not be needed for God's presence—implying that the religious seeker needed to find God everywhere, even in places where the seeker might not expect. The different pieces of the Hindu landscape, writes Eck, are ultimately all part of "a wider peripheral vision" in which each pilgrimage path and temple is "ultimately numberless, limited not by the capacity of the divine to be present, but by the capacity of human beings to discover and to apprehend the divine presence" (Eck 1999: 26). The attention outsiders gave to material qualities of the slum environment distracted them from seeing anything valuable in the ramshackle *jhuggīs*.

More than place, the capacity to recognize potential in environment mattered. This was lost on people who saw potential in terms of a wealth of options. In her casual tone, Sarala explained that rich and poor people not only ate differently, but thought differently about the meaning of their food. "Look, rich people see beauty differently. They could have thirty-six types of snacks—'I like this,' or 'I want that.' 'This is what I like, so this is what I need.'" For them, they could sit in their car, drive around, and eat whatever they wanted wherever they wanted. She paused to encourage my field assistant's three-year-old son as he made imaginary *roṭīs* with the handle of the water jug. But, she contrasted, "Us poor people, we eat *dāl*, *roṭī*, and vegetables. We do not stay in tension. Okay, so today I will make this, tomorrow, I will make that. In a week, you'll eat something or another. We make by what suits." She summarized, "They have wealth, so they eat it; we don't, so we eat *dāl-roṭī*." But then she made a distinction, "There is no difference between the wealthy and the poor. There are differences between the things."[2] For Sarala, wealthy and poor people were essentially equal. What differentiated them were the things they had: feasts procured from the windows of their cars and *dāl-roṭī* eaten on improvised tables inside homes. Like Durga's son, who saw God's presence in the physical space of a temple, the rich people that Sarala described found beauty in all of the different types of food they could have whenever they wanted.

The "knower of the field," as the *Bhagavad Gita* puts the self, is "the source of all light in the field," illuminating the land's potential as much as the light within (Easwaran 2007). In the same way, as Durga enriched her view of the environment with the spiritual presence she found, this process of knowing indicated something about the capacity of her self to recognize the generative capacity of this place. Here, people did not look toward the environment as a moral guide, as some anthropologists have shown (Basso 1996), but instead looked toward *themselves* as the moral guides who must interpret a denigrated physical environment, often in varied ways. South Asia is replete with examples of the spiritual endorsement of stigmatized physical spaces. The Hindu god Shiva can be found on the stigmatized cremation ground (Fuller 1992), and Mariamman, the goddess of smallpox, protects those who live in poor, dirty, crowded conditions, rather than the rich (Egnor 1984). Environmental symbols of lower-caste pollution are transformed to signify removal from worldly desires and thus greater spiritual power. Though Durga's home mattered, just as did the temples in her village, what mattered more was her ability to make light in any place.

In expressing the generative potential of the environment, slum residents called for a revaluation of meaning—for judging value on potential rather than physical appearance. Both accounts of lower-caste groups (Khare 1984; Vincentnathan 1993) and South Asian religion more generally (Babb 1983a; Narayan 1989; Shweder et al. 1997) indicate how the "real" interior self is covered by superficial outside appearances. The ability to retrain one's emotional response to physical reality, "to overcome feelings of repulsion and terror at the sight of that which to the uninitiated is ugly and terrifying, is the sign of a true devotee" (Das and Addlakha 2001: 518). It is true faith—something inculcated, not given—that can make even the most polluted filth be experienced as sacred (Babb 1983a: 309–10). Because only a developed self can perceive the potential of the environment, the cultivation of the physical is intertwined with the cultivation of the self.

Neetu knew that people passing by their neighborhood on the way to factories judged their neighborhood and its residents as filthy. "Many rich people say that the *jhuggīs* are only germ-ridden gutters (*nālās*)—but have you seen our *jhuggīs?*" Imitating such visitors to the *jhuggīs* and the people who must talk to me about my time in the *jhuggīs*, she asked, puffing herself up: "Why do you go to the *jhuggīs?* Good people don't live there! Look how those people *live!*" She broke her frame and asserted angrily: "No! That's the wrong way to think." Turning to them in her imagined court before her, she answered their allegations: "Your fate is a good place. So why do you say that to someone? It's possible that your fate will be revealed to be the same. Right?" Neetu separated material conditions from personhood. "Good place" was due not to good character, but to fate (*nasīb*), which was entirely in the hands of God.

While Neetu acknowledged that it was her responsibility to accept this environment as her fate (*nasīb*), her comments on beauty pointed toward a more active orientation toward the physical. "God sends us [into life] with so much unique beauty," she insisted. "These days, ladies want a face with the beauty of *Durgā-mā*.[3] They spend one hundred thousand rupees, twenty thousand, ten thousand, two thousand on makeup—for the purpose of beauty, right? To have beauty, [in such thinking] you need to put on makeup. But in giving us our own unique appearance, God gave only beauty. So there is no need to put on so much makeup. It is merely adornment. From God's adornment is beauty."

Homes, faces—these things were dressing that overlaid the real beauty at the core, beauty that must be known before it could be recognized. Neetu contended that through the divine gift of "unique beauty," there is essential equality. But women mistakenly perceive their unique beauty as unequal forms of beauty. Neetu argued that, as women try to alleviate their perceived disadvantages, their efforts are not only misguided; they cannot identify their divine potential. Wealth was inherent in what they had rather than what they could become. Durga urged that "God has given us such a precious body; our biggest wealth is this thing, our body."[4] Both Neetu and Durga commented on how beauty was obscured by an ignorant focus on immediate physicality—whether of the body or the environment. And, in both cases, they show that environmental value is equally available, if only people develop the capacity to recognize it.

Men did not talk with me about environmental potential in the same way. There was certainly inequality in environmental circumstances, Akshay said, but his account had a trickster undercurrent. Akshay said that his factory had a drinking water filter with three different spouts. One was for foreign visitors; one for the workers; and one for water to wet the material they used. Of course, the water for foreigners was the highest quality. Akshay speculated that it was some 1,500 rupees a glass! Sometimes, he revealed slyly, he and his friend took a few cups of the best water and disappeared to the roof to hang out. He laughed as he pointed out that he elevated his own status through taking on the habits of the foreigners who were supposedly in charge. He also speculated about the water I must drink at home and bring with me to his and Saraswati's house. He guessed it was Bisleri, using the brand name that I had heard used often in the slum to describe high-end bottled water. I admitted that it was; my housemate insisted on it. You know, he said, often people filled up those Bisleri containers with any water they found and resold it to make a big profit. In both cases, Akshay questioned the continued salience of this status symbol that signified access to better health and cleaner bodies. He, whose lower-class digestive system was deemed universally disease-resistant by the middle class, could and should drink expensive water in leisure. Yet I, whose foreign digestive system was deemed fragile by the middle class, could be throwing away money to drink the same water that people drank in the *jhuggīs*. Rather than divine equality, Akshay inverted class hierarchy through breaking rules of environmental exclusivity and exposing their false fronts. In contrast, Aamir focused on environmental inequality that was alive and well. He became irate when I asked him about the causes of illness, condemning the government for environmental negligence: "Our country and people would benefit if this filth was far from here. Our children would stay healthy, everything would be fine. We appeal to the government for this—that no matter how many problems there are, that they are resolved!"[5] Aamir emphasized that environmental inequality could only be answered with immediate social action. To him, environmental potential was not an issue.

Durga and Neetu held that the inequality of material circumstances masks an essential equality of selves. Material circumstances appear to be all-powerful—as indicators of social identity and value, as well as beauty and health. But these women asserted the greater importance of cosmological equality, represented in the capacity to recognize God in any landscape, see one's divinely granted beauty, or develop strength. In each case, women described how their ability to resee their environment reverberates in their self—as closer to God or as wealthy. Those who were able to "know the field" of their environment, bodies, and health with their own source of light found obscured value in unlikely places. Women's perceptions of their environment also move the boundaries of inclusion to be based less around consumerism. Even though their environments are without beautiful temples, with humble homes and food they are made to be signs of their moral substance, a type of inclusion made through individual effort rather than external acceptance.

UNLIKELY STRENGTH FROM UNEXPECTED SOURCES

For a whole week, Jyoti had been immobilized with a fever; the doctor she had seen in the neighborhood had given her medicine, but it had done nothing, she said. Usually, she moved gingerly around as she did her day's work, making food, pausing to breast-feed her youngest one, stepping into the shared washing space between apartments to wash clothes. Now, she was stuck on the *chārpāī* (cot), stretched out in a way that I never had seen in her constant bending and moving. When I asked about going to the government hospital, her husband dismissed my suggestion with a wave: "It's useless. You have to wait so long." They were afraid to go to another neighborhood doctor. Too many times they had gone when their children were sick over the years—once with dengue fever, once with severe diarrhea—and they wound up with bills worth three times their monthly income. Jyoti's pattern of bad health seemed not unlike accounts of other women living in South Asian slums, in which they refer to their health as weak, "dried-up" (Unnithan-Kumar 2003), and riddled with tension (Rashid 2007b). It all sounded so far from the portrait of environmental abundance advocated in the generative philosophy of South Asian agriculture and health outlined above. Research on women's health care–seeking practices too confirms the lack of control women like Jyoti experience in regard to their health. For women to seek the expertise of a doctor beyond the slum, they often need the permission of their husbands, help in arranging child care, and financial commitment from their families (Das, Das, and Das 2012; Das and Das 2006; Ramasubban and Rishyasringa 2008). Many women in slums fear that doctors will make judgmental comments or uncover serious health conditions (Ramasubban and Rishyasringa 2008: 238).

When Jyoti's husband stepped out of their room, Saraswati shared her suggestion: "If the medicine from that doctor does not make a difference, then don't go back." Instead, she recommended the doctor around the corner from her. There she would not have to spend much, and the medicine was good. Furthermore, Saraswati directed, "You should drink water with salt to clean out your throat and then drink only boiled water—not cold water, and only once it is cooled down. And don't drink chai, since it leaves an acidic feeling in your stomach. Once in a while, turn off the fan and let your body sweat as much as you can stand to bring the fever out." Hearing about the repeated rounds of failed medicine and her husband's outright rejection of the hospital even though the situation seemed dire left me feeling hopeless. I really only trusted medical establishments because they felt more real to me. I focused more on the serious diagnoses that would not be followed up on, then the potential risks and long-term financial obligations that repelled Jyoti's husband. But Saraswati momentarily replaced the lurking health despair and fatigue from unpromising medical options with her expertise, the healing regime that Jyoti could steer herself, and the strength of her endurance.

A theme to all of these efforts was endurance, a quality that indicated a strong self and enabled a health regime that was in their hands. Home practices of health focused on building bodily strength through awareness and careful management of the vulnerability posed by weather, a theme central to South Asian medicine (Kurin 1983; Nichter 1989; Pool 1987). The extremes of heat and cold, people explained, caused weakness, nausea, diarrhea—everything! Women described how the microenvironment of the *jhuggīs* accentuated the extreme seasons in South Asia, each of which poses a different type of vulnerability to the body (Zimmermann 1980). Here, in summer, fans spun lackadaisically because of the area's intermittent electricity supply. The lack of trees, the heat produced by air conditioning units, the buildings, Geeta pointed out, all made Delhi hotter than her rural village. On cold winter days in the *jhuggīs*, men still bathed outside, and Neetu fought with her son about the cost of heating water. If the wealthier neighbors heated up water for their daughters' baths, he argued, then why did *he* have to use cold water?

Durga was not alone in her belief that "people should live according to the season." To live according to season meant protecting oneself from the extremes of climate. When a friend and I appeared sweater-less in December in the settlement, our naked arms horrified Geeta and her neighbors. "You are asking to be sick," they said. Explaining our bizarre comfort amid the cold, Geeta remarked to her neighbor, "We're weak (*kamzor*), so we need these shawls, but they're young (*javān*) and strong, so they don't need them." Many women explained that, by eating, drinking, and traveling according to season, they adapted their bodies to their surrounding changing weather (see also Kurin 1983; Pool 1987; Nichter 1989). Because of the risk such intense weather posed to the body, women limited their exposure to the elements. In the summer, women restricted their heavy work to the morning and evening. In the monsoon, they avoided walking in the rain because cold rain clung to wet clothes, endangering warm bodies as their temperatures mixed. When I had to go out anyway, Saraswati carefully adjusted my *dupaṭṭā* (scarf) over my head to seal out the water. And, in the depths of winter, children appeared as sweaters in human shape, with faces poking through their small holes, betraying their inner contents. These subtle techniques mitigated the external forces of weather that made the body susceptible to illness by stabilizing the body's internal temperatures.

Padma laughed at the lengths to which people went to protect themselves. "You can do anything, but if you're going to get sick, you're going to get sick. Everyone thinks that whether it is hot, cold, or whatever season, I am going to save my body [from sickness]," she said, "but even in trying to save it, you won't!" To her, sickness was going to happen as regularly as the seasons changed. Like weather's cycles, "many forms of sickness are regarded as having a natural course" (Lambert 1992: 1071). Therefore, "damage limitation" was the ideal response to illness, using "measures of containment and encouragement intended to ensure an uncomplicated, speedy and ultimately harmless passage of the sickness through the body of the patient" (Lambert 1992: 1071).

But many people abstained from such practices because they shunned the uncomfortable endurance that they required. Geeta claimed that Sunita's refusal to accept weather put her at a disadvantage. "She has three fans going on her from all sides, and she is *still* complaining she's hot," she whispered disdainfully. "Look in here," proclaimed Geeta quietly, "I sit here without fans and enjoy the breeze coming through the door." Geeta elaborated a practice of protection from harsh weather that was combined with endurance. By bearing the hot weather, she trained her body to tolerate a broader range of temperatures. Durga felt the same frustration with me. When I whined in reaction to her suggestion that I drink hot tea before leaving at the peak of the day's 105-degree heat, she snapped in response: "If you drink cold things as soon as you come inside or right before you leave to go out in the heat, then you will get sick." Comparing my ignorance to a child's, she continued, "Drinking cold things that way, you stop your body from letting out all of its heat." She pointed to the pores on my skin and said that it was through these that heat and sweat came out and whose function was necessary to create bodily equilibrium. By drinking tea, I would encourage the body's gradual process of adjustment, rather than simply leaving it to make its own transitions (Alter 1999: s51). All of these therapeutic techniques used climate force that was part of the Indian landscape and therefore freely available to those in the slum. Residents answered for themselves when to tolerate extremes to build bodily strength, when to protect the body, and when simply to alleviate discomfort through quick, but potentially dangerous, fixes.

Slum residents emphasized that amenities to ameliorate the harsh climate—like regular electricity, refrigeration, and air conditioning—were more freely available in the city and were used particularly by rich people, *baṛhe log*.[6] But residents warned there were deceptive consequences to the increased use of such climatic amenities to make separate modern urban environments. Though poverty made residents more vulnerable to illness, they claimed that in some ways, it built stronger bodies. While Neetu had described equal physical beginnings, Dilip pointed out the physical differences that emerged through long-term exposure to different environments. Even though poor people took precautions to protect themselves from weather, they faced the weather more immediately than the rich. "Rich people stay inside. They don't come outside. If they come out, they become hot and will get sick. Unlike that, we keep on moving." He continued, "That's why poor people's blood is like this." Withstanding the weather enriched blood that enabled movement, ability, and strength.

Residents indicated that certain aspects of the body were determined at birth, but others could be altered through adjustment (see also Nichter 1980: 227). Sure, Saraswati said, wealthy people could run from the heat as they passed from air-conditioned car to air-conditioned home to air-conditioned restaurant, but at a certain point, their insulated tunnel would run out, and they would be violently struck by what they had tried to avoid. Saraswati pointed out how they disposed of built-in bodily techniques in favor of total, yet futile, environmental separation.[7] By using a strong will to embrace harsh environmental forces, they promoted intertwined physical and self-development. When women insulated themselves entirely from the weather, their fitness diminished. Certain aspects of the body were determined at birth, but others, through adjustment, could be altered, "the way a rice eater adjusts to be able to digest wheat after some periods of time" (quoted in Nichter 1980: 227). But if people made no effort to build stamina, they would be left suffering, like Sunita and her fan fortress. When Neetu's friend visited her in her new apartment, her infant began wailing. "She has an air cooler *ādat* (nature)," the friend explained, laughing, "She can't endure any heat and always must be in front of a cooler." Sarala said the same thing about me to Saraswati. I surely could not spend the night with her, Sarala reasoned as I stood watching their interchange—I simply could not endure an evening without air conditioning in the middle of the summer. Endurance (*bardāsh karnā*) of weather and sickness built bodily capacity.

Much environmental knowledge espoused in the slum was similar to what is heard in middle-class urban South Asian households or in rural India, whether it concerned exposure to weather or proper eating habits (Gupta 1998; Kurin 1983). Yet Dilip's and Saraswati's comments about the weakness engendered by insulated environments indicted the urban rich, this whining anthropologist, and sometimes their neighbors as well. When it came to climate, their language emphasized how physical difference was not caused by original difference or unequal environmental conditions alone. Rather, the physical endurance that slum residents highlighted more generally echoed the indifference to illness, pain, and sensual temptation that indicates moral capacity and resilience (Khandelwal 2004).

MAKING A HOME: CREATING MICROENVIRONMENTS

"If you were to grow vegetables in the water that flows in these *nālās*,"[8] said Dilip as we sat outside his *jhuggī*, "stink would come from them. No matter how much you wash it, how much you clean it, still no good taste would come from it. Those from the fields in the village have good taste and nourishment (*poshak āhār*) that you cannot get in the vegetables here." The taste and quality came from the substance it had absorbed in the process of growing. Washing vegetables grown in the *jhuggīs* never made a difference because the substance of the vegetable was contaminated by the polluted water and land in which it grew. In South Asia, it is understood that vegetables' and fruits' intimate relationship with the environment makes them absorb the qualities of the water and dirt that they were grown in. In Ghaziapuram, it was harder to ascertain the qualities of the dirt that made its way into their homes, the water that unreliably flowed from bore wells, or food from the market and ration shops. Their origins could be as anonymous as those of their neighbors, who appeared to be one thing but were actually something else. If there was so much stink in this environment, how could it be anything but soiled?

Women said that they manipulated aspects of the wider slum environment to diminish its overall disadvantages and to delineate a separate micro-environment. They drew on South Asian medical-agricultural philosophy to trace how environmental qualities flow through the wider environment into its constituent parts. In this medical-agricultural philosophy, espoused similarly within the slum, the environment is conceptualized in terms of moving—and changing—elements. Whether air, water, dirt, or food is hot or cold, stagnant or moving, its characteristics make their way into the body (Gupta 1998: 280; Kurin 1983: 286). In Ghaziapuram, residents traced circulating environmental qualities and the flow of substances that made their way into their homes, streets, and their bodies that nestled within.

From the microscale of germs and soil to the macroscale of sewage systems and urban air flow, residents narrated how they regulated the substances within their environment, increasing the outflow of bad substances and maximizing the quality of what they needed. To begin with, there was water. The soil (*miṭṭī*) of land cleared of trees, like that in the industrial area, Geeta had said, made the groundwater salty. Thus, it was unfit for drinking, made women's hair break, and stained the skin. Though water in the slum was generally of poor quality, Geeta emphasized that this quality had a gradient. In general, she explained, the groundwater that many pumped to supplement tanker water was salty because the soil (*miṭṭī*) it came from was industrial land cleared of trees. But she pointed out how she trekked to a different neighborhood to wash her clothes. The trees there, she said, made that water sweeter than what was available at the treeless public toilet block in her own neighborhood where others did their washing.

Even those lucky enough to have access to piped water were suspicious of it. Women told me, Who knows what maze of pipes the water flowed through, how long the water sat in them, or how well they were connected![9] It simply did not have the quality of water that freely flowed from hand pumps to be used immediately. Saraswati had other techniques to improve water quality. She explained to me that the quality of the water delivered by the municipal tanker truck was suspect. Because the truck arrived hours and sometimes even *days* late, she had to store it in jugs in her house. But the longer it sat in the jugs, the greater the chance of contamination by germs or mosquitoes. Thus, whenever the municipal water tanker truck came, she ran to empty all the remaining buckets of water and rushed to the truck to refill as many as possible with fresh water. She reasoned that though her technique was more work, the water stood stagnant for less time. Both women were reassured by these small, yet important, alterations they made to the water they consumed, even if it remained far from the ideal. Instead of accepting their environment as a given, these women improved their microenvironments by isolating qualities to change (Alter 1999: s51).

Replacing inferior water with sweeter and fresher water was part of a larger pattern of substitution. Many residents of the *jhuggīs* depended on poor-quality government-subsidized rations of basic staples, particularly wheat flour and rice, for the bulk of their diet. They explained that the shopkeepers at the ration store set aside the high-quality supplies to sell on the black market and sold the poor-quality ones to slum residents at the subsidized price (Venkatesan 2010). Some ration shops, reported Mohan's son, were only open once a month, leaving an entire community to throng around the store to accommodate delayed needs from the previous weeks. Even what was available had to be fought for. Many people did not have the paperwork to get the ration cards they were technically eligible for; others struggled after demolition to get new ration cards for their new addresses, having to turn away from unwieldy crowds. Like other South Asian slum dwellers, these urban migrants faced higher food insecurity in the city—and thus higher malnutrition—in contrast to the food and livestock production they directed in the village (Hassan and Ahmad 1991; Izutsu et al. 2006; Unnithan-Kumar 2003).

In Delhi, residents were exposed to neighbors and rich people (*baṛhe log*) who ate all varieties of food. With vicarious pleasure, Neetu and Saraswati separately mentioned to me the ghee they knew Durga ate regularly. When I underestimated Durga's age, Neetu corrected me and insisted, "She's at least 70! She eats ghee that keeps her looking strong." It was not as if women did not know the potential of certain foods to make their bodies stronger, but they had to accept that such substances were not available to nourish their bodies. Durga's physical presence was a reminder to most people in the *jhuggīs* that they simply could not eat like her.

Sunita said the doctor's advice to eat certain fruits to improve her health was nothing she did not already know, but she was too embarrassed to admit to the doctor that the reason she was not eating them was because she could not afford them. Instead, Geeta said, poor people used cheap foods, like oil that made their bodies small and ruined their stomachs over time. Geeta tried to reduce her use of bad oil so that her stomach was not completely ruined, but we both knew the reasons why I stood like a giant beside all the women: my body, always nourished by good expensive foods, was bigger and stronger. By limiting their intake of harmful foods, women might not eat like me, but they were able to improve the food that their budget determined and buffer the long-term negative impacts of cheap foods. And in other ways, women made do with what they had. Sarala declared that, "[When] there are no vegetables in the house, no *dāl*, but there is *roṭī*—with pickle (*achār*), you can eat *roṭī*." There was no nutritional benefit to eating it, she cautioned; but in eating the pickle, "taste comes to your mouth."[10] Sarala balanced her awareness about their limitations with an acceptance about what they could still eat. "We eat, but we eat according to what we wish. But take note—what we don't have, we can't just bring it from anywhere. What we don't have, why would we try to get it? Look *clear,* what I'm saying is that what we don't have, we don't feel that, 'Okay, we have flour, we have potatoes, so we'll make something from *that* vegetable there.' Eat, lay in your home! That's how we think."[11]

Women mocked the heroic, yet always incomplete, efforts they took to make up for these disparities. Mrinalini, like many others, unveiled her cache of food from the village with a hushed wonder that almost felt illicit, as if she hid stolen treasure. But Mrinalini contorted her usual stately, larger, middle-aged body into a shape that echoed a street performer's as she imitated herself at the railway station, balancing these things with every appendage, "Whenever we come from the village, we bring some of this, some of that, but really, how much can you carry up the stairs in the railway station?" The extent to which a woman with achy joints would compromise herself to bring as much village food as possible through the teeming crowds of the Delhi station was comical. She was under no illusion that she could feed her family in Delhi with the same food they might have eaten in the village. That was not their life anymore, no matter how much their heavy loads seemed to indicate otherwise. But, with laughter at how ridiculous her efforts appeared at times, she commented on the feeling that motivated her environmental cultivation, even though it never would result in total transformation.

Even still, nearly every home made a point of displaying the jars filled with special foods that they had brought from the village: flours of roasted chickpea and barley, rice from one's family fields, pickle (*achār*) of hand-picked mangoes, and clarified butter (*ghī*). And because those supplies were limited, people sought out foods that felt close to homegrown, like the more expensive milk Saraswati bought for her son from her neighbor's water buffalo because it was *ghar kā*, of the home. "You never know what they put into the milk sold in bags," she said, "or how much they have watered it down." These foods for special occasions or flavor were not abundant enough to diminish rampant malnutrition. However, they suggested imagery of agricultural abundance in an environment of insecurity and connected now-urban women to their rural environments.

Durga liked to comment on how rich people possessed little awareness about their food. They did not see the value of knowing what was in their food. "They don't like homemade food; they like restaurant food[12] better," Durga explained, "That's why rich people fall sick." Her point was particularly directed at me. I had become sick from bad street food I ate before our trip to her village. As I vomited repeatedly out of the bus window on the long journey with her, she had no kind words for ignoring such basic advice. With one hand she held my hair and then cleaned up the mess I left and with the other she gestured wildly to indicate her indignation: "What did I tell you?! Outside food is bad! They put in too much oil! How many times have I told you not to eat that food? And what do you do? You eat that food!" As my body violently expelled the food, Durga's incensed disapproval indicated that I should pay more heed to the substance of what I put in my body—lest my body would have to do the job as it was now. To me, eating out was easier—food at home was surely healthier, but it was time that meant more. Having someone else buy the vegetables, cook them, and clean up liberated me from many more tasks I wanted nothing to do with. But food was not only an energy input, as I thought. Durga's attention to its specific aspects forced me to look at how the food would transform my body in the immediate (painful) present, as much as over the long term. Though I was willing to impart my environmental decisions to the random cook who made my takeout, Durga urged that I must take responsibility for learning what environmental substances I consumed. If I took no interest in how much oil was in my food or whether the cook washed his hands or not, then why should the cook bother? Earlier, in her elaboration of the need to build bodily endurance, Durga had supported softening the modern boundary between public and private. Yet in asserting the importance of her home, she advocated for the creation of a separate microenvironment by furnishing it with substances whose origins were known. Durga created an environment whose boundaries were marked less by physical space—because she and others indeed welcomed in food from afar—but more by the familiar origin of its contents.

Women argued that their daily routines—cooking homemade food, scrubbing laundry, sweeping, mopping, and bathing—built a level of protection from the external, and more contaminated, environment. Saraswati maintained that the degree to which she was able to keep her home and body clean directly improved her chances for good health. Yet this required vigilance of her home, as well as the ways it was linked with the broader environment. She growled that as she swept the last pile of dust out the door, her son ran inside, his head crawling with lice that she knew came from children on the street. Neighborhood dirtiness (*gandagī*) quickly became *her* son's bodily dirtiness as surrounding dirt, house dirt, and bodily dirt combined and multiplied. Even when her environmental knowledge did not impact the environment, she used it to publicly remark on her self—a self dissociated from environmental squalor by her creation of microenvironment.

"In the village," she remembered with a tinge of romance, "people go out first thing in the morning and walk. But I have to stay in my room all day long working to keep it clean." There was a sense that, in the city, without the broader environment to call their own, women were charged with creating safe home environments in the midst of large piles of uncollected trash, backed-up *nālās*, unswept streets, and hidden contaminants. Sometimes no amount of planning could make a difference. That was the case for Jyoti, who anxiously watched the declining water line in her water drums. When the water did not come regularly in the building where they moved after demolition, they had to take the containers to the public toilets to fill them. They could not even use the shared latrine on their floor without water to flush the squat toilet. She knew that it was not good for anyone's health because they couldn't bathe as regularly, wash clothes, or wash the dishes—but what could she do? She was rationing the rest of the water because it was all they had left for drinking.

To the extent that they were successful in creating such a microenvironment, women felt the results of their labors through the reduced illness in themselves and their families. In contrast to their gossip about neighbors' dirty children and forgotten piles of food-encrusted dishes, women's descriptions of their own cleanliness marked the extent to which they worked to create a microenvironment that was ideal, from the food they ate to the drains outside their front door. In the water quality, neighborhood characteristics, and cleanliness that their attention enabled them to distinguish, women saw the contours of an environment that outsiders knew as universally contaminated.

Men's efforts helped fuel these efforts as well, and they came with their own frustrations of managing errant family members. On a hot afternoon, Geeta's son Dev lay sprawled on the floor of their *jhuggī*. His night shifts as a guard in a wealthy neighborhood meant that by the afternoon, when he was supposed to be studying, he often folded into bizarre contortions as his fatigue overcame him. (Usually, his mother and I liked to imitate his body pretzels for fun, but that day I was similarly passed out.) He sprang to life when his father angrily appeared at the door, informing him that water was finally flowing through the pipes and Dev was not present to collect any of it. Half asleep and cranky, Dev ran to meet his father who waited for him by the pump with a pile of jugs. Their collective emptiness provoked his dad's urgency as much as his anger that Dev had missed part of the brief window to fill them.

As a government demolition drive of their homes loomed, residents selected the best places to make homes. Good landlords maintained the plaster and paint on walls, sprayed for pests, and regulated unruly tenants. Bad landlords built rooms of intolerable size without regard to ventilation; they neglected maintenance so drastically that it stymied even the most diligent cleanliness campaigns. Women ranked rooms based on the extent to which they furthered the flow of water, air, and waste in the broader landscape. They described how, when water streamed out of washing areas, air flowed freely through windows and doors, and waste moved unimpeded through open sewer drains, bad substances would flow out (i.e., Egnor 1983: 937) or be transformed through drying and breakdown (Rosin 2000).[13] People agreed that the worst rooms bordered wide community *nālās* where germs (*kīṭāṇu*) collected. It was preferable to be uphill of where *nālās* ended, so that community waste would not accumulate right outside the door. In other less desirable neighborhoods, water buffalo manure was left on streets. Instead of being used as fuel or for cleaning, as is common practice in the village (Khare 1976: 32), manure left like this attracted mosquitoes and trapped *gandagī* (dirt) underneath. People also tried to avoid rooms on narrow alleys (*galīs*) that shut out sunlight and breeze. Any room was hot in the summer, but without at least a well-placed door or a small window, hot air became suffocating. Although endurance of heat was important, experiencing heat in confined spaces was different. Padma was horrified after seeing the bright red pustules (*gamoriyān*) that had appeared all over her former neighbor Kaamla when she saw her for the first time, weeks after demolition. Her new room was an oven, so the heat was trying to escape the body, women explained. Dark buildings and neglect of public areas prevented washing and latrine water from drying. In such places, no one wanted to work.

Rooms on large streets open to breezes and light were preferred. There, many women brought their laundry outside, scrubbing their clothes on shared slabs of concrete. This allowed women with smaller homes to segregate cooking and worshiping places from cleaning wastewater (Khare 1976: 30). When they were done with their work, women cleared away their dirty water and remnants of food with large coarse brooms. Residents praised the community policing of *nālās,* which forbade the addition of trash that prevented waste flow. When young children squatted in the lanes to relieve themselves, their mothers ideally threw away their fecal matter and rinsed the area with water. Wind slapped fat drops of water out of wet clothes hung to dry. Pans of rice and *dāl* were cleaned outside, because the breeze caught the stones, bugs, and dust within. These purifying processes circulated air, carried out waste, and transformed toxins. Neighborhoods with these environmental characteristics were praised not only for their health-giving potential, but also for fact that neighbors had sustained an environmental order collectively. This was no small feat when fights constantly broke out about how to manage the use of resources shared between too many people within too small a space. This shared space was not an open public, but a limited one whose boundaries were maintained as if it mimicked a larger estate connected to their homes.

Women contextualized their efforts within a broader landscape. While they celebrated the potential that they created in their environment through their individual determination, they realized their homes were not just islands in a unified slum environment. The daily environmental practices of women in slums confirmed that individual behaviors to mitigate risks within homes and upgrade infrastructure can make a difference in health (Asthana 1995; Cairncross et al. 2010). Having recognized the diversity of this landscape, residents did not vilify it as a whole but identified where they were most likely to cultivate potential. There were surely eyesores amongst the rooms that they toured before selecting their own, but residents' careful ranking demonstrated how an array of landlords, the state, negligent neighbors, and geography produced the dilapidation at the root of slums' definition. Residents' discourse on this cast conveyed how the slum landscape was not shaped by a singular subaltern logic, but built by multiple actors with varying interests, whose individual decisions made up the smaller pieces that women negotiated in making their home environments.

As women visited each other in the months following demolition, they compared their new environments. Neetu pointed out the *gandagī* of Durga's new room, gesturing toward the flies outside, and Durga reciprocated, remembering the pile of dishes left in the shared washing area that Neetu had outside her new room in a lower-middle-class neighborhood. "Water is so easy here," noted Durga; there was supply water in the evening and another source right next door. "It is for me too," defended Neetu, explaining the pipe that faithfully delivered water to their floor every evening. Even as women agreed with their former neighbors about the shortcomings of their current dwellings, they defended their decisions to choose the rooms they did, and, when achieved, the collective efforts they had accomplished with their neighbors to improve local flow. When their exhaustion subsided, women reflected on the creative process of building their homes and temporarily left aside the physical boundaries they marked in their daily work. At the beginning of my fieldwork, residents had asked what I thought of their houses, emphasizing their small size and fragile materials. But as I grew to know their homes, they asked me to acknowledge that they built them "just right." In her new room, bounded by the railroad tracks and insulated from the fresh air and sunshine of the main road, Padma told me to verify her claims about her old house to her new neighbors. In her small yard (*āngan*), she explained, by day she ground spices and cooked food, and at night she slept outside on her cot under the overhang. The chickens that she kept there had received her exuberant praise when they paused to surreptitiously pull bits of vegetables from the vegetable seller's cart. There, Geeta told her neighbors on the opposite side of Ghaziapuram, the *jhuggīs* were lined up neatly on either side of the road, and the roads were dry and clean because everyone swept their space. Her own home had two large rooms, perfect for storing her husband's supplies for his *jalebī* (a kind of sweet) vending. Her kitchen was built around a tree that, though no longer living, was used to mark the landscape after demolition—that was where Geeta lived, people would say.

Gradually, many women refurbished rooms they had initially disparaged, turning them into warm home spaces. They charted the fresh newspaper they pasted on walls, the bright, neatly cut decorations for Diwali (the Hindu New Year), the improved placement of fans to circulate air, and the new space that was opened by rearranging trunks of belongings. As they acknowledged these small alterations to their environments, women did not romanticize one ideal environment before demolition, but demonstrated their capacity to convert environments into the right space.

At other moments, women laughed at the fragility of the boundary that separated their carefully assembled homes from the wider slum's contamination. As we stood waiting to fill water buckets at the municipal tanker truck, Saraswati shrieked in horror when I accidentally knocked one bucket into a *nālā* filled with thick, gray water. We leapt to save it with seemingly heroic abilities. Then we doubled over laughing. In all likelihood, the unseen remnants of the muck on the bucket would leave Saraswati's family with diarrhea. But somehow in that moment, we still laughed anyway. Attempting to transform a seemingly hopeless environment was a superhuman task.

These narratives on microenvironments challenge the simple classification of environmental substances as contaminated or healthy (within public health), or as polluted or pure (within caste ideology). Here, women emphasized that environmental substances should be classified within a complex spectrum of qualities. They emphasized how they found better options than what was readily available, though often these substances could not be said to be pure. They focused on how their efforts could sometimes improve qualities of environmental substances and how they could mitigate contamination, even if they could not eliminate it (Trawick 1992a). At a larger level, women's work to create boundaries to their homes asserted a physical space that protected them from contamination, while obliquely differentiating themselves from neighbors. Women's warm feelings about their established homes acknowledged their success in creating environments of their own from environmental potential.

FEELING DIFFERENTLY

For slum outsiders and residents alike, it was easy to feel that when it came to the field of the slums, the environment was self-evident—and what was evident provoked revulsion. To judgmental outsiders, including me, the harsh state of their environment led to the conclusion that this *jhuggī* environment was homogeneous. For Durga's sons in the village or outsiders, it did not matter which lane you were on, or which house you were in, it was still the polluted *jhuggīs*. For those indicting the inequality of their environment, like me, the *jhuggīs* were homogeneous in a different way. When I told women it was not fair to criticize certain neighborhoods, or even castes of people, for having an environment that was dirtier, they rebuffed me. To them, my righteous analysis of structural inequality was wrong—what people did in their environments did make a difference.

Political-economic analysis has well illuminated the macroscale of environmental inequality experienced by people living in slums (Chaplin 1999; Dupont 2005; Karn, Shigeo, and Hideki 2000; McGranahan 1993). Though the research on environmental inequality has been motivated by the goal of enacting social change, it has created a body of literature in which people living in slums are known first and foremost for their lack of toilets, ramshackle housing, and feeble health, inadvertently reproducing dangerous social stigma (Yang et al. 2007). The efforts of people living in poverty to live within their environments have been constructed above all as survival, with the meaning of their environment seen as less "real" (Dickey 2000: 481). So while this "global" scale generates valuable recommendations to reform urban and social policy, it cannot translate localized experiences within these environments (Ingold 2000; West 2005: 639). With the goal of understanding women's environmental experiences within slums, I have examined the cocreation of self and environment through exploring perception, physical and moral transformation, and communication.

The level of perception reveals how women learn from and receive information from the environment (Milton 2005: 35). Part of this relationship to environment includes the emotions that emotional geographers have shown shape our sense of place and who we are (Bondi, Davidson, and Smith 2007; Davidson and Milligan 2004: 524). While perceptions of the environment come from immediate experience, emotions about the environment are learned (Milton 2005: 36). Here, I have illustrated the strenuous process through which emotional reactions to the environment are manipulated and relearned. In this community, women see their process of relearning their emotions to environment, and the daily practices through which they manipulate the environment, as "forms of vigorous self-development" (Alter 1999: s51). In the slums to which they migrated, they not only had to learn ways to live in a drastically different environment but to cope with the fact that they were known for their stigmatized environment.

Like the generative transactions through which human-environment interaction can produce identity (West 2005), women described how changing their environment produced changes in their self. I have used self-transformation, rather than identity, to indicate how women pose a moral challenge to themselves while responding to stigma and differentiating themselves from others. Women's processes of self-transformation were tense and conflicted, echoing the contradictory processes that face Indians living in contemporary slums (Das 1994; Fuchs 2005). Although opportunities for mobility and increased autonomy inspire hope, low-income women's immense caregiving responsibilities, a degraded slum environment, and poverty perpetuate their exclusion from society.

Through comparisons, women remarked on the tension of choosing between different interpretations of the same environment. These choices involved the fortitude to reimagine places, hard physical labor, and uncomfortable physical endurance. In making new rooms, in choosing to sit in the absence of a fan, in choosing not to wish for a temple of the village, women challenged themselves to transform space, body, and self dialectically. Rather than measure the degree to which women in this slum have achieved inclusion, I have focused on how women perceive the struggle of defining their selves as moral work.

It was evident from women's descriptions of their environments to particular audiences that part of their task of self-improvement was social comparison. In this setting where identity claims are always made to specific audiences (Chandola 2010: 57–58; Fuchs 2005: 110), women used their environment to differentiate themselves as educated, socially superior, or spiritually elevated. This type of communication reinterprets South Asian literature on substance flow (Busby 1997; Daniel 1984; Lamb 2000; Lambert 2000) that new kinship studies has integrated into its studies on culturally variable models of relatedness (Carsten 2001). The theory of substance flow postulates that in South Asia a shared environment generates "a locality-specific social identity" that is "affected by the qualities of the water and soil of their particular locality" (Lambert 2000: 84). In this model of environmental flow, qualities circulate without direction, and the local environment is shared rather than shaped into multiple environments.

This model, applied previously in village contexts, has deeper ramifications when applied to people living in slums. It would suggest that the contaminated substances available within would solely determine the physical substance of people living in slums. Yet in Ghaziapuram, women claimed their responsibility for channeling flow. Their efforts reveal the complex web of environmental characteristics in the slum landscape from which they made choices of certain *types* of water, *types* of circulation, and *types* of food to produce environmental differences. In this case, women did not frequently measure the physical difference in their bodies that resulted in the environmental flow they directed, but instead they measured their bodies against those of their neighbors. Yet in the case of weather, women did claim the physically distinct identity of slum residents in contrast to the wealthy. But here, rather than pointing to their locality as the basis of difference, women argued that bodily practices to endure shared harsh weather created physical difference. As women communicated their self-improvement to different audiences, the meaning of environment shifted as much as the type of environment in which women want to be included. These contextual variations about environment should provoke analytical restraint in privileging any single description of a relationship to place and draw attention to the points of comparison. While outcomes-centered approaches to health chart women's progression from ill health to well-being, what mattered here to women was that they were able to define some of the terms of their environment, even if it did not always make them healthier.

Geeta's initial criticism of Sunita's frustration with their slum environment appears to offer two conflicting perspectives on space: that of environmental inequality and that of environmental potential. Yet in their daily environmental practices, women living in slums interpret the bridging of this gap as a moral accomplishment that, if successful, can effect change within their selves. As they contrasted their environmental practice from that of their neighbors and middle-class residents, women isolated the moral spirit through which they found potential in a land that no one else was able to recognize. Women here were not miracle farmers who grew plentiful fields out of nothing. But even still, women reached for the potential that lay right before the horizon.

Conclusion

Though most of my goodbyes in the field were bittersweet, the last visit to say goodbye to my field assistant, Saraswati, was not. To escape the heat of their room, which remained stifling even in October, Saraswati, her husband, Akshay, her small son, her sister, and I sat on the flat roof of her room, nestled by the rugged brick walls of the slum homes all around us. After I had written down all of my contact information in the United States and we had worked through the mechanical details of country codes and time differences, Saraswati added, "Well, there will be no reason for me to get a visa to visit, because as soon as you leave, I'll just die and then my soul (*ātma*) can come to visit you in America. No need for a passport or a visa."

She laughed. I tried to laugh too, but my attempts were weak. I felt like she mocked her fragile health. And I resented it. Moments before I pointed out to her how much weight she had lost recently by wrapping my fingers around her wrist to the point where the girth of her arm stopped me from going further. The ring I had made with my fingers went up to her elbow. Weeks of a diminished appetite had left their mark, as had the tension of caring for a mercurial husband and switching rooms to escape a neglectful landlord. She responded by pointing to the diminished color under

Figure 6. Rajiv Gandhi Setu. Photo by Mayank Austen Soofi.

my fingernails. I was weak too, she pointed out. I could not understand why this was a laughing matter. As much as I wanted to fight the stereotype of slum-dwellers as fatalistic and apathetic, to me, Saraswati seemed ready to discount what was so urgently there before her—her physical health.

I had come to her neighborhood a year earlier to learn about women's pressing efforts for health, to explore the homes and families they created to provision health. I thought about the bruises that women showed me and the never-ending sickness they told me about. It seemed impossible to talk about their well-being without forwarding their suffering. I had focused on the people that Saraswati said had let her down—her husband, her politicians, her neighbors, and me too—and felt negligence manifested in her thin wrists, wrists which should not be mocked. The inequality and lack of accountability that resulted in her poor health seemed foremost. What she needed, what people in poverty needed, was massive social transformation to alleviate the poverty that generated her sickness (Baer, Singer, and Susser 1997; Farmer 2005; Lockhart 2008). Past research on poor people in India has asserted the profound lack of control that poor urban people have over their health (Das and Das 2004; Das and Hammer 2007; Karn, Shigeo, and Hideki 2000; Shukla, Kumar, and Ory 1991; Garg, Sharma, and Sahay 2002) and their lives more generally (de Neve 2005; Cross 2010; Haider 2000; Pinney 1999). Researchers and development officials have hoped to decrease poverty, extend the protections of citizenship, and expand women's autonomy so that the frantic work of basic survival is replaced by stabilizing social conditions for health.

These goals were oriented toward better health for women—but who they were did not really matter. In this research, I have tried to capture women's own techniques for stability. I was slow to notice women's relational techniques that built well-being because they struck me as incredibly apolitical. What did they have to do with the scale of change that their health disparities required? Women, by and large, did not want to join together to protest demolition. They stood by family members who threatened them physically, socially, and financially. They freely critiqued those whose social circumstances seemed to me to be in solidarity to their own. From the perspective of larger social structures, women's actions that I have described here seem too inadequate to make any difference. Regardless of whether Saraswati could give, she would still be with an abusive husband. Her cleaning was pointless when she was enveloped by so many environmental hazards. Her prayers would only offer temporary comfort.

As many other researchers have so enthusiastically celebrated in their studies of organizing and resistance (Appadurai 2002; Holston 2009; Chatterjee 2004; Ray 1999; Scott 1985), I wanted women in Ghaziapuram to "raise their fists," as Durga had chided me. Instead, they had indicated other more seemingly humble, but actually lasting, transformations. Indeed, not all powerful social movements seek to change social institutions (Babb 1984). Through all of our fights, debates over research, and frustrations with each other, Saraswati offered something else, something that was not always attached to this slum or her survival in it. She offered tactics to navigate the social relationships that shaped her health, tactics that often did not result in the scale of change that researchers hope for, but that generated inner well-being that enabled her to persist.

Geeta refused to accept her environment as poisoned water that suffused her body and a shack that threatened to crumble on top of her.

Affirming the water she found and the home that she built tempered her environment to her terms. Women who endured neglect and modeled caregiving for their family members reminded themselves of their own tenacity, even when their family members disappointed them. Saraswati suspended trust of Neetu to ensure a feeling of autonomy and guard against potential judgment. When politicians forgot their promises and state protections faded away, Mrinalini's vision of getting ahead would not wait for them to be restored and fulfilled. The way that women dealt with the familial, community, state, and environmental relationships shaped the way they experienced the social conditions that threatened their health.

The self-affirmation, autonomy, endurance, and vision that women generated through these approaches to relationships demonstrated their capacity for action within their circumstances. According to South Asian spiritual principles, their personhood, body, and birth were signs of their current existence. As much as they did not determine this position, their actions in everyday life did much to define how they experienced it (Khare 1993; Khare 1984: 53). Neetu and Padma rejected jealousy of the wealth that they "could not have." Instead, they asserted their responsibility toward affirming their own *roṭī* and salt: perhaps they were poor, but they still had the capacity to act. Geeta and Dilip argued that perhaps their environments were insufficient, but they must still develop the capacity of their bodies and homes. On the eve of demolition, Durga looked toward her hands and concentrated on the bodily capacity that would persist even after her home did not. "Living for others" furthered women's awareness of their moral capacity—while ensuring that their frustration with their families would not determine their own character. Their approaches contrasted with the future-oriented perspectives of public health research and reform that stress what *could* and *should* be with proper social change. Like reformers, women imagined what could and should be, but lived with the circumstances that they had now. They could change the meaning of their inequality through their moral perspective, even if they did not change their immediate health and social conditions.

Women's approaches to their own action emphasized the sentiment with which they enacted agency. They aspired to detachment from the results of their actions and articulated the need for acceptance of circumstances. These orientations toward action made even provisional efforts meaningful. Even if Durga's continued giving never shamed her sons into reciprocity, she argued that she still gained by giving without attachment. Residents argued that they would persist in their efforts to get ahead despite the government's failure to recognize their contribution to society. Intentions, not just actions, mattered (Babb 1983b: 180). Their actions may have sent the message of resistance, just as did Gandhi's hunger strikes, but women argued that ultimately their actions were to build their selves.

Over the course of their lifetimes, explained Durga, the sentiments of their actions were cumulative, and would be known to the world. Women asserted the important differences that existed between their neighbors, their family members, broader society, and themselves to assert the different actions through which they lived their lives. Their allegiance to any one grouping was tenuous—be it their caste, their family, the community, or the powerful. Unlike Dalits' struggle for civil rights (Khare 1984), the movement for nationalism (Rudolph and Rudolph 2003; 2006), or spiritual reform (Babb 1984), women could not rally around shared goals or even leadership. I have structured this book around the moral values that they shared and discussed with one another. However, as shared as these values were, women drew back to their individual selves to enact these values within their own lives.

Far from their daily struggles, women described an otherworldly spiritual plane in which all people were "intrinsically related and equal" (Khare 1984: 53), rejecting the differences that stigmatized them. Neetu pointed to the inner beauty with which everyone was born and the chance that anyone could be born in the *jhuggīs*. On this plane, women accepted the limits of their action. Mrinalini said that regardless of what she did, she knew that she should have faith in what came ahead, accepting her life rather than being incapacitated by her tension. Geeta argued that, ultimately, as much as she tried through household techniques, her health and the security of her home was up to God—even when God irritated her. In these ways, women looked past their ability to act, beyond their immediate circumstances, and beyond social distinctions. In so doing, they released their striving for ideals. On this plane, as they released their individual feelings, physical needs, and social distinctions, women argued, they could find peace.

Women tacked back and forth between this world and that, individual and social needs, social distinctions and no distinctions (Khare 1993). By investing their efforts in their selves, they argued for longer-term justice that could be granted through their accountability to their selves, unmediated by others (Khare 1984: 151). By referring back to God's awareness of their decisions, they grounded their investment in themselves with the awareness that eventually justice would be enacted, even if not now (Khare 1998: 178). I have placed women's passionate reflections on their ideals alongside the tense negotiated moments in which they tried to realize them. Women did tire and question their faith in themselves—as when Saraswati slumped down after endless cleaning or when she proclaimed her desire to become a *sādhu* (ascetic).

I offer this as a culturally specific exploration of mental health resilience, a term that researchers have used to explore how people in poverty persist in spite of chronic difficulty (Mullings 2005; Mullings and Wali 2001; Canvin et al. 2009). By redefining the risks through which women framed their priorities, this research suggests that critical medical anthropology and political-economic approaches to poverty give more priority to emic categories. Furthermore, this book has stressed how well-being is intimately related to how individuals navigate their relationships. I have reoriented attention from effects that relationships have on health to focus on the process of negotiating these relationships and the subsequent impacts this process has on well-being.

FROM EXPERIENCE NEAR TO POLICY

This book has concentrated primarily on women's lived experiences of their efforts to further their inner well-being. In this microview, I have purposefully made development, health care, biomedical health, and public policy wait on the sidelines of my writing. These fields are vital—and, even in spite of my own focus, all of these elements are present in the experiences I presented here. Development programming is marked by the NGOs that are embedded in local power configurations. The medication that women frequently took to ease their illness came from providers in nearby lanes and more distant, crowded hospitals. Women's fragile health shows up in the tension, weakness, and poor reproductive health that made their days difficult. Women's experience of public policy has been evident in the retreat of resettlement programming, ration card entitlements that are woefully inadequate, and the unemployed husbands who stay at home as jobs decline. I have argued that women's relational techniques and definition of inner well-being are not oriented toward structural change, but toward enabling their resilience. But nonetheless, the small scale of women's efforts have effects on fighting stigma, promoting family-based care, and strengthening women's sense of self-efficacy—thereby inadvertently offering directions for programming and policy. Having emerged from the complex choices that women face, women's relational techniques account for a broader definition of well-being. After all, physical health is only one of many priorities that women living in poverty face. Here, I suggest several implications that this research has for policy and future research related to health in urban slums.

1. NGO and Development Programming

NGO FUNDING PRIORITIES

With few state urban health programs in India, social welfare services in slum communities are primarily provided by nongovernmental organizations of varying sizes. Frequently, in order to receive international funding, organizations must offer programming that addresses global funding priorities—even when they do not address local needs. This has resulted in programming that changes every few years to respond to development trends, often reproducing particular "best practices" across vastly different locations. In the part of Delhi where I did this research, many NGOs had special programming devoted to HIV/AIDS prevention and awareness despite the fact that HIV/AIDS incidence was remarkably low in poor urban communities. Meanwhile, there was comparatively little programming to attend to domestic violence prevention, malnutrition, reproductive health care access, and clean water access—all issues that shaped the overall health of women daily. The gap between NGO work and women's needs alienated many women from the area NGO—and, after demolition, from other NGOs. International funding for NGO programming could facilitate greater social change if it allowed local organizations more leeway in defining programming objectives and adapting best practices to fit their needs.

WOMEN'S COLLECTIVES

In recent years, microfinance and anti–domestic violence work has been promoted through women's collectives, a common tool to promote empowerment and shared ownership in low-income international communities (Galab and Rao 2003; Hossain et al. 2004; Magar 2003; Roy, Jockin, and Javed 2004). Using a feminist philosophy that encourages group empowerment, these groups are composed of women from low-income communities who work together. *Mahilā pañchāyats*, women's councils, are one type of women's collective. Women facing domestic violence, dowry harassment, or lack of support can bring their husbands before a community-based council to have their dispute heard and receive recommendations for its resolution. With the legal system operating at a sluggish pace and police a threat more than a resource, *mahilā pañchāyats* are often the lead institutional players in adjudicating family disputes for low-income urban families (Grover 2011; Magar 2000).

Yet neighborly and community relationships, as we have seen, can be as fraught as they are intimate. Like the community relationships that surround them, women's collectives can be forums where the community members in leadership positions can reinforce their caste and regional positions (Grover 2011: 184, 188). Furthermore, researchers have noted that as many women who utilize this tool, many more do not, in spite of their need. Women with secondary marriages, in particular, may face additional scrutiny and stigma (Grover 2011). In Ghaziapuram, many women were hesitant to use these community resources because they were wary of having locally powerful women adjudicate their fragile intimate lives. While women might benefit from these services, as long as they remain entrenched in hierarchical community relationships with the same women who are supposed to advise them, they will avoid these forums. *Mahilā pañchāyats* would be more effective if they served women with whom they had no previous relationship, such as women from adjacent communities. Making disclosure of relationship a preliminary step in *mahilā pañchāyat* proceedings would promote greater anonymity and restrict power conflicts. Without knowing the caste or social reputation of the women they advised, *pañchāyats* could more effectively focus their deliberations on arbitrating conflict between couples.

SANITATION EDUCATION

By and large, public health and urban planning research has stressed that systemic development of sanitation facilities and water access is the first step to improve the health of people living in slums. In addition, it has been emphasized that several health behaviors, including hand washing with soap and reducing open defecation, need to be further promoted (Chambers and Medeazza 2013). Yet public health practitioners need to account for the impact that recommended health behaviors will have on household routines. How such recommendations fit into daily use are matters of convenience and comfort that determine whether technologies are adopted (Thurber et al. 2013)—but they are also matters of *feasibility*. For instance, hand-washing education does not address the fact that washing with soap increases the amount of water women must collect daily. For many households, using extra water to wash hands with soap multiple times per day would eliminate water for other uses—whether for bathing, cooking, or cleaning. Before promoting a particular behavior, practitioners should understand whether it is knowledge that is the barrier or whether other issues—such as water access—need to be addressed first.

Community-level environmental management is also significant in determining health outcomes. As I have described, women considered themselves lucky when they lived on lanes with cooperative efforts to keep public areas clean. However, in other situations, local power configurations override women's individual hygiene practices. Dr. Renu Khosla, director of Delhi's Centre for Urban and Regional Excellence, explained to me how this took place in one community. One man would spread the waste of the water buffaloes he kept in several places through the community to avoid being caught. The result was that this waste backed up the open drains carrying household wastewater. Everyone knew and disapproved of his habits. Yet his alliance with the police meant that his habits could not be regulated. Campaigns to promote better community-level sanitation will benefit from understanding the role of powerful individuals in shaping regional environments.

2. Community Activism

Anthropologists have celebrated the efforts of many residents of Indian slums to change the conditions in which they live—resisting demolition, securing water access, and demanding toilet facilities (Appadurai 2002; Chatterjee 2004; Harriss 2005; Holston 2009). Similarly, community-based participatory methods, now mainstream in the field of public health, identify shared challenges and collectively act to change social conditions (Mullings et al. 2001; Sabo et al. 2013; Silverstein et al. 2010). But what if communities reject, or lack the will for, collective action?

First, organizations that successfully do collective work in slums acknowledge the immediate and long-term needs of people living in poverty. Sadre Alam, of the Centre for Community Support and Social Development, has worked in Delhi's slum communities for over fifteen years. He explained that "people come to the city to work—not to do political work." Or, as Amita Baviskar writes, "Driven by the desire to secure legal housing and a stable foothold in the uncertain economy of the city, slum-dwellers abandon their collective struggle for individual gain" (2003: 96). For Sadre, in achieving his goals to better the conditions in which the poor live, he is mindful that it is not the priority of poor communities to assemble for protest. Workers in community-based organizations, he explained, can be overwhelmed by residents' requests for help with their individual—not collective—problems: their electricity, availability of rations, and anything that needs an immediate response. Successful community organizations have strategies to accommodate these repeated emergencies while budgeting time and effort for their long-term collective change operations.

Second, those interested in initiating community advocacy should learn of existing power relationships and hierarchies in communities before beginning their work. Although important advocacy work can be achieved collectively, as Appadurai (2002) and Chatterjee (2004) point out, exclusions and unfair advantages may equally be part of this work. Cleavages within communities should not be dismissed as petty histories, but taken seriously as indicators of cultural patterns. The shared "we" that may be asserted to outside researchers when they first arrive may turn out to be tenuous, and individuals may prefer self-protection. In communities

with entrenched political hierarchies, community activism can be a vehicle to further power and may not result in equitable outcomes.

3. Health Care

This research supports other findings that health interventions would do
well to develop health care options that respond to women's articulations
of their health problems (Kostick et al. 2010; Trollope-Kumar 2001).
Women are more likely to seek help for conditions that impact their reproductive health—and to receive support from their families (Ramasubban
and Rishyasringa 2008). Though it is their physical symptoms that receive
legitimacy as a health complaint, women's articulations of their illnesses
intertwine with social and moral concerns. Women's physical complaints
may not always match up to biomedical conditions; however, their complaints indicate vulnerable health. Therefore, women's tendency to seek
assistance for their reproductive health can be an opportunity to provide
them with a broad array of services, including for mental health and
domestic violence (García-Moreno et al. 2005; Kostick et al. 2010).

Who should provide these services? Widespread research has pointed
out that community-based registered medical practitioners (RMPs) offering private medical services are the primary health care service provider for
people living in India's slums (Das and Hammer 2007; Das and Das 2006;
de Zoysa et al. 1998; Kamat and Nichter 1998). Health care quality researchers have debated whether public policy and development should support
the work of RMPs or whether they should concentrate on improving the
quality of care and access to public hospitals, which only a third of people
living in slums use as their primary source of health care (Gupta, Arnold,
and Lhungdim 2009). On the one hand, RMPs have immense variations in
their level of education and competence; some argue that their orientation
is more toward profit, leading to improper and dangerous pharmaceutical
use (Kamat and Nichter 1998). On the other hand, RMPs are often the
most comfortable source of health care to women living in slums: they do
not demand invasive exams, they use familiar language about health, they
charge predictable fees, they are close by, and they provide immediate service (Ramasubban and Rishyasringa 2008). RMPs often combine biomedical knowledge with Ayurvedic and religious concepts—thus using health

language that more closely aligns with the customers they are serving. I agree with other researchers who have argued that working with RMPs, instead of against them, is preferable. Providing further training could make them effective community health workers (Kafle et al. 1992).

To the extent that public health workers and NGO outreach workers could partner with RMPs, they could utilize community-based health infrastructure and fit into women's existing treatment-seeking patterns. Meanwhile, using free referrals for further services provided at the same location, public health workers could offer services that women would not seek out on their own. Public health workers could benefit from interventions that fit the cultural context of slums, where well-being is deeply social and spiritual. First, they could utilize interventions that have been used to help women decrease the health risks that arise within their relationships through motivational interviewing, a counseling style that encourages behavior change (Leukefeld et al. 2012; Staton-Tindall et al. 2011). In a setting where women are committed to improving their family relationships, and living independently is extremely difficult, health interventions that help women to protect themselves are more feasible than those that encourage them to escape abuse or neglect. This book has shown that women cannot always shape their family relationships, but they use multiple ways to communicate their desire for change. Second, while faith-based interventions have been used in the United States to help survivors of family violence or those suffering from illness (Gillum, Sullivan, and Bybee 2006; Kreidler 1995), paradoxically, these methods have not been utilized in South Asia, where morality and faith are integrated within concepts of health (Khare 1996). Health workers could use faith-based counseling to help women balance the meaning they derive from family life (Raval 2009) with their individual needs for care. Promoting health through the relationships that women prioritize builds on the techniques they already use to further well-being, while being realistic about the constraints that they face in caring for themselves.

4. Research Directions and Methods

This qualitative study has identified substantive themes to be explored further and offers methodological suggestions to strengthen existing lines of research.

URBAN ENVIRONMENT

Environmental surveys of slums have done well in documenting the differences in household type (as *kacchā* [dirt] or *pakkā* [brick]), access to toilets, and patterns in water use. Other measures, however, could account for community-level factors impacting health—for instance, the microenvironment of single lanes, degree of cooperation between neighbors, and power arrangements shaping environmental conditions. Further studies could explore the experience of climate within dwellings, which varies considerably according to type of settlement, building, and surrounding homes. How do efforts to select particular indoor environments and endure climate conditions shape physical vulnerability? Environmental researchers need to be more sensitive to the ways that their work may inadvertently reproduce stigma. In a society where lower caste and class status are stereotyped as filthy, researchers must be cognizant of how their line of questioning and research products may inadvertently reproduce this association. Following community-based participatory strategies, researchers would benefit from considering community *assets* as well— whether environmental knowledge, cooperative hygiene practices, or strategies to manage limited resources. Including these assets within investigations does not have to detract from assessing inequity, but it will begin to provide positive environmental representations—which, as researchers know, are integral to the way that policy is made (i.e., Mann 2007; Prashad 2001).

RESIDENTIAL STRATEGIES AND ECONOMIC STATUS

Many quantitative measures have explored the physical security of people living in slums through their housing type, income, and slum status (as notified or not notified). Yet identifying the residential strategies of people living in slums may be a better guide to assessing their perception of their physical security. What reasoning guides them to select particular housing, and how does it fit with their long-term plans for mobility? These strategies determine which types of communities people live in, the location of the community, and how long they plan on living there (see also Cavalcanti 2007; Chandola 2010). Residents may choose more insecure housing in the present as a strategy to save for more permanent housing;

in other cases, insecure housing is simply an indication of limited resources. Residential strategies shape individuals' orientations toward in-slum development or community organization. As much as they may be frustrated with community conditions, if they plan on moving in the near future, they will not perceive community organizing efforts as worthwhile. Identifying family goals for mobility will elucidate how families allocate their resources over time. Immediate sacrifices—like having children work in menial jobs—may be part of a larger plan to save money for other mobility goals, such as having younger children attend private schooling. Therefore, studies on economic status and mobility would benefit from measuring respondents' residential histories as well as their orientation toward the future.

FAMILY AND HOUSEHOLD MEMBERSHIP

This study has shown that long-term research can uncover kinship patterns and practices that will likely not appear in short-term and interview-based methods (see also Burton et al. 2009). I recognize the invasive elements of my own participant observation–based research. But I suggest that, like my interlocutors, many women are eager to discuss their frustrations with their families when confidentiality is ensured and judgment is suspended (i.e., Menon and Shweder 1998; Ring 2006). Future researchers could consider participatory-action research approaches in which local women define the goals and methods of kinship research. Due to the stigma of leaving husbands (even if abusive), surveys are unlikely to uncover accurate self-reports about women's marital histories. However, researchers may be more successful in gauging the extent of this demographic trend if they ask respondents to estimate the number of neighbors who have secondary marriages. Having more data on this practice is essential, because of the way that marital status appears linked to women's negotiating power—including for access to health care, food consumption, and vulnerability to domestic violence. Considering the great fluctuations in household membership that spanned the period of my fourteen months of fieldwork, I suggest that further research could detail these trends quantitatively. What impact do they have on available household resources, relationship dynamics, and health status?

FINAL THOUGHTS

Four years after saying goodbye to Saraswati, I remain troubled about her well-being. She laughed when I told her a year later how worried I had been after our farewell. Was I right to worry? Not unlike those who emphasize the suffering of those living in poverty, I keep thinking of Saraswati's wrists and the ending she cynically forecast. But to listen to Saraswati meant seeing beyond just her weakness, to—as she liked to point out with her wry smile—all the things that I could not do. In her daily feats, she reduced her dependencies, highlighted her moral high ground, and contrasted her endurance with what was temporary. Saraswati still doesn't have a visa, but she keeps asking me if she should get one. Her health is okay, but probably could be better. But she was right when she said her soul would visit me.

Notes

1. "*Har chīz ām ādmī paise ke picche bhāgtā hai.*"
2. "*Bhagvān dukh kam karenge kāienge, Bhagvān ke hī hāth jorke prārthnā karte hain. Bhagvān denevālle tum ho, kāinevālle tum hī ho, hamāre bacche ke, hamāre ādmi ke, hamāra dukh karnevālle āta. Isiliye Bhagvān ke darvāze par jāte hain. Bhagvān ke chaunkat damā detā hai, ādmi Bhagvān ki bharosa pe. Kyonki janm dene vālle vah hai. Isīliye Bhagvān ke nām marte kā time bhī aur jīte kā time bhī. Bhagvān kā nām hī bāt-vālli hai aur denevālle tum bhī ho. Dukh hamāra tum hī kāioge, mārogi tum hī, aur acchā karogī, tum hī. Tumhāra hī sab din hai, jaise jis karm men tum rakho hamen. Yah hī ādmi badosa kā Bhagvān kartā, bhāī.*"
3. "*Bhagvān to tabiyat ko kyā karen? Bhagvān kuch nahīn kartā hai. Uske hī marzī hai, sab. Vah kyā hai . . . ki sab unhī ke hāth men hai. Vahīn khush rakten, vahīn nārāz karte hain. Hai to sab unhī ke hāth men hai. Sab Bhagvān ke hāth men hai. Insān ke hāthon men kuch bhī nahīn hai.*"
4. "*Bhagvān hamen kaī taraf se janm diyā, to Bhagvān karm bhī karne ki bolā, ki janm de rahā hūn, to karm isī hāth men karm karo. Kisī kā burāi na karo, kisī kā chulāi na karo, kisī ko dekhke jalen mat, kisī kā chori na karo . . . roṭī -namak cāhie jisse usī men* time-pass *karo, usī men khushi raho, Bhagvān ne yah bolā.*"

231

5. *"Isīliye kahete hain hāth se kisī ko de do na to vah hī apne āge ā jātā hai. Tum kisī ko ek doge to Bhagvān tumhein das degā. Sahī batā rahe hain yah bāt tumhein. Kisī ko ek rupyā tum darvāze par doge Bhagvān tumhen das degā. Agar tum us ek ko bhī rakh loge na to koī bhī kahegā, dekh le yār . . . bara kharāb ādmī hai. Ise khā le sāle, tu zindagī bhar bhūkhā hī maregā. Aise kah dete hain."*

6. *"Amīr-gharīb men fark nahīn hai. Har ek cīz men fark hai."*

7. Though some scholars have emphasized how realizing this otherworldly self fully frees individuals from the cycle of reincarnation, I follow those who show the otherworldly self as an ideal that people strive to approximate, rather than an ideal that is fully achieved (Khandelwal 2004).

8. *"Bhagvān kā nām lene men ātmā ko bahut shānti miltī hai . . . Bhagvān har sankat men sāth dete hain. Har sankat men, dukh men, sukh men, vah sab men mere Bhagvān hain. Sab kā Bhagvān hain."*

9. Though much of the literature discussed in the following four chapters discusses changes in India following economic liberalization in the early 1990s, I also include other studies that pre-date liberalization, particularly Khare (1984). While liberalization has profoundly transformed contemporary India, I believe that by tying contemporary shifts in social dignity (for better or worse) to liberalization alone may obscure some of the preexisting shifts that may have been already set in motion. Some scholars (Gupta and Sharma 2006) challenge how significant the shift between welfare-development state and neoliberal India really has been. For the works on kinship, I use ethnographies of working class urban South Asian families in conjunction with a few classics. Most of these studies come from India; however, the work of Wilce, Jasmin and Salway, and Rashid comes from Bangladesh; Ewing's work is from Pakistan.

10. Much kinship literature for South Asia has focused on the changing morphology of the household, charting how its membership shifts, particularly as to which and how many family members live together. Here I mostly focus on the specific changes in form impacting poor urban families or those impacted by migration.

11. *Dalit* is a term used to describe the various castes of people formerly classified as untouchables. It is now preferred to *untouchable* because the word *dalit* (suppressed) references the struggles they face.

12. Leatherwork was considered a particularly demeaning task because Dalits were forced to carry and handle animal carcasses, work that was not only considered to be impure but that was extremely demanding physical work.

13. "On average in India, over 60 percent of slum dwellers vote in contrast to the 30 percent from the rest of the city" (Connors 2007: 96).

14. Chamar is the name of one Dalit (untouchable) caste, and they have historically been identified as leather makers.

CHAPTER 1: "YOU SHOULD LIVE FOR OTHERS"

1. In her study of domestic violence in Delhi slums, Magar (2000: 65) notes that usually when a man begins seeing another woman and spending money on her, there is "an escalation of wife battering from the time the illicit affair begins." This has impacts on women's health, as men's violence increases the risk that they will transmit STDs to their wives (Martin et al. 1999).

2. In India, many women call their husbands by an alternate title than their name. Here Padma simply referred to her husband as "Deepak's father."

3. Navratri is a nine-day Hindu festival to worship the goddess Durga that comes in early autumn. Some people break the nine days of fasting by feeding a group of local children.

4. Shankar Ramaswami's (2006) work, however, does an amazing job of capturing some of men's perspectives on family life in the same region of Delhi.

5. "*Aurat kī tabiyat isīliye kharāb hotā hai ki* gents *apnī aurat ko sambhāl nahīn pātā thik hai. Pahle vāle* gents *ab nahīn hain ki aurat kī dekhbhāl kar sake.*"

6. "*Jo apne sehat kā khyāl karte hain, khāte-pīte hain, unkī to koī bāt hī nahīn rahtī hai.*"

7. As in the statement, "*Abhī ham javān hain aur jo ham ne bachpan se mā-bāp ne khilāyā pilāyā hai uskī tākat hai hamāri andar.*"

8. Das and Das importantly continue: "and fear that intervention by the state to stop violence might be more harmful to their lives than one might think" (2004: 44).

9. Most all of this research has been conducted by anthropologists. However, there are a few exceptions. Sonia Jesmin and Sarah Salway (2000) are in development and public health; Ananya Roy (2003) is in urban and regional planning. However, their intimate perspectives on and similar conclusions about poor South Asian families make their research congruent with the scholarly conversation I present here.

10. "*Sab se baṛī kamzorī ghar kī hai.*" Here, I have translated *ghar*, which also means home, as family because of the larger context of the interview.

11. "*Dillī men paisā bahut kam hai, kām nahīn hai, rozgāri ki kami kī vajah se sāri duniyā ulṭī phūltī bimār paṛ jātī hai.*"

12. "*Aurat ko to sab cīz kā dukh sahanā paṛtā hai . . . hai? Bacche kī parishānī ho, ghar kī parishānī ho, tension ho, to sab cīz ke tension ho, to aurat ko zyādā parishānī hotī hai. Zyādā kamzorī hotī hai, to usko khānā khānā khāyā, davāī khātoge, to sharīr men nahīn lagtā. Tension zyādā hotā hai. Isī vajah se nahīn lagtā hai ki kuch bhī de ho.*" Durga said similarly, "Tension is because of the troubles of the home. Some people have tension from their children, some from their husbands. Some husbands don't keep their wives well; this also causes tension."

13. In Hindi, they would say, "*Mujhe* tension *hai*" (I have tension) or "*Mujhe* tension *lag rahā hai*" (I am feeling tension).

14. Men, too, use *tension* to describe their difficulties. Ramaswami (2006: 221) and Halliburton (2005: 133) elaborate how *tension* is used to describe the difficulty of providing.

15. *"Yahān par gharīb log zyādā hain, aur mehnat karne vāle nahīn, nashe khāne vāle ādmī hain. Apne nashe se paisā bachegā tabhī to apne bacche ko ṭhīk karegā."*

16. *"Jo ādmī dusrī kī madad kartā hai, sab se baṛā dharm ho hī yah hai. Jo apne liye jītā hai, vah ādmī nahīn hai. Jo dusre ke liye jītā hai, us ādmī ko accha ādmī ko kahatā hai. Jo dusre ke liye jītā hai, us ādmī ko accha ādmī ko kahatā hai."*

17. And, in fact, Grover (2009) argues that love marriages, though more likely to stay together than arranged marriages, often dissolve into bitter conflict because they do not receive the support of their families.

18. For a further exploration of how magic is used to control and harm the body, see Dwyer (2003).

19. I had refused to stay the night, completely frustrated at the prospect of sitting with her and her sister hoping that Akshay would return when I thought it was futile, and I momentarily hated him, as much as I knew I should not. In turn, Saraswati was so mad at me that we did not even talk the whole next week.

20. Haridwar is a pilgrimage center in the foothills of the Himalayas closer to the headwaters of the Ganges.

21. I comment on the methodological impacts of this in the introduction.

22. Durga did eventually return to the village to live because several months after demolition her business had significantly declined and she had a hard time continuing to afford rent. However, from what I had heard, she kept an independent household from her sons—a rare occurrence for a woman of her age.

23. One exception was that several people critiqued Shaista's care for her youngest son, who was adopted. Several women told me that they felt she treated him like a servant. I do not explore this as fully here, because by and large, I was taken aback by the number of positive things that people had said about her child rearing more generally, in a place where neighbors had few nice comments to spare about each other.

24. In most neighborhoods in Delhi, and particularly in poor ones, water only flows for a few hours a day. This requires people to stand waiting with buckets at the right time. See Sengupta (2006).

25. She expressed it as *"apnā kām nikalkar phir na pahachānā."*

CHAPTER 2: LET THE DIRTINESS GO

1. These are all states from which area residents hail: Bihar, West Bengal (Bengali can also refer to Bangladeshis who have migrated illegally), and Rajasthan.

2. "Tuitions" in Indian English.

3. *Roṭī* is a round flatbread made from wheat flour that, along with rice, is a staple grain that forms a typical meal with lentils and vegetables across North India.

4. One hundred thousand rupees. A very substantial sum for even a middle-class person in India.

5. Tripta Chandola (2010: 80–86), who also conducted research in a Delhi slum, writes a powerful account of Geeta, who does not openly admit the many sources of income she has because of her need to present herself politically to outsiders for her poverty.

6. Many married Hindu women in North India place *sindūr* (a type of red powder) in the part of the hair and a dot (*bindī*) on the forehead to indicate their marital status.

7. *Rajpūt* is a higher caste (Kshatriya) that is found in Rajasthan, Uttar Pradesh, and other areas of North India. Though women sometimes may assume the caste of their husband following marriage, this has recently been the subject of court action in 2010, which declared that women's caste status remains the same after marriage.

8. Witsoe similarly found in his study of Bihar (a poor eastern state): "Many people with whom I spoke commented on the increased number of these local leaders. As one villager in Rajnagar put it, 'There is only politics here. In this village even children are politicians (*bacche log bhī netā hai*). There is only politics here, nothing else'" (2011: 79).

9. *Pūrī* is a fried bread often served at celebratory occasions including political rallies.

10. This sentiment was not unique to the slum. A middle-class friend also told me that taking any public action was dangerous because it threatened the powers that be.

11. Other stories came up during my fieldwork that indicated how wide this police-*pradhān* nexus was. In 2009, police shielded illegal bootleggers whose bad liquor was responsible for the deaths of fourteen residents in one Delhi slum. During my fieldwork it was reported that some 2,503 children went missing in the Delhi area, primarily from poor and lower-caste families, who suspected that they might be used in trafficking or begging trades; this was the type of act that required complex coordination between the underworld and the local world.

12. Six of the nine families (not counting Sunita's) with whom I did my research told me versions of this story about Sunita's local rise to power.

13. *"Us ne apne āp banāyā."*

14. In Hindu cremations, the eldest son typically is responsible for releasing the spirit from the body by cracking the skull during the cremation (Parry 1994).

15. It is hard for me to say something conclusive about how these groups change over the long term because my research spanned a period of fourteen

months: three months in 2007 and twelve months in 2008–09. During the first span of my research I was unaware of these groupings and therefore did not make detailed observations about the composition of these groups. I outline here only what I can say conclusively from my own research. Certainly the shifts that I observed were motivated in part by where people moved after demolition. Future research projects could chart these changing dynamics over time.

16. This is based on the idea that the left hand should be used to clean after defecation.

17. Closing the curtain blocks the evil eye [*nazar*] of passing neighbors and establishes privacy.

18. Here, I am not referring to a specific Hindi word that approximates "introspection." This is my phrasing.

19. *"Jaise ham ne karm kare, us ke hisāb se ham ko phal milegī. Jo ham ab karenge, ham ko āge milegī. Isī liye ham kah jātā hai, kisī ko būrā mat karo! Būrā mat kaho! Būrā mat bolo!"*

20. *"Agar koī ādmī burāī dikhāī dekhkar us se picche haṭ jāo.* [Repeats.] *Hamāre bhī thoṛe din kī zindagī hai."*

21. *"Marne ke bād to yah kahate hain ki bahut burā ādmī thā, acchā ho gayā! Pacchīs bār yah bolegā. Agar vah acchā ādmī the, to sārī duniyā royegī. Kyon mar gaye, bhāī? Kyon chalā gayā, ham ko ḍukhī ho gaye. Acchā to duniyā yād kartī hai. Būre ko bhī yād karte hai. . . . Par acche ko duniyā rotī hai, to Bhagvān bhī rotā hai. Būre ko duniyā sirf būrāi hī kahate hain."*

CHAPTER 3: "GETTING AHEAD" AS MORAL CITIZENSHIP IN THE FACE OF DEMOLITION

1. *"Us se pahle yahān kuch bhī nahīn thā. Patthar hī patthar the. Kuch nahīn thā aur na hī yahān ādmī the na itnī rahan-sahan thī na itnī bhīṛ-bhadkā thī."*

2. *"Ek mazburī kī vajah se yahān paṛe hain kyonkī gāov men itnā paisā nahīn hai. Yahān kamāte aur khāte hain, peṭ bharte hain. Gāov men itnā dhan na hai kheti men itnā paidā bhī nahīn hotā. Isīliye matlab gāov kā pānī bhī hai khānā bhī hai; harek cīz acchī hai."*

3. *"Ab āke huā hai idhar ye pānch sāl ke bhītar hī bhītar jo kuch huā hai yah ab huā hai, us se pahle to kuch nahīn thā."*

4. Bhan writes that ousted residents of the Yamuna Pushta region in Delhi, one of the largest demolitions in its history, used similar imagery as they described how they built their neighborhood. "Many families in the area tell the story of filling in the vacant marshy embankment, considered 'too soft' to build on, with leftover sand and brick from construction sites, slowly turning it into a habitable settlement" (2009: 128).

5. People still use bikes to haul water, but over a much shorter distance.

6. *"Āte rahe, baṛhāte rahe. Āte gaye, baṛhāte gaye. Jhuggī-jhonpṛī banāte gaye, āte gaye. Āte gaye, banāte gaye."*

7. Jervis Read, in her research on a resettlement colony in East Delhi, notes a similar atmosphere there: "Several people refer to the demolitions and early days of the colony as a time of *ātank*, of acute fear, apprehension, even terror" (Jervis Read 2012: 93).

8. The Delhi Development Authority (DDA) has built flats all over the city for a variety of income levels, but primarily for middle-class people. There is a block of DDA flats directly north of Shikhar Colony, now the largest slum in the Ghaziapuram Industrial Area.

9. These were small metal tokens to identify the homes that were present at that time. Residents showed them to denote the length of their tenure in the settlement. Ghertner (2010) describes how the purpose of the tokens was to provide residents with proof of their presence that formalized "their right to resettlement in case their slum was removed."

10. Dilip argued that this bore-well water was salty and the water from their community-installed hand pumps was better. According to him, the government work had ruined their pumps.

11. *"Mūlī hai, pālak hai, yah sare . . . subah men bec detī hai phir khā lete hain. . . . Bore kā pānī chal rahā hai, dhote hain usmen banātī hai, usmen gandagī nahīn hotī, shudhd hotī hai. Use khāne se bhī svād ātā hai."*

12. "Tension *hotā hai mere ghar-vāllāh dārū pītā hai. Dārū kī vajah se* tension *to merā roz hī dimāg men rahatā hai. Kabhī* tension *utārtā nahīn mere dimāg se. Kyon merā ādmī che-che bacche hain dārū pītā hai. Ghar kī koī zimmedārī janatā hī nahīn ki kyā hotā hai, kyā nahīn. Yahīn baṛā laṛkā hai usī ke ūpr sārā bojh hai. Main bhī koī kām-dhandhā kartī nahīn hūn. Ghar men baiṭhī rahatī hūn. Ab ek hī laṛkā kī kamāī se ghar cal rahā hai. Ab is bāt ke liye* tension *main hī to lūngī. Ādmī ke to koī* tension *hai nahīn.* Tension *to janani kī hotī hai.* Tension *kī vajah se merā dimāg men lagtā hai ki cakkar khāke gir jaūngī.* Tension *ke māre merā dil ghabarāne lagtā hai ki kahīn* heart fail *ho jāyen merā aise aise hone lagtā hai."*

13. Checking is the final inspection of goods to make sure they are properly manufactured before sending them for export.

14. Bhan (2009: 127) states: "Between 1990 and 2003, 51,461 houses were demolished in Delhi under 'slum clearance' schemes. Between 2004 and 2007 alone, however, at least 45,000 homes were demolished, and since the beginning of 2007, eviction notices have been served on at least three other large settlements. Fewer than 25 per cent of the households evicted in this latter time period have received any alternative resettlement sites." See also Ghertner (2010) on changing meaning of resettlement.

15. *"Dekho us samay jab ham āye the us samay koī* company *nahīn thī. Log vahān ghar ghar men āte the bulāne ke liye: "Calo, hamāre yahān kām karvāne*

ke liye."Aur āj kal to ham jākar seal *mārte hai tab bhī koī nahīn detā hai* company *men. Ādmī baṛhāhai kām utnā nahīn baṛhā. . . . Aur āj bhī berozgārī bahut hai."*

16. In fact, the public interest litigation (PIL) ruling, *MC Mehta vs Union of India* decreed as early as 1984 that large and medium industries should be moved outside city limits (Bhan 2009: 133).

17. Indeed, now the court thought of slums as "large areas of public land . . . usurped for private use free of cost" (quoted in Ramanathan 2006).

18. Sonia Gandhi is the chair of the Congress Party. I was confused when Vijay said this. "But Sonia Gandhi isn't the prime minister," I said. "Yes she is," Vijay insisted. "Well, what about Manmohan Singh?" I asked. "He is just the puppet that she stands behind—she tells him what to say, what to do, and he goes and does all the meetings. But she is the real leader." Vijay was echoing a popular sentiment about the prime minister from that period and continuing to the present. I should note that actually Vijay's speculation happened after demolition, but I include it here because it is relevant to the discussion.

19. *"Jaise āye zabardastī toṛ diye abhī koī ḍanḍā se zor se jīttā hai . . . log ṭūṭne kā to koī matlab nahīn thā. Bas ṭūṭ gaye . . . thāne men ghusā dete hai. Thāne vallon ko khilā dete hai."*

20. A Hindu spring holiday when people throw colored powder and water at each other. They had ordered an extra tanker at the time to have enough water to wash all of the colors off.

21. Thanks to Dr. Cyril Robin, a former scholar at Centre de Sciences Humaines, in Delhi for this insight, based on his work on caste associations and urban governance.

22. Chatterjee openly acknowledges what his view of political society leaves out: "Besides, let us not forget that a local political consensus is also likely to be socially conservative and could be particularly insensitive, for instance to gender or minority issues . . . political society will bring into the hallways and corridors of power some of the squalor, ugliness and violence of popular life." (2004: 74)

23. As described in chapter 2, *pūrīs* are fried flatbread that are considered more special than everyday food and are frequently given out by politicians. Sweets are also given to voters to woo them.

24. *"Ham na kisī kā pānī pīte hain na kisī kā khānā khāte hain. Janatā kī jo ham se banātī hai. Vah sevā karāte hain bāki kuch nahīn hai. Hamāre yahān hamārā yahīn itihās hai."*

25. *"Kis-kisī ke dekhke jalā jāyen, to hamen vah kām nahīn karnā cāhie. . . . Ki ham aise pahanen, aisa khāyen."*

26. *"Ham to bas ek jagah rahete hain, das jagah jāne kī zarurat nahīn hai. Hamen na sharāb cāhie na* meat *cāhie na paise cāhie na pūrī cāhie. Kuch bhī nahin cāhie. Din bhar jūṭhī* plate *dhotī hūn roṭī lagātī hūn peṭ ke liye ārām se bhojan apne baccon ko detī hūn."*

27. *"Ham yah samajhtī hūn ki hamāre nasīb men yah sonā nahīn, hamāre nasīb men aise kapṛe nahīn hain, hamāre nasīb men aise gāṛi men nahīn ghūm saktī, aise mahal men nahīn rah saktī."*

28. *"To isī vajah se ham ne apne nasīb samajhte hain jab hamāre Bhagvān ne nasīb nahīn diyā hai, to ham kisī ko dekhte jalte nahīn hain. Hamen Bhagvān ne itnā diyā jitnā ham roṭī khāte hain, apne ghar men so saken, jaise bacce khā saken, jaise ham kām kar saken."*

29. *"Māldār to yār, ek baccā paidā ho gayā, kothī-vāle ke to bas band karvāo. Gharīb ādmiyon ke to das bacce paidā hai das ṭhīk hai. Unke pās nahīn hai, kacce ke hai, unke pās. Ek ke pās kacce nahīn hain, to baniyān hai, ek ke pās kamīz nahīn hai, māldār log kahete hain. Are, agar uske nahīn hai to kyā tumse bhīkh māngne to nahīn jā rahā koī . . . dekhā nahīn māldār hī to the vah log, hamāri jhuggī hī tuṛvā dī bahan-chod ne. Tamārā kām hī sāf karvā diyā bahan-chod ne. Māldār logon ne dekhā hai gharīb log kahān jayenge? Nahīn, unhein to apnī māldārī par ghamaṇḍ hai. Ek din jab marenge nā to sirf cūṭiyā par hāth rakhke jāyenge, sab yahīn choṛke cale jāyenge."*

CHAPTER 4: TO KNOW THE FIELD

1. In this industrial region, the government had set up a few public latrines that had varying degrees of cleanliness.

2. *"Dekho bhaīyā, amīr log ke alag-alag dekhne se hī khūbsūrtī ātī hai. Lagtā hai usmen 36 rang kā nāshtā . . . hamārā pasand yah hai, to hamko yah cāhie. Hamārā pasand yah hai to hamko yah cāhie . . . ab gharīb men dekho ham vahīn dāl, roṭī, sabzī khāte hain. Hamen koī* tension *nahīn rahatā hai. Calo, ham āj yah banāyen, āj vāh banāyen. Man kiyā to calo, hafte men kabhī-kabhār kuch na kuch banāte hain. To hisāb se banāte hain. . . . Unke pās daulat hai to vah khā rahe hain, hamāre pās nahīn hai to ham dāl-roṭī khā rahe hain. Amīr-gharīb men fark nahīn hai. Har ek cīz men fark hai."*

3. This term refers to the Hindu goddess Durga.

4. *"Bhagvān ne itnā kīmtī sharīr hamko diyā hai aur sab se zyādā dhan-daulat yahīn cīz hai, apnā sharīr."*

5. *"Hamāre desh ko fāydā hogā, hamāre apne ko fāydā hogā aur jab hamārī gandagī dūr hogī, to hamāre bacce bhī svasth rahenge. Har cīz sahī rahegī aur ham sarkār se yah* appeal *karte hain ki hamārī jitnī bhī samasyā hai, unkā samādhān karen."*

6. There were certainly families I knew in the slum who had small refrigerators and heaters and, in one case, an air conditioner. But these were not commonplace.

7. To further illustrate the critique that people chose habits that built their strength, Saraswati's husband argued that he and his neighbors in the slum were

far weaker than their village relatives who worked outside all day in the sun. In comparison, he explained, he had grown weak and could only work in the fields at night when he visited his family's rural village.

8. *Nālā* doesn't translate well. It is the drain or channel that flows between streets and homes to carry wastewater in many urban areas in India. In slums, it is frequently not covered. In addition to water, it may carry raw sewage and trash—what is put into the *nālā* often determines how well it flows, but this is also determined by how often it is cleaned by municipal workers. Adults do not defecate into *nālās*, but waste from households flows into them, and young children may use them as latrines.

9. Indeed some studies (Tovey 2002) show that water pipes in slums dip into *nālās* that carry sewage.

10. *"Achār khāne se lābh nahīn hotā hai. Jībh kā svād hotā hai. Jaise mān lo achār banā liyā. Māno hamāre ghar men sabzī nahīn hai, dāl nahīn hai, rotī hai to use khā lete hain."*

11. *"Khāte hain, ham apnī icchā anusār khāte hain. Lekin ab mān lo, jo hamāre pās jo nahīn hai use kahān se lāyenge? Jo cīz hamāre pās nahīn hai, ham use kyon lāye? Dekho clear, hamārā kahene kā matlab yah hai ki jo hamāre pās hai nahīn, usko ham anubhav nahīn karte ki calo hamāre pās āṭā hai, ālū hai, to usi ki sabzī banā lo. Khā lo, apne ghar par paṛe raho. To yah sochte hain ham."*

12. Also referred to as outside food, *bahār kā khānā*.

13. Prior to demolition, most of the women with whom I worked lived in freestanding *jhuggīs* they had built or purchased. However, after demolition, most women moved into rooms that were in larger buildings—often more cramped.

Bibliography

Agarwal, Siddharth, Aravinda Satyavada, S. Kaushik, Rajeev Kumar, R. G. Khayat, P. C. Saxena, A. N. Sharma, P. Dwivedi, T. Wahed, and A. Bhuiya. 2007. "Urbanization Urban Poverty and Health of the Urban Poor: Status Challenges and the Way Forward." *Demography India* 36 (1): 121–34.

Aklujkar, Vidyut. 1992. "The Divine Feast: Evolution of Food Metaphor in Marathi Sant Poetry." In *The Eternal Food: Gastronomic Ideas and Experiences of Hindus and Buddhists*, edited by R. S. Khare, 95–116. Albany: State University of New York Press.

Alderman, Harold, Peter F. Orazem, and Elizabeth M. Paterno. 1996. "School Quality, School Cost, and the Public/Private School Choices of Low-Income Households in Pakistan." In *Impact Evaluation of Education Reforms*, edited by Policy Research Department Poverty and Human Resources Division. Washington, DC: World Bank.

Ali, Kamran Asdar. 2010. "Voicing Difference: Gender and Civic Engagement among Karachi's Poor." *Current Anthropology* 51 (S2): S313–S320. doi: 10.1086/653422.

Almedom, Astier M. 2005. "Social Capital and Mental Health: An Interdisciplinary Review of Primary Evidence." *Social Science & Medicine* 61 (5): 943–64. doi: 10.1016/j.socscimed.2004.12.025.

Alter, Joseph. 1999. "Heaps of Health, Metaphysical Fitness: Ayurveda and the Ontology of Good Health in Medical Anthropology." *Current Anthropology* 40 (supplement): s43–s66.

Anand, Nikhil. 2011. "Pressure: The Politechnics of Water Supply in Mumbai."
  Cultural Anthropology 26 (4): 542–64.
Anand, Nikhil, and Anne Rademacher. 2011. "Housing in the Urban Age:
  Inequality and Aspiration in Mumbai." *Antipode* 43 (5): 1748–72.
Anjaria, Jonathan. 2011. "Ordinary States: Everyday Corruption and the Politics
  of Space." *American Ethnologist* 38 (1): 58–72.
Appadurai, Arjun. 2000. "Spectral Housing and Urban Cleansing: Notes on
  Millenial Mumbai." *Public Culture* 12 (3): 627–51.
———. 2002. "Deep Democracy: Urban Governmentality and the Horizon of
  Politics." *Public Culture* 14 (1): 21–47.
Asthana, Sheena. 1995. "Variations in Poverty and Health between Slum
  Settlements: Contradictory Findings from Visakhapatnam, India." *Social
  Science & Medicine* 40 (2): 177–88.
Babb, Lawrence. 1983a. "The Physiology of Redemption." *History of Religions*
  22 (4): 293–312.
———. 1983b. "Destiny and Responsibility: Karma in Popular Hinduism." In
  Karma: an Anthropological Inquiry, edited by Charles F. Keyes and E.
  Valentine Daniel, 161–81. Berkeley: University of California Press.
———. 1984. "Indigenous Feminism in a Modern Hindu Sect." *Signs* 9(3):
  399–416.
Banerjee, Biswajit, and S. M. Kanbur. 1981. "On the Specification and Estima-
  tion of Macro Rural–Urban Migration Functions: With an Application to
  Indian Data." *Oxford Bulletin of Economics and Statistics* 43 (1): 7–29. doi:
  10.1111/j.1468–0084.1981.mp43001002.x.
Bang, Rani, and Abhay Bang. 1994. "Women's Perceptions of White Vaginal
  Discharge: Ethnographic Data from Rural Maharastra." In *Listening to
  Women Talk about Their Health: Issues and Evidence from India*, edited by
  Joel Gittelsohn, Margaret E. Bentley, Pertti J. Pelto, Moni Nag, Saroj
  Pachauri, Abigail D. Harrison, and Laura T. Landman, 79–94. Delhi:
  Har-Anand Publications.
Baer, Hans, Merrill Singer, and Ida Susser. 1997. *Medical Anthropology and the
  World System*. Westport, CT: Greenwood.
Baruah, Bipasha. 2007. "Gendered Realities: Exploring Property Ownership
  and Tenancy Relationships in Urban India." *World Development* 35 (12):
  2096–109. doi: 10.1016/j.worlddev.2007.02.003.
Basso, Keith. 1996. *Wisdom Sits in Places: Landscape and Language among the
  Western Apache*. Albuquerque: University of New Mexico Press.
Baviskar, Amita. 2003. "Between Violence and Desire: Space, Power, and
  Identity in the Making of Metropolitan Delhi." *International Social Science
  Journal* 55 (175): 89–98.
———. 2006. "Demolishing Delhi: World Class City in the Making." *Mute
  Magazine* no. 5.

Bear, Laura. 2007. *Lines of the Nation: Indian Railway Workers, Bureaucracy, and the Intimate Historical Self.* New York: Columbia University Press.

———. 2013. "'This Body Is Our Body': Vishwakarma Puja, the Social Debts of Kinship and Theologies of Materiality in a Neo-Liberal Shipyard." In *Vital Relations: Kinship as a Critique of Modernity,* edited by F. Cannell and S. McKinnon. Santa Fe, NM: School for Advanced Research Press.

Berkman, Lisa F., Thomas Glass, Ian Brissette, and Teresa E. Seeman. 2000. "From Social Integration to Health: Durkheim in the New Millennium." *Social Science & Medicine* 51 (6): 843–57. doi: 10.1016/S0277-9536(00)00065-4.

Berkman, Lisa F., and S. L. Syme. 1979. "Social Networks, Host Resistance, and Mortality: A Nine-Year Follow-Up Study of Alameda County Residents." *American Journal of Epidemiology* 109 (2): 186–204.

Bhan, Gautam. 2009. "'This Is No Longer the City I Once Knew.' Evictions, the Urban Poor and the Right to the City in Millennial Delhi." *Environment and Urbanization* 21 (1): 127–42. doi: 10.1177/0956247809103009.

Bhatt, Amy, Madhavi Murty, and Priti Ramamurthy. 2010. "Hegemonic Developments: The New Indian Middle Class, Gendered Subalterns, and Diasporic Returnees in the Event of Neoliberalism." *Signs* 36 (1): 127–52. doi: 10.1086/652916.

Biehl, João Guilherme, J. Byron, and Arthur Kleinman. 2007. *Subjectivity: Ethnographic Investigations.* Berkeley: University of California Press.

Blom Hansen, Thomas. 2005. "Sovereigns beyond the State: On Legality and Authority in Urban India." In *Sovereign Bodies: Citizens, Migrants, and States in the Postcolonial World,* edited by Thomas Blom Hansen and Finn Stepputat, 169–81. Princeton, NJ: Princeton University Press.

Bodenhorn, Barbara. 2000. "'He Used to Be My Relative': Exploring the Bases of Relatedness among Inupiat of Northern Alaska." In *Cultures of Relatedness: New Approaches to the Study of Kinship,* edited by Janet Carsten, 128–48. Cambridge: Cambridge University Press.

Bondi, Liz, Joyce Davidson, and Mick Smith. 2007. "Geography's 'Emotional Turn.'" In *Emotional Geographies,* edited by Joyce Davidson, Liz Bondi, and Mick Smith, 1–16. London: Ashgate.

Boo, Katherine. 2012. *Behind the Beautiful Forevers: Life, Death, and Hope in a Mumbai Undercity.* New York: Random House.

Bose, Sugata. 1997. "Instruments and Idioms of Colonial and National Development: India's Historical Experience in Comparative Perspective." In *International Development and the Social Sciences: Essays on the History and Politics of Knowledge,* edited by Frederick Cooper and Randall Packard. Berkeley: University of California Press.

Bourgois, Phillippe, and Nancy Scheper-Hughes. 2004. "Comment on 'An Anthropology of Structural Violence,' by Paul Farmer." *Current Anthropology* 45 (3): 317–18.

Browne-Yung, Kathryn, Anna Ziersch, and Fran Baum. 2013. "'Faking til You Make It': Social Capital Accumulation of Individuals on Low Incomes Living in Contrasting Socio-Economic Neighbourhoods and Its Implications for Health and Wellbeing." *Social Science & Medicine* 85 (0): 9–17. doi: 10.1016 /j.socscimed.2013.02.026.

Burton, Linda M., Diane Purvin, Raymond Garrett-Peters, Glen H. Elder, and Janet Z. Giele. 2009. "Longitudinal Ethnography: Uncovering Domestic Abuse in Low-Income Women's Lives." In *The Craft of Life Course Research*, edited by Glen H. Elder and Janet Z. Giele, 70–92. New York: Guilford.

Busby, Cynthia. 1997. "Permeable and Partible Persons: A Comparative Analysis of Gender and Body in South India and Melanesia." *Journal of the Royal Anthropological Institute* 3: 261–78.

Butt, Leslie. 2002. "The Suffering Stranger: Medical Anthropology and International Morality." *Medical Anthropology* 21 (1): 1–24. doi: 10.1080 /01459740210619.

Cairncross, Sandy, Caroline Hunt, Sophie Boisson, Kristof Bostoen, Val Curtis, Isaac C. H. Fung, and Wolf-Peter Schmidt. 2010. "Water, Sanitation and Hygiene for the Prevention of Diarrhoea." *International Journal of Epidemiology* 39 (suppl 1): i193–i205. doi: 10.1093/ije/dyq035.

Canvin, Krysia, Anneli Marttila, Bo Burstrom, and Margaret Whitehead. 2009. "Tales of the Unexpected? Hidden Resilience in Poor Households in Britain." *Social Science & Medicine* 69 (2): 238–45. doi: 10.1016/j. socscimed.2009.05.009.

Carsten, Janet. 1995. "The Substance of Kinship and the Heat of the Hearth: Feeding, Personhood, and Relatedness among Malays in Pulau Langkawi." *American Ethnologist* 22 (2): 223–41. doi: 10.1525/ae.1995.22.2.02a00010.

———. 2001. "Substantivism, Antisubstantivism, and Anti-Antisubstantivism." In *Relative Values: Reconfiguring Kinship Studies*, edited by Susan McKinnon and Sarah Franklin. Durham, NC: Duke University Press.

———. 2004. *After Kinship*. Vol. 2. Cambridge: Cambridge University Press.

Caughy, Margaret O'Brien, Patricia J. O'Campo, and Carles Muntaner. 2003. "When Being Alone Might Be Better: Neighborhood Poverty, Social Capital, and Child Mental Health." *Social Science & Medicine* 57 (2): 227–37. doi: 10.1016/S0277-9536(02)00342-8.

Cavalcanti, Mariana. 2007. *Of Shacks, Houses, and Fortresses: An Ethnography of Favela Consolidation in Rio de Janeiro*. PhD diss., University of Chicago.

Chakrabarty, Dipesh. 2002. *Habitations of Modernity: Essays in the Wake of Subaltern Studies*. Chicago: University of Chicago Press.

Chambers, Robert, and Gregor von Medeazza. 2013. "Sanitation and Stunting in India." *Economic & Political Weekly* 48 (25).

Chandola, Tripta. 2010. *Listening in to Others: In between Noise and Silence.* PhD diss., Faculty of Creative Industries, Queensland University of Technology, Queensland.

———. 2012a. "Listening in to Water Routes: Soundscapes as Cultural Systems." *International Journal of Cultural Studies* 16(1): 55–69.

———. 2012b. "Listening into Others: Moralising the Soundscapes in Delhi." *International Development Planning Review* 34 (4): 391–408.

Chaplin, Susan E. 1999. "Cities, Sewers and Poverty: India's Politics of Sanitation." *Environment and Urbanization* 11 (1): 145–58.

Charsely, Simon. 1996. "'Untouchable': What Is in a Name?" *Journal of the Royal Anthropological Institute* 2 (1): 1–23.

Chatterjee, Partha. 1989. "Colonialism, Nationalism, and Colonized Women: The Contest in India." *American Ethnologist* 16 (4): 622–33.

———. 1993. *The Nation and Its Fragments: Colonial and Postcolonial Histories.* Princeton, NJ: Princeton University Press.

———. 2004. *The Politics of the Governed: Reflections on Popular Politics in Most of the World.* New York: Columbia University Press.

Chatterji, Roma, and Deepak Mehta. 2007. *Living with Violence: An Anthropology of Events and Everyday Life.* Delhi: Routledge India.

Chaturvedi, Santosh K., Prabha S. Chandra, Mohan K. Issac, and C. Y. Sudarshan. 1993. "Somatization Misattributed to Non-Pathological Vaginal Discharge." *Journal of Psychosomatic Research* 37 (6): 575–79. doi: 10.1016/0022--3999(93)90051-G.

Chowdhry, Prem. 2007. *Contentious Marriages, Eloping Couples: Gender, Caste, and Patriarchy in Northern India.* New Delhi: Oxford University Press.

Chua, Jocelyn Lim. 2012. "The Register of 'Complaint.'" *Medical Anthropology Quarterly* 26 (2): 221–40. doi: 10.1111/j.1548-1387.2012.01202.x.

Cohen, Lawrence. 1998. *No Aging in India: Alzheimer's, the Bad Family, and Other Modern Things.* Berkeley: University of California Press.

Collier, Jane, Michelle Rosaldo, and Sylvia Yanagisako. 1992. "Is There a Family? New Anthropological Views." In *Rethinking the Family: Some Feminist Questions,* edited by Barrie Thorne and Marilyn Yalom, 31–51. Boston: Northeastern University Press.

Connors, Genevieve. 2007. *Watering the Slums: How a Utility and Its Street-Level Bureaucrats Connected the Poor in Bangalore.* PhD diss., Department of Urban and Regional Planning, MIT, Cambridge, MA.

Cross, Jamie. 2010. "Neoliberalism as Unexceptional: Economic Zones and the Everyday Precariousness of Working Life in South India." *Critique of Anthropology* 30 (4): 355–73. doi: 10.1177/0308275x10372467.

Dabral, Shweta, and S. L. Malik. 2004. "Demographic Study of Gujjars of Delhi: I. Population Structure and Socio-Cultural Profile." *Journal of Human Ecology* 16 (1): 17–24.

Daniel, E. Valentine. 1984. *Fluid Signs: Being a Person the Tamil Way.* Berkeley: University of California Press.

Das, Jishnu, Ranendra Kumar Das, and Veena Das. 2012. "The Mental Health Gender-Gap in Urban India: Patterns and Narratives." *Social Science & Medicine* 75 (9): 1660–72. doi: 10.1016/j.socscimed.2012.06.018.

Das, Jishnu, and Jeffrey Hammer. 2007. "Location, Location, Location: Residence, Wealth, and the Quality of Medical Care in Delhi, India." *Health Affairs* 26 (3): w338-w351. doi: 10.1377/hlthaff.26.3.w338.

Das, Veena. 1976. "Masks and Faces: An Essay on Punjabi Kinship." *Contributions to Indian Sociology* 10 (1): 1–30.

———. 1994. "Modernity and Biography: Women's Lives in Contemporary India." *Thesis Eleven* 39: 52–62.

———. 2006. *Life and Words: Violence and the Descent into the Ordinary.* Berkeley: University of California Press.

Das, Veena, and Rena Addlakha. 2001. "Disability and Domestic Citizenship: Voice, Gender, and the Making of the Subject." *Public Culture* 13 (3): 511–31.

Das, Veena, and Ranendra K. Das. 2004. The Interface between Mental Health and Reproductive Health of Women among the Urban Poor in Delhi. In *Occasional Research Paper Series.* Delhi: Institute of Socio-Economic Research on Development and Democracy.

———. 2006. "Pharmaceuticals in Urban Ecologies: The Register of Local." In *Global Pharmaceuticals: Ethics, Markets, Practices,* edited by Adriana Petryna, Arthur Kleinman, and Andrew Lakoff, 171–205. Durham: Duke University Press.

Das Gupta, Monica. 1995. "Life Course Perspectives on Women's Autonomy and Health Outcomes." *American Anthropologist* 97 (3): 481–91. doi: 10.1525/aa.1995.97.3.02a00070.

———. 2005. "Public Health in India: Dangerous Neglect." *Economic and Political Weekly* 40 (49): 5159–65. doi: 10.2307/4417485.

Dash, Dipak Kumar. 2013. "By 2017, India's Slum Population Will Rise to 104 Million." *Times of India,* August 20.

Datta, Ayona. 2007. "'Samudayik Shakti': Working-Class Feminism and Social Organisation in Subhash Camp, New Delhi." *Gender, Place & Culture* 14 (2): 215–31. doi: 10.1080/09663690701213818.

———. 2011. "'Mongrel City': Cosmopolitan Neighbourliness in a Delhi Squatter Settlement." *Antipode* 44 (3): 745–63. doi: 10.1111/j.1467-8330.2011.00928.x.

Davidson, Joyce, and Christine Milligan. 2004. "Embodying Emotion Sensing Space: Introducing Emotional Geographies." *Social & Cultural Geography* 5 (4): 523–32. doi: 10.1080/1464936042000317677.

Davidson, Joyce, Mick Smith, and Liz Bondi, eds. 2007. *Emotional Geographies.* Farnham, UK: Ashgate.

Davis, Mike. 2006. *Planet of Slums*. London: Verso.

Dean, Melanie. 2013. "From 'Evil Eye' Anxiety to the Desirability of Envy: Status, Consumption and the Politics of Visibility in Urban South India." *Contributions to Indian Sociology* 47 (2): 185–216. doi: 10.1177/0069966713482999.

de Neve, Geert. 2011. "'Keeping It in the Family': Work, Education and Gender Hierarchies among Tiruppur's Industrial Capitalists." In *Being Middle-Class in India: A Way of Life*, edited by Henrike Donner, 73–99. New York: Routledge.

Derne, S. 1995. *Culture in Action: Family Life, Emotion, and Male Dominance in Banaras, India*. Albany: State University of New York Press.

De Silva, Mary J., Kwame McKenzie, Trudy Harpham, and Sharon R. A. Huttly. 2005. "Social Capital and Mental Illness: A Systematic Review." *Journal of Epidemiology and Community Health* 59 (8): 619–27. doi: 10.1136/jech.2004.029678.

de Zoysa, Isabelle, Nita Bhandari, Naseema Akhtari, and Maharaj K. Bhan. 1998. "Careseeking for Illness in Young Infants in an Urban Slum in India." *Social Science & Medicine* 47 (12): 2101–11. doi: 10.1016/S0277-9536(98)00275-5.

Dhar, Aarti. 2009. "India Shifting to Urban Centers." *The Hindu*, February 5.

Dhar, Debotri. 2011. Beyond the Binary: Rape, Suicide and the State in Contemporary India. In *Yale Modern South Asia Workshop*. New Haven, CT.

Dickey, Sara. 2000. "Permeable Homes: Domestic Service, Household Space, and the Vulnerability of Class Boundaries in Urban India." *American Ethnologist* 27 (2): 462–89.

Domínguez, Virginia R. 2000. "For a Politics of Love and Rescue." *Cultural Anthropology* 15 (3): 361–93. doi: 10.2307/656607.

Donner, Henrike. 2008. *Domestic Goddesses: Maternity, Globalization and Middle-Class Identity in Contemporary India*. Farnham, UK: Ashgate.

Dumont, Louis. 1980. *Homo Hierarchicus: The Caste System and Its Implications*. Chicago: University of Chicago Press. First published 1970.

Dupont, Veronique. 2005. "Residential Practices, Creation and Use of Urban Space: Unauthorized Colonies in Delhi." In *Urbanization and Governance in India*, edited by Evelin Hust and Michael Mann, 311–42. Delhi: Manohar.

———. 2011. "The Dream of Delhi as a Global City." *International Journal of Urban and Regional Research* 35 (3): 533–54.

Easwaran, Eknath. 2007. *The Bhagavad Gita (translation)*. Berkeley, CA: Blue Mountain Center of Meditation.

Eck, Diana. 1999. "The Imagined Landscape: Patterns in the Construction of Hindu Sacred Geography." *Contributions to Indian Sociology* 32 (2): 165–88.

Edelman, Brent, and Arup Mitra. 2006. "Slum Dwellers' Access to Basic Amenities: The Role of Political Contact, Its Determinants and Adverse Effects." *Review of Urban & Regional Development Studies* 18 (1): 25–40. doi: 10.1111/j.1467-940X.2006.00109.x.

Egnor, Margaret. 1980. "On the Meaning of Sakti to Women in Tamil Nadu." In *The Powers of Tamil Women*, edited by Susan Wadley, 1–34. Syracuse, NY: Syracuse University.

———. 1983. "Death and Nurturance in Indian Systems of Healing." *Social Science & Medicine* 17 (14): 935–45.

———. 1984. "The Changed Mother, or What the Smallpox Goddess Did When There Was No More Smallpox." *Contributions to Asian Studies* 18: 24–45.

Ewing, Katherine P. 1990. "The Illusion of Wholeness: Culture, Self, and the Experience of Inconsistency." *Ethos* 18 (3): 251–78. doi: 10.2307/640337.

———. 1991. "Can Psychoanalytic Theories Explain the Pakistani Woman? Intrapsychic Autonomy and Interpersonal Engagement in the Extended Family." *Ethos* 19 (2): 131–60. doi: 10.1525/eth.1991.19.2.02a00010.

Farmer, Paul. 2004. "An Anthropology of Structural Violence." *Current Anthropology* 45 (3): 305–25. doi: 10.1086/382250.

———. 2005. *Pathologies of Power: Health, Human Rights, and the New War on the Poor*. Berkeley: University of California Press.

Farquhar, Judith, and Qicheng Zhang. 2005. "Biopolitical Beijing: Pleasure, Sovereignty, and Self-Cultivation in China's Capital." *Cultural Anthropology* 20 (3): 303–27.

Fernandes, Leela. 2006. *India's New Middle Class: Democratic Politics in an Era of Economic Reform*. Minneapolis: University of Minnesota Press.

Firdaus, G., and A. Ahmad. 2013. "Relationship between Housing and Health: A Cross-Sectional Study of an Urban Centre of India." *Indoor and Built Environment* 22 (3): 498–507. doi: 10.1177/1420326x12443846.

Foucault, Michel. 1981. *The History of Sexuality*. Vol. 1, An Introduction. Harmondsworth, UK: Penguin.

Frøystad, Kathinka. 2003. "Master-Servant Relations and the Domestic Reproduction of Caste in Northern India." *Ethnos* 68 (1): 73–94. doi: 10.1080/0014184032000060371.

Fuchs, Martin. 2005. "Slum as Achievement: Governmentality and the Agency of Slum Dwellers." In *Urbanization and Governance in India*, edited by Evelin Hust and Michael Mann, 103–26. New Delhi: Manohar.

Fuller, C.J. 1992. *The Camphor Flame: Popular Hinduism and Society in India*. Princeton, NJ: Princeton University Press.

Fullilove, M. 2004. *Root Shock*. New York: Ballantine.

Furstenberg, F. F. 1993. "How Families Manage Risk and Opportunity in Dangerous Neighborhoods." In *Sociology and the Public Agenda*, edited by William Julius Wilson, 231–58. Newbury Park, CA: Sage Publications.

Galab, S., and N. Chandrasekhara Rao. 2003. "Women's Self-Help Groups, Poverty Alleviation and Empowerment." *Economic and Political Weekly* 38 (12/13): 1274–83. doi: 10.2307/4413378.

Ganguly-Scrase, Ruchira, and Timothy J. Scrase. 2008. *Globalisation and the Middle Classes in India: The Social and Cultural Impact of Neoliberal Reforms.* Vol. 17. London: Routledge.

García-Moreno, Claudia, HAFM Jansen, Mary Ellsberg, Lori Heise, and Charlotte Watts. 2005. *WHO Multi-Country Study on Women's Health and Domestic Violence against Women.* Geneva: World Health Organization.

Garg, Suneela, Nandini Sharma, and Ragini Sahay. 2002. "Socio-Cultural Aspects of Menstruation in an Urban Slum in Delhi, India." *Reproductive Health Matters* 9 (17): 16–15. doi: 10.2307/3776394.

Ghannam, F. 2002. *Remaking the Modern: Space, Relocation, and the Politics of Identity in a Global Cairo.* Berkeley: University of California Press.

Ghertner, D. Asher. 2010. "Calculating without Numbers: Aesthetic Governmentality in Delhi's Slums." *Economy and Society* 39 (2): 185–217. doi: 10.1080/03085141003620147.

Gibson-Graham, J.K. 2006. *The End of Capitalism (as We Knew It): A Feminist Critique of Political Economy.* Minneapolis: University of Minnesota Press.

Gillum, Tameka L., Cris M. Sullivan, and Deborah I. Bybee. 2006. "The Importance of Spirituality in the Lives of Domestic Violence Survivors." *Violence Against Women* 12 (3): 240–50. doi: 10.1177/1077801206286224.

Go, Vivian F., Sethulakshmi C. Johnson, Margaret E. Bentley, Sudha Sivaram, A.K. Srikrishnan, David D. Celentano, and Suniti Solomon. 2003. "Crossing the Threshold: Engendered Definitions of Socially Acceptable Domestic Violence in Chennai, India." *Culture, Health & Sexuality* 5 (5): 393–408. doi: 10.2307/4005345.

Gonzalez de la Rocha, Mercedes. 1994. *The Resources of Poverty: Women and Survival in a Mexican City.* Oxford, UK: Blackwell.

Gooptu, Nandini. 2007. "Economic Liberalisation, Work and Democracy: Industrial Decline and Urban Politics in Kolkata." *Economic and Political Weekly* 42 (21): 1922–33.

Green, Linda. 2004. "Comment on 'An Anthropology of Structural Violence,' by Paul Farmer." *Current Anthropology* 45 (3): 319–20.

Greenough, Paul. 2009. "Asian Intra-Household Survival Logics: The 'Shen Te' and 'Shui Ta' Options." In *History of the Social Determinants of Health: Global Histories, Contemporary Debates,* edited by Harold J. Cook, Sanjoy Bhattacharya, and Anne Hardy, 27–41. Hyderabad, India: Orient Blackswan.

Grover, Shalini. 2009. "Lived Experiences: Marriage, Notions of Love, and Kinship Support amongst Poor Women in Delhi." *Contributions to Indian Sociology* 43 (1): 1–33. doi: 10.1177/006996670904300101.

———. 2011. *Marriage, Love, Caste and Kinship Support: Lived Experiences of the Urban Poor in India New Delhi.* New Delhi: Social Science Press.

Gupta, Akhil. 1995. "Blurred Boundaries: The Discourse of Corruption, the Culture of Politics, and the Imagined State." *American Ethnologist* 22 (2): 375–402. doi: 10.1525/ae.1995.22.2.02a00090.

———. 1998. *Postcolonial Developments: Agriculture in the Making of Modern India.* Durham, NC: Duke University Press.

———. 2012. *Red Tape: Bureaucracy, Structural Violence, and Poverty in India.* Durham, NC: Duke University Press.

Gupta, Akhil, and Aradhana Sharma. 2006. "Globalization and Postcolonial States." *Current Anthropology* 47 (2): 277–307. doi: 10.1086/499549.

Gupta, Akhil, and K. Sivaramakrishnan. 2010. "Introduction: The State in India after Liberalization." In *The State in India after Liberalization: Interdisciplinary Perspectives,* edited by Akhil Gupta and Kalyanakrishnan Sivaramakrishnan, 3–27. London: Routledge.

Gupta, Indrani, and Arup Mitra. 2002. "Rural Migrants and Labour Segmentation: Micro-Level Evidence from Delhi Slums." *Economic and Political Weekly* 37 (2): 163–68. doi: 10.2307/4411601.

Gupta, Indrani, and Swadhin Mondal. 2014. "Urban Health in India: Who Is Responsible?" *International Journal of Health Planning and Management.* doi: 10.1002/hpm.2236.

Gupta, Kamla, Fred Arnold, and H. Lhungdim. 2009. Health and Living Conditions in Eight Indian Cities: National Family Health Survey (NFHS-3) India 2005–06. Mumbai: International Institute for Population Sciences.

Haider, S. 2000. "Migrant Women and Urban Experience in a Squatter Settlement." In *Delhi: Urban Space and Human Destinies,* edited by Veronique Dupont, Emma Tarlo, and Denis Vidal, 29–50. Delhi: Manohar.

Halliburton, Murphy. 2005. "'Just Some Spirits': The Erosion of Spirit Possession and the Rise of 'Tension' in South India." *Medical Anthropology* 24 (2): 111–144. doi: 10.1080/01459740590933849.

Han, Clara. 2011. "Symptoms of Another Life: Time, Possibility, and Domestic Relations in Chile's Credit Economy." *Cultural Anthropology* 26 (1): 7–32. doi: 10.1111/j.1548–1360.2010.01078.x.

Hancock, Mary. 1999. *Womanhood in the Making: Domestic Ritual and Public Culture in Urban South India.* Boulder, CO: Westview Press.

Haraway, Donna. 2007. *When Species Meet.* Minneapolis: University of Minnesota Press.

Harper, Edward B. 1964. "Ritual Pollution as an Integrator of Caste and Religion." *Journal of Asian Studies* 23 (s1): 151–97.

Harriss, John. 2005. "Political Participation, Representation and the Urban Poor: Findings from Research in Delhi." *Economic and Political Weekly* 40 (11): 1041–54.

————. 2007. "Bringing Politics back into Poverty Analysis: Why Understanding Social Relations Matters More for Policy on Chronic Poverty Than Measurement." In *CPRC Working Paper 77*. Vancouver: Chronic Poverty Research Centre, School for International Studies, Simon Fraser University.

————. 2010. "'New Politics' and the Governmentality of the Post-Liberalization State in India: An Ethnographic Perspective." In *The State in India after Liberalization: Interdisciplinary Perspectives*, edited by Akhil Gupta and Kalyanakrishnan Sivaramakrishnan, 91–108. London: Routledge.

Hassan, N., and K. Ahmad. 1991. "The Nutrition Profile of the Slum Dwellers: A Comparison with the Rural Poor." *Ecology of Food and Nutrition* 26 (3): 203–14. doi: 10.1080/03670244.1991.9991202.

High, Holly. 2011. "Melancholia and Anthropology." *American Ethnologist* 38 (2): 217–33. doi: 10.1111/j.1548-1425.2011.01302.x.

Hindu News Group. 2009. "52 Per Cent of Delhi Lives in Slums without Basic Services." *The Hindu*, December 17.

Holmström, Mark. 1999. "A New Map of Indian Industrial Society: The Cartographer All at Sea." *Oxford Agrarian Studies* 27 (2): 165–86. doi: 10.1080/13600819908424172.

Holston, James. 2009. *Insurgent Citizenship: Disjunctions of Democracy and Modernity in Brazil*. Princeton, NJ: Princeton University Press.

Hosagrahar, Jyoti. 2005. *Indigenous Modernities: Negotiating Architecture and Urbanism*. New York: Routledge.

Hossain, S. M. Moazzem, Abbas Bhuiya, Alia Rahman Khan, and Iyorlumun Uhaa. 2004. "Community Development and Its Impact on Health: South Asian Experience." *British Medical Journal* 328 (7443): 830–33.

House, J. S., K. R. Landis, and D. Umberson. 1988. "Social Relationships and Health." *Science* 241 (4865): 540–45. doi: 10.1126/science.3399889.

Husain, N., F. Creed, and B. Tomenson. 1997. "Adverse Social Circumstances and Depression in People of Pakistani Origin in the UK." *The British Journal of Psychiatry* 171 (5): 434–38. doi: 10.1192/bjp.171.5.434.

Ingold, T. 2000. *Perception of the Environment: Essays in Livelihood, Dwelling and Skill*. London: Routledge.

Islam, M., M. Montgomery, and S. Taneja. 2006. *Urban Health and Care Seeking Behavior: A Case Study of Slums in India and the Philippines*. Bethesda, MD: The Partners for Health Reform Project, Abt Associates Inc.

Israel, Barbara A., Stephanie A. Farquhar, Amy J. Schulz, Sherman A. James, and Edith A. Parker. 2002. "The Relationship between Social Support, Stress, and Health among Women on Detroit's East Side." *Health Education & Behavior* 29 (3): 342–60. doi: 10.1177/109019810202900306.

Izutsu, Takashi, Atsuro Tsutsumi, Akramul Md Islam, Seika Kato, Susumu Wakai, and Hiroshi Kurita. 2006. "Mental Health, Quality of Life, and Nutritional Status of Adolescents in Dhaka, Bangladesh: Comparison between an Urban Slum and a Non-Slum Area." *Social Science & Medicine* 63 (6): 1477–88. doi: 10.1016/j.socscimed.2006.04.013.

Jackson, John L., Jr. 2010. "On Ethnographic Sincerity." *Current Anthropology* 51 (S2): S279–S287. doi: 10.1086/653129.

Jacobs, David E. 2011. "Environmental Health Disparities in Housing." *American Journal of Public Health* 101 (S1): S115–S122. doi: 10.2105/AJPH.2010.300058.

Jeffery, Patricia, Roger Jeffery, and Andrew Lyon. 1989. *Labour Pains and Labour Power: Women and Childbearing in India.* London: Zed Books.

Jeffrey, Craig. 2010. "Timepass: Youth, Class, and Time among Unemployed Young Men in India." *American Ethnologist* 37 (3): 465–81. doi: 10.1111/j.1548-1425.2010.01266.x.

Jejeebhoy, Shireen J. 1998. "Wife-Beating in Rural India: A Husband's Right? Evidence from Survey Data." *Economic and Political Weekly* 33 (15): 855–62. doi: 10.2307/4406642.

Jejeebhoy, Shireen J., and Leila Caleb Varkey. 2004. "Maternal Health and Pregnancy-Related Care." In *Looking Back, Looking Forward: A Profile of Sexual and Reproductive Health in India,* edited by Shireen J. Jejeebhoy, 44–87. Jaipur, India: Rawat Publications.

Jervis Read, Cressida. 2012. "A Place in the City: Narratives of 'Emplacement' in a Delhi Resettlement Neighbourhood." *Ethnography* 13 (1): 87–101.

Jesmin, Sonia, and Sarah Salway. 2000. "Marriage among the Urban Poor of Dhaka: Instability and Uncertainty." *Journal of International Development* 12 (5): 689–705. doi: 10.1002/1099-1328(200007)12:5<689::aid-jid7043.0.co;2-2.

Jha, Saumitra, Vijayendra Rao, and Michael Woolcock. 2007. "Governance in the Gullies: Democratic Responsiveness and Leadership in Delhi's Slums." *World Development* 35 (2): 230–46. doi: 10.1016/j.worlddev.2005.10.018.

Joshi, Chitra. 1999. "Hope and Despair: Textile Workers in Kanpur in 1937–38 and the 1990s." *Contributions to Indian Sociology* 33 (1 & 2): 171–203.

Kabra, Harish, and Soma Wadhwa. 2004. "I Know, so I Am." *Outlook India Magazine,* Sept. 13.

Kafle, K. K., R. P. Gartoulla, M. S. Pradhan, A.D. Shrestha, S. B. Karkee, and J. D. Quick. 1992. "Drug Retailer Training: Experiences from Nepal." *Social Science and Medicine* 35 (8): 1015–25.

Kakar, Sudhir. 1978. *The Inner World: A Psycho-Analytic Study of Childhood and Society in India.* Oxford: Oxford University Press.

———. 1989. "Health and Medicine in the Living Traditions of Hinduism." In *Healing and Restoring: Health and Medicine in the World's Religious Traditions,* edited by Lawrence Sullivan. New York: Macmillan.

Kamat, Vinay R., and Mark Nichter. 1998. "Pharmacies, Self-Medication and Pharmaceutical Marketing in Bombay, India." *Social Science & Medicine* 47 (6): 779–94.

Kanani, S., K. Latha, and M. Shah. 1994. "Application of Qualitative Method-
ologies to Investigate Perceptions of Women and Health Practitioners
Regarding Women's Health Disorders in Baroda Slums." In *Listening to
Women Talk about Their Health: Issues and Evidence from India*, edited by
Joel Gittelsohn, Margaret E. Bentley, Pertti J. Pelto, Moni Nag, Saroj
Pachauri, Abigail D. Harrison, and Laura T. Landman, 116–30. Delhi:
Har-Anand Publications.

Kapur, Devesh, Chandra Bhan Prasad, Lant Pritchett, and D. Shyam Babu.
2010. "Rethinking Inequality: Dalits in Uttar Pradesh in the Market Reform
Era." *Economic & Political Weekly* 45 (35): 39–49.

Karn, S. Kumar, and H. Harada. 2002. "Field Survey on Water Supply, Sanitation and Associated Health Impacts in Urban Poor Communities: A Case
from Mumbai City, India." *Water Science & Technology* 46 (11): 269–75.

Karn, Sunil K., Shikura Shigeo, and Harada Hideki. 2000. "Living Environment and Health of the Urban Poor: A Study in Mumbai." *Economic and
Political Weekly* 38 (34): 3575–86.

Karp, Ivan. 2002. "Development and Personhood: Tracing the Contours of a
Moral Discourse." In *Critically Modern: Alternatives, Alterities, Anthropolo-
gies* edited by Bruce Knauft. Bloomington, IN: Indiana University Press.

Kaviraj, Sudipta. 1997. "Filth and the Public Sphere: Concepts and Practices
about Space in Calcutta." *Public Culture* 10 (1): 83–113.

Kawachi, Ichiro, Bruce P. Kennedy, Kimberly Lochner, and Deborah Prothrow-
Stith. 1997. "Social Capital, Income Inequality, and Mortality." *American
Journal of Public Health* 87 (9): 1491–98.

Khan, Sameera. 2007. "Negotiating the Mohalla: Exclusion, Identity and
Muslim Women in Mumbai." *Economic and Political Weekly* 42 (17):
1527–33. doi: 10.2307/4419519.

Khandelwal, Meena. 2004. *Women in Ochre Robes*. Albany: State University of
New York Press.

Khare, R. S. 1976. *The Hindu Hearth and Home*. New Delhi: Vikas.

———. 1984. *The Untouchable as Himself: Ideology, Identity, and Pragmatism
among the Lucknow Chamars*. Cambridge: Cambridge University Press.

———. 1992. "Food with Saints: An Aspect of Hindu Gastrosemantics." In *The
Eternal Food: Gastronomic Ideas and Experiences of Hindus and Buddhists*,
edited by R. S. Khare, 27–52. Albany: SUNY Press.

———. 1993. "The Seen and the Unseen: Hindu Distinctions, Experiences and
Cultural Reasoning." *Contributions to Indian Sociology* 27 (2): 191–212.

———. 1995. "The Body, Sensoria, and Self of the Powerless: Remembering/'Re-
Membering' Indian Untouchable Women." *New Literary History* 26 (1):
147–68. doi: 10.2307/20057273.

———. 1996. "Dava, Daktar, and Dua: Anthropology of Practiced Medicine in
India." *Social Science & Medicine* 43 (5): 837–48.

———. 1998. *Cultural Diversity and Social Discontent: Anthropological Studies on Contemporary India.* New Delhi: Sage.

Kim, D. , S. V. Subramanian, and I. Kawachi. 2008. "Social Capital and Physical Health: A Systematic Review of the Literature." In *Social Capital and Health,* edited by I. Kawachi, 139–90. New Yorker: Springer.

Knox, Sarah S., and Kerstin Uvnas-Moberg. 1998. "Social Isolation and Cardiovascular Disease: An Atherosclerotic Pathway?" *Psychoneuroendocrinology* 23 (8): 877–90. doi: 10.1016/S0306–4530(98)00061–4.

Koenig, Michael A., Saifuddin Ahmed, Mian Bazle Hossain, and A. B. M. Khorshed Alam Mozumder. 2003. "Women's Status and Domestic Violence in Rural Bangladesh: Individual- and Community-Level Effects." *Demography* 40 (2): 269–88. doi: 10.2307/3180801.

Koenig, Michael A., Rob Stephenson, Saifuddin Ahmed, Shireen J. Jejeebhoy, and Jacquelyn Campbell. 2006. "Individual and Contextual Determinants of Domestic Violence in North India." *American Journal of Public Health* 96 (1): 132–38. doi: 10.2105/AJPH.2004.050872.

Kolenda, Pauline. 1967. "Toward a Model of the Hindu *Jajmani* System." In *Tribal and Peasant Economies,* edited by G. Dalton. Garden City, NY: American Museum of Natural History.

———. 1968. "Region, Caste, and Family Structure: A Comparative Study of Indian 'Joint' Family." In *Structure and Change in Indian Society,* edited by Milton Singer and Bernard S. Cohn, 339–96. New York: Wenner-Gren Foundation.

Kostick, Kristin M., Stephen L. Schensul, Kalpita Jadhav, Rajendra Singh, Amruta Bavadekar, and Niranjan Saggurti. 2010. "Treatment Seeking, Vaginal Discharge and Psychosocial Distress Among Women in Urban Mumbai." *Culture, Medicine, and Psychiatry* 34 (3): 529–47. doi: 10.1007/s11013-010-9185-8.

Krause, Inga-Britt. 1989. "Sinking Heart: A Punjabi Communication of Distress." *Social Science & Medicine* 29 (4): 563–75. doi: 10.1016/0277-9536(89)90202-5.

Kreidler, Maryhelen C. 1995. "Victims of Family Abuse: The Need for Spiritual Healing." *Journal of Holistic Nursing* 13 (1): 30–36. doi: 10.1177/089801019501300105.

Krishna, Anirudh. 2010. "Poverty Knowledge and Poverty Action in India." In *The State in India after Liberalization: Interdisciplinary Perspectives,* edited by Akhil Gupta and Kalyanakrishnan Sivaramakrishnan, 111–32. London: Routledge.

Kumar, Shuba, Lakshmanan Jeyaseelan, Saradha Suresh, Ramesh Chandra Ahuja, and IndiaSAFE Steering Committee. 2005. "Domestic Violence and Its Mental Health Correlates in Indian Women." *The British Journal of Psychiatry* 187 (1): 62–67. doi: 10.1192/bjp.187.1.62.

Kumar, Usha. 2001. "Indian Women and Work: A Paradigm for Research." In *New Directions in Indian Psychology*, edited by Ajit K. Dalal and Girishwa Misra, 366–85. New Delhi: Sage Publications.

Kundu, Amitabh. 2007. "Mobility of Population." In *The Oxford Companion to Economics in India*, edited by Kaushik Basu, 350–53. Delhi: Oxford University Press.

Kurin, Richard. 1983. "Indigenous Agronomics and Agricultural Development in the Indus Basin." *Human Organization* 42 (4): 283–94.

Kutty, Omar. 2006. "Balmiki Critique of Modernity." *Seminar* 558: 39–44.

Laidlaw, James. 2002. "For an Anthropology of Ethics and Freedom." *Journal of the Royal Anthropological Institute* 8 (2): 311–32. doi: 10.1111/1467-9655.00110.

Lamb, Sarah. 2000. *White Saris and Sweet Mangoes: Aging, Gender, and Body in North India*. Berkeley: University of California Press.

Lambert, Helen. 1992. "The Cultural Logic of Indian Medicine: Prognosis and Etiology in Rajasthani Popular Therapeutics." *Social Science & Medicine* 34 (10): 1069–76.

———. 2000. "Sentiment and Substance in North Indian Forms of Relatedness." In *Cultures of Relatedness: New Approaches to the Study of Kinship*, edited by Janet Carsten. Cambridge: Cambridge University Press.

Leonard, Karen. 1997. "Finding One's Own Place: Asian Landscapes Re-Envisioned in Rural California." In *Culture, Power, Place: Explorations in Critical Anthropology*, edited by Akhil Gupta and James Ferguson, 118–36. Durham, NC: Duke University Press.

Lessinger, Johanna. 2002. "Work and Love: The Limits of Autonomy for Female Garment Workers in India." *Anthropology of Work Review* 23 (1–2): 13–18. doi: 10.1525/awr.2002.23.1–2.13.

Leukefeld, Carl, Jennifer Havens, Michele Staton Tindall, Carrie B. Oser, Jennifer Mooney, Martin T. Hall, and Hannah K. Knudsen. 2012. "Risky Relationships: Targeting HIV Prevention for Women Offenders." *AIDS Education and Prevention* 24 (4): 339–49. doi: 10.1521/aeap.2012.24.4.339.

Lin, Nan, and Alfred Dean. 1984. "Social Support and Depression." *Social Psychiatry* 19 (2): 83–91. doi: 10.1007/bf00583819.

Lockhart, Chris. 2008. "The Life and Death of a Street Boy in East Africa: Everyday Violence in the Time of AIDS." *Medical Anthropology Quarterly* 22 (1): 94–115. doi: 10.1111/j.1548-1387.2008.00005.x.

Lukose, Ritty A. 2009. *Liberalization's Children: Gender, Youth, and Consumer Citizenship in Globalizing India*. Durham, NC: Duke University Press.

Luthra, Sangeetha. 2003. "Educating Entrepreneurs, Organizing for Social Justice: NGO Development Strategies in New Delhi Basti." In *Regional Modernities: the Cultural Politics of Development in India*, edited by K. Sivaramakrishnan and Arun Agrawal. New Delhi: Oxford University Press.

Lynch, Caitrin. 1999. "Good Girls or Juki Girls? Learning and Identity in Garment Factories." *Anthropology of Work Review* 19 (3): 18–22. doi: 10.1525/awr.1999.19.3.18.

Magar, Veronica. 2000. *Reconceptualizing Domestic Violence in Delhi Slums: Multidimensional Factors and Empowerment Approaches.* PhD diss., Maternal and Child Health, College of Public Health, University of North Carolina, Chapel Hill, NC.

———. 2003. "Empowerment Approaches to Gender-Based Violence: Women's Courts in Delhi Slums." *Women's Studies International Forum* 26 (6): 509–23. doi: 10.1016/j.wsif.2003.09.006.

Maitra, Shubhada, and Stephen L. Schensul. 2008. "Reflecting Diversity and Complexity in Marital Sexual Relationships in a Low-Income Community in Mumbai." In *Reproductive Health in India: New Evidence,* edited by Michael A. Koenig, Shireen Jejeebhoy, John C. Cleland, and Bela Ganatra, 339–57. Jaipur: Rawat Publications.

Mankekar, Purnima. 2010. "Becoming Entrepreneurial Subjects: Neoliberalism and Media." In *The State in India after Liberalization: Interdisciplinary Perspectives,* edited by Akhil Gupta and Kalyanakrishnan Sivaramakrishnan, 213–31. London: Routledge.

Mann, Michael. 2007. "Delhi's Belly: On the Management of Water, Sewage and Excreta in a Changing Urban Environment during the Nineteenth Century." *Studies in History* 23 (1): 1–31.

Manuel, Jennifer I., Melissa L. Martinson, Sarah E. Bledsoe-Mansori, and Jennifer L. Bellamy. 2012. "The Influence of Stress and Social Support on Depressive Symptoms in Mothers with Young Children." *Social Science & Medicine* 75 (11): 2013–20.

Markus, Hazel R., and Shinobu Kitayama. 1991. "Culture and the Self: Implications for Cognition, Emotion, and Motivation." *Psychological Review* 98 (2): 224–53. doi: 10.1037/0033-295X.98.2.224.

Marriott, McKim. 1968. "Caste Ranking and Food Transactions: A Matrix Analysis." In *Structure and Change in Indian Society,* edited by Milton Singer and Bernard S. Cohn, 133–71. Chicago: Aldine.

———. 1976. "Hindu Transactions: Diversity without Dualism." In *Transaction and Meaning: Directions in the Anthropology of Exchange and Symbolic Behavior,* edited by B. Kapferer, 109–42. Philadelphia: Institute for the Study of Human Issues.

Marriott, McKim, and Ronald Inden. 1977. "Toward an Ethnosociology of South Asian Caste Systems." In *The New Wind: Changing Identities in South Asia,* edited by Kenneth H. David, 227–38. Paris: Mouton.

Marris, Peter. 1962. *Family and Social Change in an African City: A Study of Rehousing in Lagos.* Evanston, IL: Northwestern University Press.

Marrow, Jocelyn. 2013. "Feminine Power or Feminine Weakness? North Indian Girls' Struggles with Aspirations, Agency, and Psychosomatic Illness." *American Ethnologist* 40 (2): 347–61. doi: 10.1111/amet.12026.

Martin, Sandra L., Brian Kilgallen, Amy Ong Tsui, Kuhu Maitra, Kaushalendra Kumar Singh, and Lawrence L. Kupper. 1999. "Sexual Behaviors and Reproductive Health Outcomes: Associations with Wife Abuse in India." *Journal of the American Medical Association* 282 (20): 1967–1972. doi: 10.1001/jama.282.20.1967.

Masson, J. Moussaieff. 1976. "The Psychology of the Ascetic." *The Journal of Asian Studies* 35 (4): 611–25. doi: 10.2307/2053674.

McFarlane, C. 2008. "Sanitation in Mumbai's Informal Settlements: State, 'Slum,' and Infrastructure." *Environment and Planning A* 40 (1): 88–107.

McGranahan, Gordon. 1993. "Household Environmental Problems in Low-Income Cities: An Overview of Problems and Prospects for Improvement." *Habitat International* 17 (2): 105–21. doi: 10.1016/0197-3975(93)90008-Z.

McHugh, Ernestine L. 1989. "Concepts of the Person among the Gurungs of Nepal." *American Ethnologist* 16 (1): 75–86. doi: 10.1525/ae.1989.16.1.02a00050.

Mendenhall, Emily. 2012. *Syndemic Suffering: Social Distress, Depression, and Diabetes among Mexican Immigrant Women.* Vol. 4. Walnut Creek, CA: Left Coast Press.

Menon, Usha. 2002. "Making Śakti: Controlling (Natural) Impurity for Female (Cultural) Power." *Ethos* 30 (1–2): 140–57. doi: 10.1525/eth.2002.30.1–2.140.

———. 2013. "The Hindu Concept of Self-Refinement: Implicit yet Meaningful." *Psychology & Developing Societies* 25 (1): 195–222. doi: 10.1177/0971333613477320.

Menon, Usha, and Richard A. Shweder. 1998. "The Return of the 'White Man's Burden': The Moral Discourse of Anthropology and the Domestic Life of Hindu Women." In *Welcome to Middle Age! (and Cultural Fictions)*, edited by Richard A. Shweder, 139–88. Chicago: University of Chicago Press.

Menon-Sen, Kalyani. 2006. "'Better to Have Died Than to Live Like This': Women and Evictions in Delhi." *Economic and Political Weekly* May 20: 1969–1974.

Menon-Sen, Kalyani, and Gautam Bhan. 2008. *Swept off the Map: Surviving Eviction and Resettlement in Delhi.* New Delhi: Yoda Press.

Milton, Kay. 1997. "Ecologies: Anthropology, Culture and the Environment." *International Social Science Journal* 49 (154): 477–95. doi: 10.1111/j.1468-2451.1997.tb00039.x.

———. 2005. "Meanings, Feelings, and Human Ecology." In *Mixed Emotions: Anthropological Studies of Feeling*, edited by Kay Milton and Maruska Svasek, 25–42. London: Berg.

Mishra, Nripendra Kishore, and Tulika Tripathi. 2011. "Conceptualising Women's Agency, Autonomy and Empowerment." *Economic & Political Weekly* 46 (11): 58–65.

Mitchell, Carey Usher, and Mark LaGory. 2002. "Social Capital and Mental Distress in an Impoverished Community." *City & Community* 1 (2): 199–222. doi: 10.1111/1540-6040.00017.

Mitra, Arup. 2004. "Informal Sector, Networks, and Intra-City Variations in Activities: Findings from Delhi Slums." *Review of Urban & Regional Development Studies* 16 (2): 154–69. doi: 10.1111/j.1467-940X.2004.00083.x.

Mody, Perveez. 2002. "Love and the Law: Love-Marriage in Delhi." *Modern Asian Studies* 36 (01): 223–56. doi: 10.1017/S0026749X02001075.

Mohanty, Chandra Talpade. 1984. "Under Western Eyes: Feminist Scholarship and Colonial Discourses." *boundary 2* no. 12/13: 333–58. doi: 10.2307/302821.

Moreno, Manuel. 1992. "Pancamirtam: God's Washings as Food." In *The Eternal Food: Gastronomic Ideas and Experiences of Hindus and Buddhists*, edited by R. S. Khare, 147–78. Albany: State University of New York Press.

Mullings, Leith. 2005. "Resistance and Resilience: The Sojourner Syndrome and the Social Context of Reproduction in Cenral Harlem." *Transforming Anthropology* 13 (2): 79–91.

Mullings, Leith, and Alaka Wali. 2001. *Stress and Resilience: The Social Context of Reproduction in Central Harlem.* New York: Springer.

Mullings, Leith, Alaka Wali, Diane McLean, Janet Mitchell, Sabiyha Prince, Deborah Thomas, and Patricia Tovar. 2001. "Qualitative Methodologies and Community Participation in Examining Reproductive Experiences: The Harlem Birth Right Project." *Maternal and Child Health Journal* 5 (2): 85–93. doi: 10.1023/a:1011397031640.

Munshi, Kaivan, and Mark Rosenzweig. 2006. "Traditional Institutions Meet the Modern World: Caste, Gender, and Schooling Choice in a Globalizing Economy." *The American Economic Review* 96 (4): 1225–52. doi: 10.2307/30034337.

Nadkarni, Vimla, Roopashri Sinha, and Leonie D'Mello, eds. 2009. *NGOs, Health and the Urban Poor.* Jaipur, India: Rawat Publications.

Nagar, Richa, and Sangtin Collective Writers. 2006. *Playing with Fire: Feminist Thought and Activism through Seven Lives in India.* Minneapolis: University of Minnesota Press.

Nair, J., and M. E. John. 2000. *A Question of Silence: The Sexual Economies of Modern India.* London: Zed Books.

Nandy, Ashis. 1995. "History's Forgotten Doubles." *History and Theory* 34 (2): 44–66.

Narayan, Kirin. 1989. *Storytellers, Saints, and Scoundrels: Folk Narrative in Hindu Religious Teaching.* Philadelphia: University of Pennsylvania Press.

———. 2004. "Honor Is Honor, After All: Silence and Speech in the Life Stories of Women in Kangra, North-West India." In *Telling Lives in India: Biography, Autobiography, and Life History*, edited by David Arnold and Stuart Blackburn, 227–51. Bloomington: Indiana University Press.

Narayan, Ravi. 2011. "Universal Health Care in India: Missing Core Determinants." *The Lancet* 377 (9769): 883–85. doi: 10.1016/S0140-6736(10)62045-4.

Naudet, Jules. 2008. "'Paying Back to Society': Upward Social Mobility among Dalits." *Contributions to Indian Sociology* 42 (3): 413–41. doi: 10.1177/006996670804200304.

Nguyen, Vinh-Kim, and Karine Peschard. 2003. "Anthropology, Inequality, and Disease: A Review." *Annual Review of Anthropology:* 447–74.

Nichter, Mark. 1980. "The Layperson's Perception of Medicine as Perspective into the Utilization of Multiple Therapy Systems in the Indian Context." *Social Science & Medicine. Part B: Medical Anthropology* 14 (4): 225–33. doi: 10.1016/0160-7987(80)90048-4.

———. 1981. "Idioms of Distress: Alternatives in the Expression of Psychosocial Distress: A Case Study from South India." *Culture, Medicine and Psychiatry* 5 (4): 379–408.

———. 1989. *Anthropology and International Health: Asian Case Studies.* Vol. 3. New York: Routledge.

Nidadavolu, Vijaya. 2004. "Domestic Violence." In *Looking Back, Looking Forward: A Profile of Sexual and Reproductive Health in India,* edited by Shireen J Jejeebhoy, 169–79. Jaipur, India: Rawat Publications.

O'Daniel, A. J. 2011. "Access to Medical Care Is Not the Problem: Low-Income Status and Health Care Needs among HIV-Positive African-American Women in Urban North Carolina." *Human Organization* 70 (4): 416–26.

Osella, Filippo, and Caroline Osella. 1999. "From Transience to Immanence: Consumption, Life-Cycle and Social Mobility in Kerala, South India." *Modern Asian Studies* 33 (04): 989–1020.

Östör, Ákos, Lina Fruzzetti, and Steve Barnett. 1982. *Concepts of Person: Kinship, Caste, and Marriage in India.* Cambridge, MA: Harvard University Press.

Palriwala, Rajni. 1993. "Economics and Patriliny: Consumption and Authority within the Household." *Social Scientist* 21 (9/11): 47–73. doi: 10.2307/3520426.

Palriwala, Rajni, and Neetha Pillai. 2008. The Political and Social Economy of Care: India Research Report 1. Geneva: United Nations Research Institute for Social Development (UNRISD).

Pandian, Anand. 2008. "Devoted to Development: Moral Progress, Ethical Work, and Divine Favor in South India." *Anthropological Theory* 8 (2): 159–79. doi: 10.1177/1463499608090789.

Papola, T. S. 2007. "Employment Trends." In *The Oxford Companion to Economics in India,* edited by Kaushik Basu, 131–36. Delhi: Oxford University Press.

Parry, Jonathan P. 1994. *Death in Banaras.* Cambridge: Cambridge University Press.

————. 2001. "Ankalu's Errant Wife: Sex, Marriage and Industry in Contemporary Chhattisgarh." *Modern Asian Studies* 35 (04): 783–820. doi: 10.1017/S0026749X01004024.

Parson, Nia. 2010. "'I Am Not [Just] a Rabbit Who Has a Bunch of Children!':' Agency in the Midst of Suffering at the Intersections of Global Inequalities, Gendered Violence, and Migration." *Violence Against Women* 16 (8): 881–901. doi: 10.1177/1077801210376224.

Patel, B. C., S. Barge, R. Kolhe, and H. Sadhwani. 1994. "Listening to Women Talk about Their Reproductive Health Problems in the Urban Slums and Rural Areas of Baroda." In *Listening to Women Talk about Their Health: Issues and Evidence from India,* edited by Joel Gittelsohn, Margaret E. Bentley, Pertti J. Pelto, Moni Nag, Saroj Pachauri, Abigail D. Harrison, and Laura T. Landman, 141–44. Delhi: Har-Anand Publications.

Patel, Vikram, and Nandini Oomman. 1999. "Mental Health Matters too: Gynaecological Symptoms and Depression in South Asia." *Reproductive Health Matters* 7 (14): 30–38. doi: 10.1016/S0968-8080(99)90004-6.

Paul, Vinod Kumar, Harshpal Singh Sachdev, Dileep Mavalankar, Prema Ramachandran, Mari Jeeva Sankar, Nita Bhandari, Vishnubhatla Sreenivas, Thiagarajan Sundararaman, Dipti Govil, David Osrin, and Betty Kirkwood. 2011. "Reproductive Health, and Child Health and Nutrition in India: Meeting the Challenge." *The Lancet* 377 (9762): 332–49. doi: 10.1016/S0140-6736(10)61492-4.

Pearson, Anne Mackenzie. 1996. *Because It Gives Me Peace of Mind: Ritual Fasts in the Religious Lives of Hindu Women.* Albany: State University of New York Press.

Peletz, Michael G. 2001. "Ambivalence in Kinship since the 1940s." In *Relative Values: Reconfiguring Kinship Values,* edited by Sarah Franklin and Susan McKinnon, 413–44. Durham, NC: Duke University Press.

Pendse, Sandeep. 1995. "Toil, Sweat, and the City." In *Bombay: Metaphor for Modern India,* edited by Sujata Patel and Alice Thorner, 3–25. Bombay: Oxford University Press.

Pinney, Christopher. 1999. "On Living in the Kal(i)yug: Notes from Nagda, Madhya Pradesh." *Contributions to Indian Sociology* 33 (1–2): 77–106. doi: 10.1177/006996679903300106.

Pinto, Sarah. 2004. "Development without Institutions: Ersatz Medicine and the Politics of Everyday Life in Rural North India." *Cultural Anthropology* 19 (3): 337–64. doi: 10.1525/can.2004.19.3.337.

Polgreen, Lydia. 2011. "High Price for India's Information Law." *New York Times,* January 22.

Pool, Robert. 1987. "Hot and Cold as an Explanatory Model: The Example of Bharuch District in Gujarat, India." *Social Science & Medicine* 25 (4): 389–99. doi: 10.1016/0277-9536(87)90277-2.

Poortinga, Wouter. 2006a. "Social Capital: An Individual or Collective Resource for Health?" *Social Science & Medicine* 62 (2): 292–302. doi: 10.1016/j.socscimed.2005.06.008.

———. 2006b. "Social Relations or Social Capital? Individual and Community Health Effects of Bonding Social Capital." *Social Science & Medicine* 63 (1): 255–70. doi: 10.1016/j.socscimed.2005.11.039.

Povinelli, Elizabeth A. 2006. *The Empire of Love: Toward a Theory of Intimacy, Genealogy, and Carnality*. Durham, NC: Duke University Press.

Prashad, Vijay. 2001. "The Technology of Sanitation in Colonial Delhi." *Modern Asian Studies* 35 (01): 113–55. doi: 10.1017/S0026749X01003626.

Pugh, Judy F. 1991. "The Semantics of Pain in Indian Culture and Medicine." *Culture, Medicine and Psychiatry* 15 (1): 19–43. doi: 10.1007/BF00050826.

Putnam, Robert D. 1993. "The Prosperus Community: Social Capital and Public Life." *New Prospect* 13 (2): 35–42.

Qadeer, Imrana. 2009. "Political and Economic Determinants of Health: The Case of India." In *History of the Social Determinants of Health: Global Histories, Contemporary Debates*, edited by Harold J. Cook, Sanjoy Bhattacharya, and Anne Hardy, 228–47. Hyderabad, India: Orient BlackSwan.

Rahman, Fazlur. 1989. "Islam and Health/Medicine: A Historical Perspective." In *Healing and Restoring: Health and Medicine in the World's Religious Traditions*, edited by Lawrence Sullivan, 149–72. New York: Macmillan.

Raj, Anita. 2011. "Gender Equity and Universal Health Coverage in India." *The Lancet* 377 (9766): 618–19. doi: 10.1016/S0140-6736(10)62112-5.

Ramachandran, Sujata. 2004. "'There Are Many Bangladeshis in New Delhi, but . . . ': Methodological Routines and Fieldwork Anxieties." *Population, Space and Place* 10 (3): 255–70. doi: 10.1002/psp.327.

Ramanathan, Usha. 2005. "Demolition Drive." *Economic and Political Weekly* 40 (27): 2908–12.

———. 2006. "Illegality and the Urban Poor." *Economic and Political Weekly* 41 (29): 3193–97.

Ramanujan, A. K. 1989. "Is There an Indian Way of Thinking? An Informal Essay." In *The Collected Essays of A. K. Ramanujan*, edited by Vinay Dharwadker, 34–51. Oxford: Oxford University Press.

Ramasubban, Radhika, and Bhanwar S. Rishyasringa. 2008. "Treatment-Seeking for Gynaecological Problems by Women in Mumbai Slums." In *Reproductive Health in India: New Evidence*, edited by Michael A. Koenig, Shireen Jejeebhoy, John C. Cleland, and Bela Ganatra, 227–51. Jaipur: Rawat Publications.

Ramasubban, Radhika, and B. Singh. 2001. "Weakness ('Ashaktapanna') and Reproductive Health among Women in a Slum Population in Mumbai, India." In *Cultural Perspectives in Reproductive Health*, edited by C. M. Obermeyer, 14–34. New York: Oxford University Press.

Ramaswami, Shankar. 2006. "Masculinity, Respect, and the Tragic: Themes of Proletarian Humor in Contemporary Industrial Delhi." *International Review of Social History* 51 (Supplement S14): 203–27. doi: 10.1017/S0020859006002665.

Rashid, Sabina Faiz. 2007a. "Accessing Married Adolescent Women: The Realities of Ethnographic Research in an Urban Slum Environment in Dhaka, Bangladesh." *Field Methods* 19 (4): 369–83. doi: 10.1177/1525822x07302882.

———. 2007b. "Durbolota (Weakness), Chinta Rog (Worry Illness), and Poverty: Explanations of White Discharge among Married Adolescent Women in an Urban Slum in Dhaka, Bangladesh." *Medical Anthropology Quarterly* 21 (1): 108–32. doi: 10.1525/maq.2007.21.1.108.

Rasu, Mayank. 2007. "Musings of a Bihari." *The Hindu,* August 26.

Raval, Vaishali V. 2009. "Negotiating Conflict between Personal Desires and Others' Expectations in Lives of Gujarati Women." *Ethos* 37 (4): 489–511. doi: 10.1111/j.1548-1352.2009.01070.x.

Raval, Vaishali V., and Michael J. Kral. 2004. "Core versus Periphery: Dynamics of Personhood over the Life-Course for a Gujarati Hindu Woman." *Culture & Psychology* 10 (2): 162–94. doi: 10.1177/1354067x04040927.

Ray, Raka. 1999. *Fields of Protest: Women's Movements in India.* Minneapolis: University of Minnesota Press.

Ray, Raka, and Seemin Qayam. 2009. *Cultures of Servitude: Modernity, Domesticity, and Class in India.* Stanford, CA: Stanford University Press.

Ring, Laura A. 2006. *Zenana: Everyday Peace in a Karachi Apartment Building.* Bloomington: Indiana University Press.

Roberts, Nathaniel P. 2008. "The Power of Conversion and the Foreignness of Belonging: Domination and Moral Community in a Paraiyar Slum." PhD diss., Columbia University.

Rodrigues, Merlyn, Vikram Patel, Surinder Jaswal, and Nandita de Souza. 2003. "Listening to Mothers: Qualitative Studies on Motherhood and Depression from Goa, India." *Social Science & Medicine* 57 (10): 1797–1806. doi: 10.1016/S0277-9536(03)00062-5.

Rosin, R. Thomas. 2000. "Wind, Traffic and Dust: The Recycling of Wastes." *Contributions to Indian Sociology* 34 (3): 361–408. doi: 10.1177/006996670003400302.

Roy, A. N., A. Jockin, and Ahmad Javed. 2004. "Community Police Stations in Mumbai's Slums." *Environment and Urbanization* 16 (2): 135–38. doi: 10.1177/095624780401600205.

Roy, Ananya. 2003. *City Requiem, Calcutta: Gender and the Politics of Poverty.* Minneapolis: University of Minnesota.

————. 2011. "Slumdog Cities: Rethinking Subaltern Urbanism." *International Journal of Urban and Regional Research* 35 (2): 223–38. doi: 10.1111 /j.1468-2427.2011.01051.x.

Rudolph, Lloyd I., and Susanne Hoeber Rudolph. 2006. *Postmodern Gandhi and Other Essays: Gandhi in the World and at Home.* Chicago: University of Chicago Press.

Rudolph, Susanne Hoeber, and Lloyd I. Rudolph. 2003. "The Coffee House and the Ashram: Gandhi, Civil Society and Public Spheres." In *Civil Society and Democracy: A Reader*, edited by Carolyn M. Elliott, 377–404. Delhi: Oxford University Press.

Saavala, Minna. 2010. *Middle-Class Moralities: Everyday Struggle over Belonging and Prestige in India.* New Delhi: Orient Blackswan.

Sabo, Samantha, Maia Ingram, Kerstin M. Reinschmidt, Kenneth Schachter, Laurel Jacobs, Jill Guernsey de Zapien, Laurie Robinson, and Scott Carvajal. 2013. "Predictors and a Framework for Fostering Community Advocacy as a Community Health Worker Core Function to Eliminate Health Disparities." *American Journal of Public Health* 103 (7): e67-e73. doi: 10.2105/ AJPH.2012.301108.

Sampson, Robert J. 1999. "What 'Community' Supplies." In *Urban Problems and Community Development*, edited by Ronald F. Ferguson and William T. Dickens, 241–92. Washington, DC: Brookings Institution.

Sangari, Kumkum. 2005. "Violent Acts: Cultures, Structures and Retradition-alisation." In *Women of India: Colonial and Postcolonial Periods*, Vol. IX, Part 3, edited by Bharati Ray, 159–82. New Delhi: Sage Publications.

Schulz, Amy J., and Lora Bex Lempert. 2004. "Being Part of the World: Detroit Women's Perceptions of Health and the Social Environment." *Journal of Contemporary Ethnography* 33 (4): 437–65. doi: 10.1177/0891241604265979.

Scott, James C. 1985. *Weapons of the Weak: Everyday Forms of Peasant Resistance.* New Haven, CT: Yale University Press.

Sen, Binayak. 2011. "Securing the Right to Health for All in India." *The Lancet* 377 (9765): 532–33. doi: 10.1016/S0140-6736(10)62182-4.

Sengupta, Somini. 2006. "In Teeming India, Water Crisis Means Dry Pipes and Foul Sludge." *New York Times* September 26: A1, A14.

Seymour, Susan C. 1999. *Women, Family, and Child Care in India: A World in Transition.* Cambridge: Cambridge University Press.

Sharani, Awadhendra. 2002. "Claims on Cleanliness: Environment and Justice in Contemporary Delhi." In *Sarai Reader 2002: The Cities of Everyday Life*, edited by Ravi Vasudevan, Ravi Sundaram, Jeebesh Bagchi, Monica Narula, Geert Lovink, and Shuddhabrata Sengupta, 31–37. New Delhi: Center for the Study of Developing Societies.

Sharma, Aradhana. 2010. "States of Empowerment." In *The State in India after Liberalization: Interdisciplinary Perspectives,* edited by Akhil Gupta and Kalyanakrishnan Sivaramakrishnan, 71–90. London: Routledge.

Sharma, K. 2000. *Rediscovering Dharavi: Stories from Asia's Largest Slum.* Gurgaon, India: Penguin Books.

Shetty, Priya. 2011. "Health Care for Urban Poor Falls through the Gap." *The Lancet* 377 (9766): 627–28. doi: 10.1016/S0140-6736(11)60215-8.

Shukla, Abhay, Satish Kumar, and F. G. Ory. 1991. "Occupational Health and the Environment in an Urban Slum in India." *Social Science and Medicine* 33 (5): 597–603.

Shweder, Richard A. 2008. "The Cultural Psychology of Suffering: The Many Meanings of Health in Orissa, India (and Elsewhere)." *Ethos* 36(1): 60–77.

Shweder, Richard A., Nancy C. Much, Manamohan M. Mahapatra, and Lawrence Park. 1997. "The Big Three of Morality (Autonomy, Community, Divinity) and the Big Three Explanations of Suffering." In *Morality and Health,* edited by Allan Brandt and Paul Rozin, 119–72. New York: Routledge.

Silverstein, Michael, Samere Reid, Kristina DePeau, Jacqueline Lamberto, and William Beardslee. 2010. "Functional Interpretations of Sadness, Stress and Demoralization among an Urban Population of Low-Income Mothers." *Maternal and Child Health Journal* 14 (2): 245–53. doi: 10.1007/s10995-009-0445-6.

Singer, Merill, and Scott Clair. 2003. "Syndemics and Public Health: Reconceptualizing Disease in BioSocial Context." *Medical Anthropology Quarterly* 17 (4): 423–41.

Singh, Andréa Menefee. 1976. *Neighbourhood and Social Networks in Urban India.* New Delhi: Marwah Publications.

———. 1977. "Women and the Family: Coping with Poverty in the Bastis of Delhi." *Social Action* 27: 241–65.

Snell-Rood, Claire. 2013. "'People Don't Think It's Possible': The Anxiety and Pleasure of Relating across Difference." Manuscript submitted for publication.

———. 2015. "Marital Discord and Appetite Loss: The Social Dimensions of Feeding amidst Food Insecurity." *Medical Anthropology Quarterly.* doi: 10.1111/maq.12184.

Srivastava, Sanjay. 2010. "'Revolution Forever': Consumerism and Object Lessons for the Urban Poor." *Contributions to Indian Sociology* 44 (1–2): 103–28. doi: 10.1177/006996671004400206.

———. 2011. "A Hijra, a Female Pradhan and a Real Estate Dealer: Between the Market, the State and 'Community.'" *Economic & Political Weekly* 46 (51).

———. 2012. "Duplicity, Intimacy, Community: An Ethnography of ID Cards, Permits and Other Fake Documents in Delhi." *Thesis Eleven* 113 (1): 78–93. doi: 10.1177/0725513612456686.

Stack, Carol B. 1974. *All Our Kin: Strategies for Survival in a Black Community.* New York: Harper & Row.

Staton-Tindall, Michele, Linda Frisman, Hsui-Ju Lin, Carl Leukefeld, Carrie Oser, Jennifer R. Havens, Michael Prendergast, Hilary L. Surratt, and Jennifer Clarke. 2011. "Relationship Influence and Health Risk Behavior among Re-Entering Women Offenders." *Women's Health Issues* 21 (3): 230–38. doi: 10.1016/j.whi.2010.10.006.

Tarlo, E. 2003. *Unsettling Memories: Narratives of the Emergency in Delhi.* Berkeley: University of California Press.

Tewari, Vinod, Mukesh Mathur, Rajesh Chandra, and Ajay Nigam. 2004. *An Evaluative Study on Environmental Improvement in Urban Slums: A Case of Delhi.* New Delhi: National Institute of Urban Affairs.

Thapan, Meenakshi. 2009. *Living the Body: Embodiment, Womanhood and Identity in Contemporary India.* New Delhi: Sage Publications.

Thurber, Mark C., Christina Warner, Lauren Platt, Alexander Slaski, Rajesh Gupta, and Grant Miller. 2013. "To Promote Adoption of Household Health Technologies, Think beyond Health." *American Journal of Public Health* 103 (10): 1736–40. doi: 10.2105/AJPH.2013.301367.

Tindall, G. 1992. *City of Gold: The Biography of Bombay.* Gurgaon, India: Penguin.

Tooley, James, and Pauline Dixon. 2007. "Private Schooling for Low-Income Families: A Census and Comparative Survey in East Delhi, India." *International Journal of Educational Development* 27 (2): 205–19. doi: 10.1016/j.ijedudev.2006.08.002.

Tovey, Kathryn S. 2002. *The Institutional Responses to the Water Needs of the Urban Poor: A Study of Collection Action in Delhi Slums.* PhD diss., Fitzwilliam College, University of Cambridge, Cambridge.

Trawick, Margaret. 1992a. "An Ayurvedic Theory of Cancer." In *Anthropological Approaches to the Study of Ethnomedicine,* edited by Mark Nichter, 207–22. Yverdon, Switzerland: Gordon and Breach.

———. 1992b. *Notes on Love in a Tamil Family.* Berkeley: University of California Press.

Trollope-Kumar, Karen. 2001. "Cultural and Biomedical Meanings of the Complaint of Leukorrhea in South Asian Women." *Tropical Medicine & International Health* 6 (4): 260–66. doi: 10.1046/j.1365–3156.2001.00699.x.

Uberoi, Patricia. 2004. "The Family in India." In *Handbook of Indian Sociology,* edited by Veena Das. Delhi: Oxford University Press.

Unnithan-Kumar, Maya. 2003. "Spirits of the Womb: Migration, Reproductive Choice and Healing in Rajasthan." *Contributions to Indian Sociology* 37 (1–2): 163–88. doi: 10.1177/006996670303700108.

Vasavi, A. R. 1994. "'Hybrid Times, Hybrid People': Culture and Agriculture in South India." *Man* 29 (2): 283–300.

Vatuk, Sylvia. 1972. *Kinship and Urbanization: White Collar Migrants in North India*. Berkeley: University of California Press.

———. 1990. "'To Be a Burden on Others': Dependency Anxiety among the Elderly in India." In *Divine Passions: The Social Construction of Emotion in India*, edited by Owen Lynch, 64–88. Berkeley: University of California Press.

———. 1995. "The Indian Woman in Later Life: Some Social and Cultural Considerations." In *Women's Health in India: Risk and Vulnerability*, edited by Monica Das Gupta, Lincoln C. Chen, and T. N. Krishnan, 289–306. Bombay: Oxford University Press.

Venkatesan, J. 2010. "Corruption Pervasive in Failed PDS." *The Hindu*, March 16.

Vera-Sanso, Penny. 1999. "Dominant Daughters-in-Law and Submissive Mothers-in-Law? Cooperation and Conflict in South India." *Journal of the Royal Anthropological Institute* 5 (4): 577–93.

Vincentnathan, Lynn. 1993. "Untouchable Concepts of Person and Society." *Contributions to Indian Sociology* 27 (1): 53–82. doi: 10.1177/006996693027001003.

Visaria, Leela. 2000. "Violence against Women: A Field Study." *Economic and Political Weekly* 35 (20): 1742–51. doi: 10.2307/4409296.

———. 2008. "Violence against Women in India: Is Empowerment a Protective Factor?" *Economic and Political Weekly* 43 (48): 60–66.

Wadley, Susan. 2008. "No Longer a Wife: Widows in Rural North India." In *Wife, Mother, Widow: Exploring Women's Lives in Northern India*, edited by Susan Wadley, 92–118. New Delhi: Chronicle. First published 1995.

Waldrop, Anne. 2004. "Gating and Class Relations: The Case of a New Delhi 'Colony.'" *City & Society* 16 (2): 93–116. doi: 10.1525/city.2004.16.2.93.

Wallace, Deborah, and Rodrick Wallace. 1998. *A Plague on Your Houses: How New York Was Burned Down and National Public Health Crumbled*. Brooklyn, NY: Verso Books.

Wasylishyn, Christine, and Joy L. Johnson. 1998. "Living in a Housing Co-Operative for Low Income Women: Issues of Identity, Environment and Control." *Social Science & Medicine* 47 (7): 973–981.

Weinstein, Liza. 2008. "Mumbai's Development Mafias: Globalization, Organized Crime and Land Development." *International Journal of Urban and Regional Research* 32 (1): 22–39. doi: 10.1111/j.1468-2427.2008.00766.x.

West, Paige. 2005. "Translation, Value, and Space: Theorizing an Ethnographic and Engaged Environmental Anthropology." *American Anthropologist* 107 (4): 632–42. doi: 10.1525/aa.2005.107.4.632.

Weston, Kath. 1997. *Families We Choose: Lesbians, Gays, Kinship*. New York: Columbia University Press.

———. 2001. "Kinship, Controversy, and the Sharing of Substance: The Race/Class Politics of Blood Transfusion." In *Relative Values: Reconfiguring Kinship Studies*, edited by Janet Carsten, Gillian Feeley-Harnik, Sarah

Franklin, and Susan McKinnon, 147–174. Durham, NC: Duke University Press.

Wikan, Unni. 1987. "Public Grace and Private Fears: Gaiety, Offense, and Sorcery in Northern Bali." *Ethos* 15 (4): 337–365. doi: 10.2307/640343.

Wilce, James M. 1995. "'I Can't Tell You All My Troubles': Conflict, Resistance, and Metacommunication in Bangladeshi Illness Interactions." *American Ethnologist* 22 (4): 927–952. doi: 10.1525/ae.1995.22.4.02a00140.

Wiser, Charlotte Viall, and William H Wiser. 1971. *Behind Mud Walls, 1930–1960.* 2nd ed. Berkeley: University of California Press.

Witsoe, Jeffrey. 2011. "Corruption as Power: Caste and the Political Imagination of the Postcolonial State." *American Ethnologist* 38 (1): 73–85. doi: 10.1111/j.1548-1425.2010.01293.x.

Yang, Lawrence Hsin, Arthur Kleinman, Bruce G. Link, Jo C. Phelan, Sing Lee, and Byron Good. 2007. "Culture and Stigma: Adding Moral Experience to Stigma Theory." *Social Science & Medicine* 64 (7): 1524–35. doi: 10.1016/j.socscimed.2006.11.013.

Yarris, Kristin Elizabeth. 2011. "The Pain of 'Thinking too Much': Dolor de Cerebro and the Embodiment of Social Hardship among Nicaraguan Women." *Ethos* 39 (2): 226–48. doi: 10.1111/j.1548-1352.2011.01186.x.

Zigon, Jarrett. 2009. "Within a Range of Possibilities: Morality and Ethics in Social Life." *Ethnos* 74 (2): 251–76. doi: 10.1080/00141840902940492.

Zimmermann, Francis. 1980. "Rtu-sa-tmya: The Seasonal Cycle and the Principle of Appropriateness." *Social Science & Medicine. Part B: Medical Anthropology* 14 (2): 99–106. doi: 10.1016/0160-7987(80)90058-7.

———. 1987a. *The Jungle and the Aroma of Meats: An Ecological Theme in Hindu Medicine.* Berkeley: University of California Press.

———. 1987b. "Monsoon in Traditional Culture." In *Monsoons,* edited by J.S. Fein and P.L. Stephens, 51–76. New York: Wiley.

Index

activism: community rights and, 90, 109; limitations of, 178, 224; perspectives on poverty, 12–13, 134, 167, 224; resistance to, 33, 167; role in research, xiv-xv, 127

agriculture, 140, 144, 205; relationship to environmental concepts in slums, 185–86, 189, 202

asceticism, 3, 20–21, 48, 49, 58–59, 64, 65–66, 71, 84, 94, 123, 169, 171-3, 218, 219, 220; detachment from neighbors and, 119, 121, 123, 129

Ayurveda. *See* health care (home remedies); South Asian medicine

body, 17, 19, 21, 42, 65, 93, 112, 125, 172, 186, 188-9, 192, 213, 217, 218; bodily difference between rich and poor, 4, 195, 200–201, 203–4, 218; embodiment, 4, 9, 16, 25, 50, 63–64, 113, 154, 182, 202, 206; strength, 3, 46, 198–201, 203; suffering/vulnerability, 9, 42, 53, 54, 63, 65–66, 171–72, 198–200. See also *kamzorī* (weakness)

care: family care, 13, 15, 24–25, 38–39, 40, 45–72, 113, 186, 189, 218; health effects of, 26, 46, 47, 51, 54–56, 62–67, 76, 84, 221; non-kin provision of, 119, 121, 149–50;

poverty's effects on, 45–46, 49, 51–54; self care, 64, 197–201, 205–6, 212; selfless ideal of, 47–50, 58–67, 77, 83–86; *sevā,* 46–47. *See also* kinship

caste, 19, 28, 30–31, 32, 89, 117, 128, 143–44, 167, 169, 177, 219, 222; Dalits and discrimination against, 30–31, 103, 185; environment and, 31, 183, 184, 188, 193–94, 210, 227; Gujjars, 109, 143; identity in contemporary urban India, 26–27, 29, 32, 91, 95–96, 98, 100, 105; methods related to, 18, 211; occupation and, 29–30, 185

citizenship, 3, 39–40, 146–51; domesticity and, 190–91; health and, 11, 184, 217; moral definitions of, 135–38, 154–60, 159–60, 171, 176–79; social entitlements related to, 133–37, 146, 161–70.

class: differences between/stratification, 9–10, 53, 134, 168, 182, 195–96, 201; identity, 26–28, 32–33, 81–82, 91, 96–98, 100–101, 128, 157, 173, 184, 190, 227. *See also* middle class

community: environmental management by, 208–9, 223, 227; local concepts of, 122–23, 127–30, 150, 177; networks, 15, 16, 39–40, 89–92, 128–29, 143–44; organizing/development, 12–13, 40–41, 115–16, 135, 224–25;

269